CARJACKED

At the boulevard stop sign, Rebecca halted and told Bruce that a red light on the instrument panel signaled a problem. The back hatch door, she said, had apparently not locked, and it was ajar. Leaving the engine running and the headlights on, she opened the driver's door, and stepped out into the shadowy night.

Bruce remained in the passenger seat, looking toward Concord and the right turn that would take them onto the freeway.

Without warning, a dark-clad figure emerged from the adjacent shrubbery, raised his right arm, leveled a handgun through the rolled down window, and pulled the trigger twice. An explosive pop was followed by the sound of shattering glass. A searing hunk of lead caught Bruce just above his upper lip, on the right side. It tore through the top part of his mouth and came out the other side of his head, just in front of the left ear.

Shocked and spurting blood, Bruce managed to push his door open, leap out, and lurch toward the vehicle's rear. He broke into a staggering run, and crossed Beswick, heading toward a driveway. The shooter followed, with less than a yard separating them, and began firing again.

HONEYMOON WITH A KILLER

DON LASSETER
with RONALD E. BOWERS

P

PINNACLE BOOKS
Kensington Publishing Corp.
http://www.kensingtonbooks.com

Some names have been changed to protect the privacy of individuals connected to this story.

PINNACLE BOOKS are published by

Kensington Publishing Corp.
119 West 40th Street
New York, NY 10018

All Kensington Titles, Imprints, and Distributed Lines are available at special quantity discounts for bulk purchases for sales promotions, premiums, fund-raising, and educational or institutional use. Special book excerpts or customized printings can also be created to fit specific needs. For details, write or phone the office of the Kensington special sales manager: Kensington Publishing Corp., 119 West 40th Street, New York, NY 10018, attn: Special Sales Department, Phone: 1-800-221-2647.

Pinnacle and the P logo Reg. U.S. Pat. & TM Off.

ISBN-13: 978-0-7860-1929-8
ISBN-10: 0-7860-1929-8

First printing: November 2009

10 9 8 7 6 5 4 3 2 1

Printed in the United States of America

Foreword

The first steps leading to murder are often set in motion by ordinary circumstances in our daily lives. What is more normal than a man and a woman, total strangers, discovering one another in a restaurant, bar, shopping mall, or any other venue where people gather? Most of us have been through similar circumstances, and have never given the slightest thought to a potentially lethal outcome.

That's exactly what happened to Bruce and Rebecca. Just a few weeks before Christmas, 1995, they met at a Southern California swap meet held on the site of an old drive-in theater.

Rebecca stood near a display of exotic bottled spices laid out on a tarpaulin. At age twenty-six, she radiated sensuality, with captivating green eyes, flaming shoulder-length auburn hair, and a thousand-watt smile. Dressed in a revealing low-cut peasant blouse and a short skirt, Rebecca turned the heads of most men strolling along colorful vendor stalls.

She certainly caught the eye of Bruce, a shy, frugal software engineer. Educated at Stanford University, still a bachelor at forty-one, and already wealthy, Bruce's experience with women could be summarized on the head of a pin. His virginity remained intact.

Seeds of their tragic story—of courtship, marriage, and murder—were planted at that moment and grew to monstrous heights as the tale played out over the next decade.

A superior court judge familiar with the facts declared,

"This should be a movie or a book. It's got everything—the love angle, the murder angle, a stripper boyfriend, the gay girlfriend, sister against sister, the innocent Mormon-mom wedding photographer, attempted seduction of a doctor, trips to Hawaii, Cabo San Lucas, and Lake Havasu. Everything!"

PART 1

Chapter 1

Gunshots
in the Night

Virginia Selva, a weary middle-aged teacher's aide, finally dropped off to sleep on a muggy, hot Friday night late in July. It had been a tough day at Lorena Street Elementary School, just a few blocks away, where she held the job title of para-educator. Most of the seven hundred–plus kids in attendance—kindergartners through fifth graders—spoke Spanish, putting Virginia in constant demand as an interpreter. Behavior problems consumed the rest of her time and patience. Stressed out from a particularly difficult Friday, she looked forward to a relaxing weekend, but she had tossed and turned after going to bed.

Cacophonous high-speed traffic on the I-5/Santa Ana Freeway—not more than eighty paces north of Virginia's front door—didn't help. Nothing buffered the rumbling din from traffic speeding in both directions on ten lanes. The steady roar flowed over a cinder block fence, crossed an open triangular field, bridged Beswick Street, and engulfed the line of homes, including Selva's two-story house. Trucks, motor-cycles, and countless cars heading to or from downtown Los Angeles never ceased, especially on Friday nights in midsummer. Even double-paned windows in the upper-floor bedroom, overlooking the street below, could barely mute the constant waves of noise.

For the most part, Virginia had learned to ignore droning engines and the deafening hum of tire traction on pavement. An hour before midnight, it all faded away for her with blessed sleep. Her respite didn't last long, though.

A little after 1:00 A.M., a sharp blast snapped her into full consciousness and sent her scrambling to the window. It sounded much more distinct than a backfiring motor, and the startled woman was convinced she had heard a gunshot. Fear mixed with curiosity gripped her when she heard shrill, angry, arguing voices. "At first, I thought it was next door," Selva later stated. "You know, that something had happened there with the neighbor girls and their boyfriends."

From her view of the outside scene, Virginia could easily make out the intersection where Beswick abutted Concord Street, two doors to the west. The street layout forced cars and trucks passing her house in the direction of Concord to halt at a boulevard stop sign, and either turn right or left. A right turn would funnel vehicles to an on-ramp and the eastbound freeway. Or they could turn left and drive south down the gentle slope of Concord through quiet residential blocks.

As Virginia gazed through streetlamp phosphorescence, trying to see what had happened, she spotted a dark-clad figure striding toward her house, away from an SUV stalled at the boulevard stop sign, with the headlights still on. The driver's door stood wide open. In his right hand, thrust forward, the man gripped a gun. As he repeatedly pulled the trigger, the weapon spit flashes of yellow-white lightning from the muzzle. At least four—maybe five—more shots pierced the night. He took a few steps backward, wheeled, broke into a gallop, raced toward Concord Street, and vanished after turning the corner and heading downhill, toward Garnet Street.

Virginia snatched her glasses from a nightstand, flew from the bedroom, and ran downstairs to a bay window. From there, her eyes zeroed in on a troubling sight—the motionless figure of a woman lying on the pavement behind the SUV's rear wheel, on the driver's side.

At that moment, a pickup truck pulled to a stop several yards behind the SUV and the prone figure. Within seconds, a taxi rounded the corner from Concord and also braked to a halt. Almost simultaneously, Virginia saw a black-and-white police cruiser arrive. Two officers jumped out. One conferred with the pickup and taxi drivers, while the other rushed toward the sidewalk next door and knelt next to something. Straining to see what had drawn the officer's attention, Virginia realized that a man lay facedown on the driveway concrete apron.

She continued to observe as a fire truck joined the other vehicles on Beswick, then an ambulance, and more police cars. Red and yellow lights flashed, casting distorted, eerie shadows of people darting to and fro on the scene. Another cop stretched yellow plastic crime-scene tape around the SUV and blocked off the adjacent driveway. Personnel in uniforms and medical garb used flashlights as they performed endless tasks.

Virginia had not turned on interior lights, which might have signaled her presence. No one knocked at her door. Eventually she went back to bed.

Because emergency vehicles arrived within moments of the incident, Virginia did not call 911. But another nearby resident, twenty-five-year-old Guadalupe "Lupe" Hernandez, who heard and saw the events from a different angle, did make the call.

As soon as an answer came, she said, "Hi. Uh, there was just some shooting outside my house, and now there's a car parked. It's just parked. I think they were shooting at the car, and it's not moving at all. The lights are on and no one is moving from there."

The 911 officer asked, "How long ago was this shooting?"

"Just like a minute ago. Like a couple of seconds."

"How many shots did you hear?"

"Ah, it was a lot." Breaking into her native Spanish language, she gasped, *"Como unos cinco verdad?"* then reverted to English. "Like five. I heard yelling, and, uh, then I saw somebody running down . . ."

"Did you see anyone?"

"I saw somebody running—it was one guy dressed in black."

"Was he white, Hispanic, black, Asian?"

"I couldn't see. I, uh, I'm [looking] from my bedroom window."

"The person was a male, wearing all dark colors? Did you see what direction he was running?"

"He was running—well, I'm located on Concord and Garnet, and he was running down the hill off of Beswick and Concord, he ran down the hill—the shooting was at Beswick and Concord." After the 911 officer repeated this for confirmation, Lupe continued to speak. "And then I heard a car, but didn't see if he got in the car. I heard it speeding off. The [other] car is still up there, and no one is moving in it."

"What color is it?"

"It's like a truck, *Es como una troca* . . . dark, like a minivan or a four-door truck." She did her best to describe an SUV, but couldn't come up with the exact words.

"And where is that minivan parked?"

"It's at the stop sign, like going into the [freeway] entrance, the I-5 south, and it's at the stop at Concord and Beswick."

"Okay, great, and the lights are on, you said?"

"Yeah, they are on."

"Do you see anybody sitting there?"

"I'm too far away to see that."

"Okay, great. Thanks for calling."

"Thank you."

Lupe Hernandez watched the buzz of activity for a while and finally went to bed.

News coverage in the next few days revealed to both Virginia and Lupe the identities of the two figures Virginia Selva had seen, a woman lying on the pavement and a man sprawled face-down on the driveway apron. They were Rebecca and Bruce Cleland.

The couple had taken their wedding vows in a magnificent Catholic church, and reveled at a country club reception, only six months and eight days before that hot summer night.

Los Angeles Police Department (LAPD) detective Tom Herman would call it the most tangled, engrossing case he ever investigated during his eleven years with the homicide team.

Chapter 2

She Definitely Had
a Way With Men

Rebecca "Becky" Salcedo's friends described her as beautiful, fun, sexy, outrageous, generous, and affectionate. Her personality acted as a magnet not only to a long parade of men, but also to numerous women. "She knows how to make you feel special," said insiders who socialized with Rebecca. Some, though, saw darker aspects in this complex woman. Words such as "deceitful" and "conniving" crept into conversations about her. She seemed to have magic powers for getting anything she wanted, especially from guys she dated. And she wanted a lot.

For Rebecca, life with a troubled mother, two older sisters, and a cowardly father had commenced in murky circumstances.

In a squalid suburb of Tijuana, Mexico, just across California's southern border, fifteen-year-old Lucy Quezada cowered on the floor of a shack. While hippies *del norte* frolicked through summers of love and flower power during those mid 1960s, Lucy's world consisted of an ongoing struggle for survival.

Screams echoed from the bedroom of Lucy's unkempt hovel, built of materials carted from scrap heaps. No one heard her or came to help. She fought her attacker with nothing more than thin, flailing arms, fingernails, and powerless kicking. No one interceded to prevent him from repeatedly raping young Lucy.

A few weeks later, she experienced a different kind of pain. Abdominal queasiness signaled pregnancy, and Lucy finally told her family that she had been violated. A quick, forced marriage to the rapist followed. The baby, named Yvonne (pseudonym), came later that year. While the infant still wore diapers, Lucy and her husband gathered their meager belongings, bundled up little Yvonne, and migrated to East Los Angeles.

Unwilling to settle for poverty, Lucy worked full-time and attended school at night to become a nurse's aide. Two years later, she gave birth to a second child and named her Dolores (pseudonym). One more baby arrived on August 15, 1969, the third and final daughter, Rebecca. Still harboring bitterness against her husband, who had initially impregnated her through rape, Lucy chose to endow all of her daughters with her maiden name, Quezada.

The irresponsible father couldn't handle family burdens. Bound by a marriage he hadn't wanted, struggling with a meager income while trying to feed a wife and three children, he buckled under the pressure and abandoned them. According to Rebecca's friends, word eventually drifted back to Lucy that he had died.

Another member of Lucy's family, her brother Arturo, had also settled in Boyle Heights. His decrepit *casa* on Fresno Street, less than a mile from the future site of a shooting at the corner of Beswick and Concord, could barely contain his brood—four daughters and two sons. Rebecca interacted well with Uncle Arturo and most of her cousins, even though Arturo drank heavily and lusted after every woman in sight.

His wife had caught him too many times, and had moved to another county. Rebecca bonded primarily with the handsome, gregarious younger boy, Alvaro, known as "Al," and easily worked her charms on the youth, four years her junior. But his brother Jose, three years older than Rebecca, kept his distance. Going by the nickname "Joe," he associated with a tougher crowd.

After the departure of Lucy's *cobarde* husband, she struggled to support her trio of daughters. Still relatively young and attractive, Lucy set out to find a husband. Pedro Salcedo filled the bill. He even adopted the kids and gave them his surname.

Pedro found a modest rental house in Maywood, an industrial community four miles southeast of Boyle Heights. Predominantly Hispanic citizens and immigrants populated the residential neighborhoods, where most structures, painted in pastels of blue and pink, or earth tones, featured chain-link fences and security grilles on windows.

Lucy worked regularly in a doctor's office. Another member of the medical staff, Patricia Medina, befriended her, and heard all about the woman's troubles. Sometimes Pedro would bring the three daughters when he came to pick up Lucy, and Medina formed a friendship with young Rebecca. As she watched the child grow into her early teens, Medina was impressed when Rebecca would occasionally show up during one of her mother's illnesses and substitute for her, performing the job like an adult.

Painful memories, stress, and damage to her psyche drove Lucy into deep depression. The ready availability of comforting drugs at her workplace proved too tempting, and she leaned heavily on them for escape. At home she sought seclusion in a darkened bedroom and spent nearly all of her time in bed. Lucy's daughters, especially Dolores, took care of the domestic chores.

Among the girls' acquaintances, one later said, "I always felt like Dolores, the middle sister, was Pedro's wife. She cooked for him, did his laundry, housekeeping, did everything for him that a woman should do, except, I guess, the physical part. Their mother, Lucy, was there for that, but nothing else. She was always ill or something, so I guess Dolores felt obligated to take care of her stepfather."

Under these circumstances, siblings sometimes unify in their struggle against the oppressive adult world. Yvonne, Dolores, and Rebecca took the opposite tack. Chaos reigned in the house. According to a couple of Rebecca's friends, "There was a lot of yelling in the family. The sisters didn't get along with each other. How could they be like that? Always bickering, always competing to see who was better than the others. They were terrible. Pedro didn't know how to talk to you, so he would just yell. Rebecca didn't care too much for him. She was always intimidated by him. I think he made decent money in some kind of maintenance work or something like that."

By the time Rebecca reached the age of thirteen, she had developed the shapely figure of an adult, and used the knowledge of how to showcase it to her advantage. She enjoyed stares from men, and encouraged them with low necklines and short skirts. Her attendance and work in school took a backseat to social activities. Low achievement in junior high required her to do corrective makeup work in the summer of 1983. Another student at the Monterey Continuation School, Bertha Araiza, age fifteen, noticed Rebecca.

Bertha, a teen Venus, with a dazzling smile, mirthful crescent-shaped brown eyes, and a sensual physique envied by women and ogled by men, had also allowed her high-school grades to slip. Today anyone meeting Bertha would immediately wonder why she had ever needed to attend a remedial school, in view of her obvious intelligence, articulate speech patterns, and upscale social skills. She later explained, "I had fallen into a pattern of getting a little crazy, hanging around with the wrong people, and started failing my classes."

Recalling it, Bertha said, "I saw Rebecca there. She was thirteen and I wondered what the heck she was doing in continuation school already. I found out she was taking a clerical and typing class so she could go to work with her mother in a medical office."

An enduring friendship between the girls came about by happenstance. As Bertha waited for a bus one morning, she saw someone waving to her from a car. Said Bertha, "Rebecca was in her mom's car, with her boyfriend driving it. She made him pull over and flagged me to see if I wanted a ride. I had seen her at school, so I accepted. From then on, she clung to me like I was her sister or something. She had a terrible relationship with her two real sisters. Sometimes she even treated me like her mother, and would listen to me. I think it was partly because I always had a good head on my shoulders and always knew what was right, and tried to do the right thing."

Rebecca's proclivity for getting whatever she wanted from men allowed her to avoid the drudgery of a full-time job, and her apathy toward formal education led to dropping out. She failed to even complete the summer courses at the continuation school, and she never bothered to enroll in high school.

Even though Bertha forged ahead and earned good grades, while Rebecca shunned classrooms, the bond between them grew. They began spending time together, doing all the things teenagers do. Looking back at it, Bertha said, "Oh, my goodness, she was always the disaster. She was thirteen, but acted like she was eighteen. We would make up these stories to our moms so we could go out and party, like I was at her house and she was at mine, but really going out and having a good time. But, with her that young, I was so shocked that she was so, uh, out there. She was already developed like a woman. She looked good, and her boyfriend was much older, too. As we started hanging out together and being friends, I got to know her family pretty well. They were very strange. Her mom was always in the bedroom and taking pills. She had access to them through her work with a doctor. Mostly she used painkillers and was always out of it."

To Bertha, her new friend's family contrasted sharply with her own.

Born in Michoacán, Mexico, on the central west coast, Bertha laughingly explained that it sounded liked "Michigan." She also pointed out that "Bertha" is a common name in Spain, and is pronounced *Bear-ta*. She first came to California as a young child, accompanying her grandmother who, with her husband, had immigrated from Spain. Bertha's family moved permanently to Southern California after her tenth birthday. Having visited Mexico only once after leaving, Bertha lost all trace of any accent, and learned to speak English with clear elocution.

The tension and conflict in Rebecca's family disturbed Bertha. "I used to think, 'Oh, my gosh, my mom is so different.' She wouldn't even take Tylenol. I thought her mom was really sad, and weird. When we wanted to borrow her car, when Becky was thirteen and fourteen, we would have to pay her mother for it! Come up with money so we could take the car, even though Rebecca wasn't even old enough to drive."

Rebecca Salcedo's mother had been raped and impregnated at age fifteen. Rebecca took a husband at the same age. But, according to a close friend of hers, neither love nor companionship had anything to do with it. Rather, she agreed to a business deal. An immigrant named Garcia paid Rebecca $2,000 for the nuptial in order to obtain his green card. The whole deal required deception, falsified documents, and calling in some favors. She never slept with the groom. He vanished from her life—the marriage no more important than a yard sale transaction.

As often as possible, Rebecca spent time in Bertha's home. "She was around our family most of her life. She even addressed our mother as 'Mom.'"

At one point in the long friendship, Bertha lived with Rebecca's family for a few months in Maywood. The experience of seeing Rebecca in the riotous, dysfunctional environment of the Quezada-Salcedo families gave Bertha deeper insight into her friend's behavior. Still, Bertha had difficulty understanding the friction between Rebecca, Dolores, and Yvonne. Mulling it over, she said, "I have four sisters and we're very, very close. I couldn't even have a little argument with them without calling later and apologizing. Those girls would do anything to hurt each other. Anything. If Dolores had a boyfriend that Becky liked, then Becky would be after that one. They slept with each other's boyfriends, and stuff like that. They did the kind of stuff that only enemies do. I thought, 'What is wrong with these girls? How could they be like that?' Always bickering, always seeing who was better than the others. They were terrible. When happy, they would act all loving. But if any one of them got upset, it was instantly ended, and pandemonium took over again."

One of Bertha's sisters, Alma Arias, agreed. "We take care of each other. It's hard to understand a family who fights all the time."

Away from the disharmony of relatives, Bertha and Rebecca resorted to typical teen stunts. Looking back, Bertha recalled, "We would show my mom Yvonne's driver's license. So my mom thought Rebecca was the age to drive. We did a lot of goofy stuff like that."

Of course, with mobility provided by a car, Rebecca and Bertha found limitless opportunity to meet guys. Even though Bertha outranked her pal in seniority, she and their other girlfriends tended to rely on Rebecca's gregarious personality to break the ice. "She knew how to talk to men. She had the sweetest voice. She was always singing and she was very sexy. Guys love that. So she could get them to do anything for her. I was always the little sidekick. We went out, but we never paid for drinks. All we had to do is let Rebecca walk in front of us. She had big boobs early, and liked to wear low necklines. And I'm not kidding, she would get us drinks all night long."

Sometimes, when Lucy Salcedo needed to use her own car, making it unavailable to the girls, Rebecca employed her feminine wiles to obtain other transportation. Bertha shared in the pleasure, but had second thoughts about that part of Rebecca's personality. "Growing up, she was fun. She was just a fun girl. But she could be very deceiving with people, and would take from Peter to pay Paul. She would take from other people, usually men, and give everything to people she cared for. If she met someone, and he had something to offer, money or whatever, she would take it and give it away. To me, she was always very generous. She was a wonderful friend. I didn't like her deceiving ways with men, though. She knew how to connive them, even from the time she was very, very young. She knew how to get her way. She always got cars. I would ask, 'Whose car is that?' 'Oh, it's so and so's car.' 'He let you borrow it?' 'Oh yeah.' Once, she had a Lamborghini at her mother's house! I don't know what she did for that one. Who knows? Maybe sexual things, I don't know. She didn't share that with me. I think she just wanted to impress me or make it seem like she was someone she wasn't. So there was a lot of stuff she wouldn't tell me, but c'mon, I knew better. She always had money, even without a job. She always had nice clothes. She even drove a motorcycle that a guy let her borrow. She definitely had a way with men. She was very attractive, but mostly had a way with men."

Gazing at a photo of young Rebecca provocatively dressed, with a low neckline, Bertha shook her head and observed, "Her boobs were always exposed."

Laughing, Alma concurred and noted, "That was nothing. She liked showing it off. She was always big, and that's what she usually looked like, so guys were always drawn to her." Pausing thoughtfully, Alma added another observation. "Rebecca liked men, but I think something else was on her mind. She and Bertha were close from the time they were young. And I think she was infatuated with Bertha."

Chapter 3

Evolution of a
Male Virgin

Harold Irvin Cleland and his wife, Theda, known as "Teddy," could be compared to one of those all-American couples portrayed in an innocent black-and-white 1950s television series. Ozzie and Harriet, or June and Ward Cleaver. Honest, moral, clean-living, and described by friends as "cute," they lived comfortably in upscale South Pasadena. Both had been born in September 1919, with Harold arriving just thirteen days before his future wife. Slim and tidy, he never grew any taller than five-nine, and she stood at least three inches shorter. Some thought they saw a resemblance in Teddy to Lucille Ball. At age thirty-one, she delivered her first baby, Patricia Ann, in April 1951. Her second and final child, Bruce, came on March 31, 1954.

March 31 natives, under the astrological sign of Aries, are said to draw controversy into their private lives, and attract eccentric, unusual types. According to a popular Web site horoscope, they may also be tricked into unwise marriages, which could end disastrously.

If a natal date can portend life's events, Bruce Cleland may have been foreordained to specialize in scientific pursuits. Several notable physicists shared March 31 birthdays, including Sin-Itiro Tomonaga, who specialized in quantum electrodynamics, Carlo Rubbia, the discoverer of W and Z particles, and Lawrence Bragg, formulator of Bragg's law of diffraction. Exactly three years before Bruce's birth, on March 31, 1951, the first commercial computer manufactured in this country, called UNIVAC I, arrived at the U.S. Census Bureau.

Bruce's father couldn't have been happier. He loved his little daughter, but eagerly anticipated the joy of a son growing up in their household. He and Teddy brought their newborn child to their one-story home on the corner of Beech Street and Fremont Avenue. The white clapboard and tan stucco exterior, with large windows trimmed by louvered shutters, sat on a slanted lot at the bottom of a sloping lane. Visitors needed to ascend a walkway, then climb seven concrete steps for access to the porch and front entrance. Giant Chinese elms shaded the garage door and second entry on the Fremont side during hot summer days. A row of Southern California's signature palm trees lined the west side of Fremont, forming a gallery that towered more than eighty feet into the smog-faded blue sky. The secure upper-middle-class neighborhood provided an idyllic childhood for the boy and his older sister.

By the time Bruce completed kindergarten, his remarkable intelligence had already manifested itself. The beaming parents realized his potential and began thinking of superior advanced educational institutions for him. Social upheaval, though, threatened to derail their dreams.

As Bruce entered elementary school, the freewheeling era of the 1960s had begun. Music on his portable plastic radio made the transition from rock and roll by Elvis and the Everly Brothers, through Chubby Checker exhorting dancers to do "The Twist," and on to the Beatles. In 1968, Bruce enrolled at South Pasadena High School (SPHS), where famous alumni included actor William Holden. Hilary Swank would be a future SPHS student. From his home, Bruce could easily walk the short distance north on Fremont Street, along the path marked by palms reaching to the sky. Dating back to 1906, the South Pasadena High campus had attracted numerous filmmakers who shot scenes there for classics such as *Gone with the Wind,* and later drew producers of *American Pie, Legally Blonde,* and *Back to the Future.*

During Bruce's tenure at SPHS, the future threat of military draft, necessary to feed the voracious meat grinder combat in Vietnam's green hell, menaced most young men. Some fled to Canada. Others joined throngs of protestors across the nation, burning draft cards and carrying signs proclaiming, *Hell no, we won't go.* It gave Bruce even more reason to prepare himself for enrollment in a good college, perform well, and keep his deferment alive.

Popular music reflected the national unrest and drug-induced escapes, ranging from folk songs to throbbing, amplified beats of the Rolling Stones and Creedence Clearwater Revival.

The quasi revolution needed an image, and it became a hirsute one. Everyone under the age of thirty grew long hair. Sideburns and mustaches became de rigueur, decorating the faces and heads of nearly every man old enough to sprout them. Bruce wore a thick, bushy mop of curls all the way down to his sloping shoulders.

Not blessed with traditionally handsome features, he grew in his mid teens to his full height of six feet. Bruce's long face, large teeth, prominent eyebrows, and hairstyle subjected him to taunting from cruel fellow high schoolers. Some compared him to a celebrity named Herbert Khaury, better known as Tiny Tim. The odd entertainer rocketed to fame by plucking a ukulele, singing his falsetto rendition of "Tiptoe Through the Tulips," and appearing frequently on the popular *Laugh-In* comedy television show. Bruce's photos in the school's yearbook, called *Copa de Oro* (Cup of Gold), show the remarkable resemblance.

Instead of reacting angrily, Bruce shielded his feelings with a sharp, self-deprecating sense of humor. His personal esteem depended heavily on the fact that no one could hold a candle to his mental agility.

Year after year, to the delight of Theda and Harold, Bruce brought home report cards with perfect scores. He earned admission to the California Scholastic Federation (CSF) in all four years of high school and wound up as a Life Member, which entitled him to a special gold seal on his diploma and transcripts. In addition, Bruce's scholastic achievements placed him with only eight other SPHS students given cash awards from a Bank of America program to recognize outstanding California high-school seniors.

Social life for Bruce consisted mostly of hanging out with his buddies or going out for his favorite meal, Mexican food. None of the school's female population showed any interest in him. Retreating into a facade of apathy toward coeds, he developed serious shyness and never worked up the courage to ask any of them for a date. Focusing his interest instead on academics—particularly math, physics, and the embryonic field of computers—he concentrated on slide rules and books. His ready smile masked the deepening timidity toward girls.

Participation in athletics held little interest for Bruce, but he loved watching football, both on television and at the Rose Bowl or Los Angeles Memorial Coliseum, adjacent to the University of Southern California (USC). Harold acquired season tickets for them so they could follow the USC Trojans. Much to their delight, Coach John McKay's squad won a national championship in 1972, and some called them the best college football team ever assembled.

Harold Cleland's relationship with Bruce transcended the usual father-son connection; they evolved into best buddies. Each spring and summer, they turned to baseball and spent weekend afternoons at Chávez Ravine's stadium, watching the Los Angeles Dodgers.

Graduation from South Pasadena High School came in

June 1972. Bruce marched to "Pomp and Circumstance" with more than two hundred classmates. That fall he entered prestigious Harvey Mudd College, in Claremont, thirty miles east of his home. The school calls itself the nation's top liberal-arts college of engineering, science, and mathematics. First opened in 1957, it states a goal of attracting the nation's brightest students and offering them rigorous scientific and technological education. Bruce Cleland fit perfectly.

Harvey Mudd is one of five undergraduate colleges, along with two postgraduate institutions, making up a consortium covering one square mile in the community of Claremont. The school chosen by Bruce is coeducational, as are most of the others. Scripps College is a private liberal-arts women's school, so opportunities for meeting and dating female students had no limits. Still, Bruce couldn't overcome his modesty, or fear of being rejected. Again he immersed himself in studies, and socialized only with male friends. He developed a taste for alcohol during this period, mostly beer. In his final semester, the editorial staff for the school's yearbook allowed seniors to select a personal photo of themselves rather than a formal portrait for inclusion in the published annual. Bruce submitted a picture of himself wearing jeans, a denim jacket, white T-shirt, and pilot-style sunglasses. With a broad grin, he is seen exiting a liquor store and lugging an aluminum keg of beer, apparently on his way to a party.

If Bruce drank more than he should have, it didn't interfere with his academic standards. In June 1976, he took his Bachelor of Science degree. His outstanding classroom performance paved the way for admission to another top educational institution for pursuit of a master's degree. Located between San Francisco and San Jose in the heart of Silicon Valley, Stanford University is recognized as one of the world's leading research and teaching schools. Bruce's previous hard work at SPHS and Harvey Mudd had prepared him well for the elevated requirements at Stanford. He sailed through the curriculum and graduated in 1978.

One of the advantages of attending a top university is the networking it provides, connecting with other future leaders in the professional world. Stanford University had long ago integrated a portion of its massive campus with high-technology corporations by setting aside a sector called Stanford Industrial Park. This not only provided a flow of income for the institution, but also paved the way for graduating students to make a simple transition into employment. Hewlett-Packard, Eastman Kodak, and General Electric participated in the program.

With his heightened expertise in software engineering, Bruce Cleland became an attractive prospect, and General Electric snapped him up. He moved to San Jose, at the southern tip of San Francisco Bay, and immersed himself in the burgeoning success of Silicon Valley.

The region's name comes from the nonmetallic element silicon, used in semiconductors related to the computer industry. "Valley" refers to the area in Santa Clara County in which high-technology companies exploded into economic success.

Living on a comfortable, residential tree-lined street, across railroad tracks from a huge industrial park, about twenty miles from the Stanford campus, Bruce dedicated himself to his new profession and prospered. Still avoiding much social life, and skipping the pain of trying to find dates, he invested his income skillfully. Having always been frugal in spending habits, he took the art to new levels. His bank account and financial portfolio grew.

After a few years with General Electric, Bruce received an offer he couldn't refuse from TRW and made the transition, joining their systems integration group. Originally known as Thompson Ramo Wooldridge, the corporation bought Electromagnetic Systems Labs (ESL) in 1977 and expanded their involvement in aerospace, data communications, software engineering, and reconnaissance technologies used by the U.S. military. Bruce's knowledge in these disciplines made him a natural for TRW.

The firm expanded, and established a huge branch in Redondo Beach, not far from Los Angeles International Airport. In 1987, Bruce transferred and moved to an apartment complex on Silverstrand Avenue, and later to Monterey Boulevard in Hermosa Beach, only a few blocks from sand and crashing surf. One of the social centers for Southern California's casual lifestyle, Hermosa Beach offers every possible opportunity for meeting sunbathing women along the strand. They also flock to all types of nightclubs and restaurants imaginable, or to parties held every night. Still, Bruce stayed inside his protective cocoon, never risking the hurt of rejection. He socialized with a few friends at work, but spent nearly every weekend with his parents in South Pasadena, or with his sister and her husband.

Patricia Cleland had started dating a painting contractor, Ed Brown, in 1984, and she married him two years later. Highly successful in his business, Brown moved his wife into an upscale home in Orange County's San Juan Capistrano, a few miles from the famous mission, where the celebrated swallows return each March. Bruce and Ed became good friends after they first met in the spring of 1985. Holidays and family celebrations brought the Clelands and Browns together.

The absence of female companionship in Bruce's life worried Ed Brown. He later described Bruce as "very introverted and quiet. He wasn't real comfortable in social settings and never dated. He was too shy." Brown also said, "He was very frugal. Tight."

For transportation from Hermosa Beach to South Pasadena, or the occasional trip to Orange County, Bruce drove a battered Jeep, nearly ten years old. When it began to sputter and stall, his father gave him a far more reliable 1973 Oldsmobile. Harold Cleland had bought it new, but put limited mileage on it. Acquaintances compared it, in good humor, to General Motors' television commercial for that line of vehicles, which tried appealing to younger customers by saying, "This is not your father's Oldsmobile." Bruce apparently felt no reluctance in driving his father's Oldsmobile.

Sometimes Bruce's job sent him on covert international junkets. The highly classified work for the U.S. military took him to several countries, but he couldn't reveal its nature to anyone, including his parents or sister. He kept his word, unlike another employee of TRW, Christopher John Boyce, one year older than Bruce. Notorious as a spy, Boyce's exploits appeared in a book and motion picture, *The Falcon and the Snowman,* in which he succumbed to greed and sold top secret information to foreign agencies.

Earning a salary at TRW in excess of $100,000 annually, a highly respectable figure at that time, investing wisely, and spending carefully, Bruce had accumulated a solid estate.

By the mid 1990s, he had matured into a reasonably handsome man in his early forties, and shed himself of the Tiny Tim image. With neatly styled dark hair, parted high on the right side, well-trimmed mustache and eyebrows, a few cosmetic dental repairs, and a pleasant smile, Bruce could have attracted any number of eligible attractive women. And many of them would have found his wealth an added enhancement. But Bruce didn't yet recognize his own appeal.

Chapter 4

She Always
Wanted What
She Couldn't Have

Bertha Araiza dreaded it when Rebecca steered them into visiting her uncle Arturo Quezada and his family at their small, decrepit house on Fresno Street. Years later, when asked to describe Arturo, Bertha and her sister Alma groaned in disgust.

Bertha explained, "He was a pig! He was Lucy's brother. I told Rebecca if he doesn't leave me alone, I'm going to file sexual-harassment charges. I am serious. He was disgusting. He was the kind of man who would just grab you and fondle you. I warned her, 'The next time your uncle tries to grab me, I'm gonna kick him where it hurts the most.' She said, 'Oh, he's just goofing around, crazy like that, harmless.' I said I meant it. At first, it was kind of funny, but after a while, it made me furious. I knew him for years, and he was always kissing me and treating me like a little daughter. As I got older, and he got older, he was all over me. He treated her other girlfriends the same way. Any girl that was near him, he would want to be all over them. He was nasty. He would say dirty words and nasty stuff. Yuck! He was a big-time alcoholic. When he was drunk, which was most of the time, he turned into an expert on any subject, especially women. He was fresh with Rebecca, too, always grabbing her breasts, kissing her. She would just laugh and tell him to stop it. He was just a dirty old man."

Arturo's daughters never seemed to be around during these visits. But Bertha and Rebecca saw a great deal of the younger son, Alvaro. Said Bertha, "When he was a kid, he was slim, and really cute, always cheerful and happy-go-lucky."

Jose, Al's brother, seldom interacted with them, circulating instead with a rough crowd of people on the law's fringes.

Shortly after Rebecca's sixteenth birthday, an event historic in crime annals took place in Boyle Heights, involving local residents who happened to be acquaintances of Bertha and her coterie of friends.

On August 31, 1985, Richard Ramirez, the notorious "Nightstalker" who would eventually be found guilty of thirteen murders, still hadn't been captured. That morning, in the Los Angeles Greyhound bus terminal, he exited a coach from Tucson, Arizona, after a short round-trip. Dressed in black pants and a short-sleeved black shirt, he passed a group of police officers in the busy downtown station who were observing outbound passengers as they boarded buses to see if any of them resembled a recently circulated photograph. The picture, a mug shot from Ramirez's 1984 arrest for car theft, had landed on the front pages of every major newspaper that morning. L.A. sheriff's detective Frank Salerno (who also investigated the John Racz case, profiled in *You'll Never Find My Body* by Don Lasseter and Ron Bowers, Kensington, 2009) had spearheaded the search for Ramirez.

Hurrying from the bus station, Ramirez headed east, toward Boyle Heights. In a liquor store, he spotted his photo on the front page of *La Opinión,* a Spanish-language paper. Panicky, he bolted, ran, and, at one point, risked his life by sprinting across the busy Santa Ana Freeway. Aboard a city bus, Ramirez thought he'd been noticed, left it, and stopped at a local market on the corner of Evergreen Avenue and Eighth Street. Glancing around, he snatched a copy of the *Herald-Examiner* from a stack and took off running again. After a block, he turned southeast on Garnet Street, trotted five blocks, and slowed in front of Lupe Hernandez's house at Garnet and Concord. Twelve years later, Lupe would play an important role in reporting a different murder. Ramirez stopped to get his breath while sitting on the front steps of a house, within a few paces of a spot where the 1997 killer would be picked up in a waiting car.

After racing another block, Ramirez turned again, rushed up to Beswick Street, and headed southeast, within yards of the site where someone would open fire on a passenger in a midnight blue SUV, and Virgina Selva would be awakened by the explosions. Dodging through alleys and zigzagging, Ramirez sped a dozen more blocks, then began scanning the curbs for a car to steal. He spotted a woman sitting alone in a vehicle with the motor running, and attempted to take it, but her boyfriend suddenly appeared and chased Ramirez away. When he reached Hubbard Street, Ramirez made another stab at carjacking, but several men realized his intent, recognized him from the news photo, and sprang toward him to prevent the theft. Outnumbered, he took off again, with a crowd of angry Latinos in full pursuit, one of them wielding a length of metal pipe. Yells of *"el matador"* echoed up the street, which literally means "the killer." Winded, Ramirez slowed and the vigilantes caught him. The man with the iron bar took a swipe at the fugitive's head and knocked him down. They kept him under control until law enforcement officers arrived to make the arrest.

It would make national headlines that the infamous Night-stalker, of Hispanic heritage, had been captured by outraged people of his own ethnicity. Some of the pursuers were friends of Bertha Araiza and Rebecca Salcedo.

* * *

As the girls grew into their later teens, they found entertainment at night clubs an exciting way to spend their evenings. Periodically, Rebecca, Bertha, and their "posse" of female friends would stop in at a place called Mr. J's to have a few drinks and watch male strippers in action. They met Dave Romero (pseudonym) there in 1986.

Romero described himself as an "independent contractor" for his duties in supplying male dancers, or strippers, to the club. He not only organized and trained the entertainers, but also performed.

Anyone seeing Romero on the street would never have guessed his profession. He certainly didn't fit the stereotypical image of a male dancer who would be expected to have washboard abs, a V-shaped torso, rippling muscles, and classic facial features, among other macho characteristics. Romero would more likely have brought to mind a young Mick Jagger. Nevertheless, he had terpsichorean skills that enabled him to please the eyes of young women. And the green eyes of Rebecca Salcedo, nearing her seventeenth birthday, followed his every move. She caught Romero's attention and invited him to join her group for a drink. He accepted.

Romero and Rebecca dated for several months. Bertha remembered it. "Dave had longer hair than Becky, and wore more makeup. I never understood what she saw in him. Maybe she thought he was a girl. Short, long hair, ugly. She would pick him up, bring him to the house, and give him a bath. They lived together, on and off, for a while. She wasn't in love with him. It was just an infatuation. I never liked him because he thought he was so good. She was into him because he really wasn't into her. She always wanted what she couldn't have."

The relationship dwindled after six months, but Rebecca remained in contact with Romero. He would dance again for her in the future, and also have an impact on the life of her good-looking young cousin, Alvaro.

Even though Rebecca always gave the impression of being ebullient, ready for a party, and happy-go-lucky, she could also fall into deep depression. At least twice, she made feeble efforts to kill herself. Most of her intimates, though, thought it more of a device for getting attention than authentic suicide attempts. Still, the first time it happened, in May 1987, she was temporarily confined in a hospital for observation.

Bertha Araiza, now working part-time and taking college courses, rented an apartment in Huntington Park, just across the south border of Maywood. It didn't take long for Rebecca to seize the opportunity to leave her chaotic family and move in with Bertha. For both young women, it provided greater social opportunities. In the complex's swimming pool, they competed among themselves and other female visitors to see who could wear the most provocative, revealing bathing suits, and posed for sexy photographs.

Discussing that period, Bertha said, "We had a party once, and a gay friend of ours, Diana Harris (pseudonym), whom I had met at work—we were like best friends—attended. She was a very sweet, nice person. She brought a woman with her, a former police officer."

According to Bertha, Rebecca seemed fascinated by the ex-cop's sparkling personality. She and Cherie Barnes (pseudonym) spent the whole evening talking together. They made plans for getting together again and keeping in touch. If it appeared that an unusual amount of physical contact had taken place between Rebecca and Cherie, Bertha thought nothing of it. "Rebecca was always hugging and kissing her friends. If there was any special attraction between them, I wouldn't have known it. She was very affectionate with everybody. Once she got to know you, she would make you feel special."

Maybe the show of affection was just another ploy for getting attention.

Rebecca always needed attention, and tried to keep her weight under control for maximum effect in displaying her body. Most young women, at one time or another, worry about adding pounds. Rebecca's curves sometimes expanded in her later teens, and her friends tried to help her. "I know that she never worked out," said Bertha. "We tried to get her to go to the gym, and she would make excuses. My little sister and I would go to the gym all the time to work out, and we'd drag her with us. She would lie down in the back room and fall asleep. And she would be doing goofy stuff, making us laugh because she was funny. She was really funny. She had a great personality and could make you feel like you were number one. No matter who she was with. She knew how to make you feel special. She was lovely and she was fun. At the gym, she would lie down. We knew she never worked out, I never saw her pick up any weights or do anything like that."

Extra body fat continued to give Rebecca trouble and efforts to correct it would create even greater difficulties.

Shortly after Valentine's Day in 1991, weight gain would turn out to be the least of Rebecca's problems. It came as a stunning shock when police officers snapped handcuffs on her wrists, transported her to jail, and pressed charges of violating drug laws. A jury convicted her on possession of cocaine with the intent to sell, and the judge handed down a sentence of three years in state prison.

Soon after Rebecca's arrival at the Valley State Prison for Women, in central California, she received another surprise. Morning sickness announced her pregnancy. And she had no idea who the father was. In her attempts to recall which sex partner it might have been, she wrote to Bertha and asked her to send a packet of photos picturing men she had been dating. When Rebecca decided which of her lovers most likely had fathered the child, she contacted him. He denied it and arranged for a DNA test, which proved him correct.

Another likely prospect, said a friend of Rebecca's, later died in a biker gang shoot-out which took place in Laughlin, Nevada, on April 28, 2002.

Rebecca's baby boy arrived on October 22, 1991, in the prison hospital. She named him Ryan (pseudonym). While her family cared for the infant, she served nearly eighteen months of her three-year sentence before being released. A few of Rebecca's friends, when visiting the baby, thought they saw a striking resemblance between him and the biker gang member. But no one ever knew, with any certainty, who had fathered the boy.

Looking for a place to live, Rebecca hooked up again with Cherie Barnes, the gay ex-cop. They had been corresponding ever since their first meeting, and Rebecca knew that Cherie had ended a relationship with another female partner. According to Bertha, "I think Becky always had a crush on Cherie. So when she got out of prison, she called her and they got together. Becky didn't have anywhere to go, so Cherie asked her to move in with her. They lived together for a couple of years."

Rebecca, the ex-con, accepted the attractive ex-cop's invitation to share her comfortable home twenty-five miles east of the old Boyle Heights area. Cherie adored the little baby boy. And Rebecca adored Cherie.

Speaking of it later, Bertha and Alma agreed that Rebecca had always treated women with much more affection than she ever gave to men. Cherie, they stated, turned out to be the love of Rebecca's life. As much as she appeared to chase males, Rebecca's heart and soul belonged to another woman. "She really loved Cherie," said Bertha. "Men were just for money and fun. She was always in love with Cherie."

Asked if Rebecca had ever shown any previous signs of being bisexual, Bertha said, "No. No. The way she was with men—who would ever think it?" Falling silent, as if reconsidering her words, Bertha admitted, "I guess, in looking back, she also had a thing for me, but she never pursued it. Or never even tried anything, because she looked up to me."

Alma, though, registered less surprise. "I think Rebecca was always infatuated with Bertha, from the time they were very young." Both sisters, in retrospect, felt certain that Rebecca had also slept with Diana Harris.

Rebecca's tenure of living with Cherie appeared to have

improved her life. The two women socialized and traveled together. Rebecca even had her female lover's name tattooed on her leg. While they partied or went away for romantic weekends, babysitting presented no problems. A middle-aged couple who lived across the street from Cherie's home often took care of little Ryan, and they grew to love him dearly.

If Rebecca thought that her existence had finally smoothed out, she soon experienced one of the most shattering events any daughter could face.

In 1994, her mother, Lucy, carried a handgun into her bathroom, put it to her temple, and pulled the trigger.

Alma recalled it. "Her mom committed suicide. She shot her brains out in the bathroom, and we had to go clean it all up. Lucy was a nurse, totally hooked on pills. I think she might have got caught up stealing stuff at the hospital. After that, Rebecca went berserk. Even crazier."

Distraught, Rebecca couldn't adjust to the blow. Her behavior turned unpredictable and disagreeable. Within a few weeks, while visiting Bertha, she ingested a handful of pills, in what appeared to be an attempt to kill herself. Her friend called the paramedics and Rebecca had her stomach pumped.

Skeptical about the so-called suicide attempt, Bertha later said, "Let me tell you about Rebecca. She was a scaredy-cat. She was a chicken and was even afraid to be at home alone. I think the thought of death frightened her silly. There's no way she would have worked up the courage to really kill herself."

Alma agreed. "If she had really wanted to die, she would have done it the other two times she supposedly tried."

Reverting to her old ways, Rebecca seemed to need men again. The love nest with Cherie unraveled. Before the year ended, Cherie could no longer stand it, and threw her roommate out.

Ever loyal, Bertha came to the rescue again, and allowed Rebecca to move in with her. Bertha even spoke to her boss at work and convinced him to give Rebecca a chance at employment, on the night shift. That, too, turned disastrous. Bertha described it. "She was working for me and she exposed herself to the president of the company. She was in the bathroom, and when she came out, her blouse conveniently popped open. Everything sprang out, and he was horrified. So he wanted her out of there. It was terrible. I got in trouble for that. He didn't want any problems. He wanted her gone, so I helped get her another job at a different place."

Rebecca's new employer imported, packaged, and distributed a variety of food and condiments, including exotic spices. The firm placed Rebecca as a clerk in their credit and collections department. Said Bertha, "She would always tell me stories that there was a lot of funny stuff going on there. She thought the owners might have been smuggling drugs with the shipments of spices. I said, 'How do you always get involved in finding these criminals?' She would laugh and say, 'I don't know.' But she always managed to get wrapped up in stuff like that."

The firm handled spices packaged in rectangular clear-glass containers, and Rebecca found a way to do a little smuggling herself. She brought samples home for Bertha, and admitted that she carried away enough to sell on the side at a swap meet.

Still behaving oddly, Rebecca stretched her best friend's patience to the limit. After six months, Bertha asked her to move out. Rebecca found a tiny, backyard house only a block up the same street, but in the city limits of Maywood, and rented it. Needing furniture for the diminutive living quarters, she relied, as usual, on various men to help. One boyfriend provided a mini-refrigerator, another came up with a bed for the little boy and a dresser for Rebecca, while others helped her pay the rent. Bertha observed, "She had different guys for all of her needs."

For Bertha, separating their living arrangements seemed the right thing to do, as she looked forward to altering her own lifestyle. The friendship could remain intact, but by this time, Bertha had entered into a serious involvement with a young man whose origins were rooted in Hawaii. She looked forward to becoming Mrs. Awana in the near future.

As 1995 neared its end, Rebecca seemed to have recovered from her mother's death. Even though her female lover and her best friend had evicted her from their live-in arrangements, both women continued to be loyal friends. At the age of twenty-six, Rebecca looked good, and still had the ability to charm men out of expensive gifts. Her moral compass had been compromised by a powerful magnet: money.

Rebecca's job in a firm's credit and collections department paid the bills, but she earned a little extra by manning a booth at the swap meet and selling purloined spices in jars. In early December, she spread her goods on a tarp, watched the crowd of shoppers stroll by, and flirted with a nice-looking man who stopped to ask some questions. Her actions would result in profound changes to several lives.

Chapter 5

What Was
He Thinking?

Bruce Cleland and his father, Harold, periodically found pleasure driving their ancient Oldsmobile from South Pasadena to a swap meet in La Mirada, a trip of about twenty-five miles. The colorful array of goods for sale, plus bargain prices, made for an entertaining day.

Held on the paved grounds of what had been the La Mirada (meaning "the view") drive-in theater from 1950 to 1990, the sprawling, gaudy marketplace occupied nearly eighteen acres. It had started in 1965, and grown over the years to feature about six hundred vendors selling everything from tires to tamales and socks to spices. Concentric curved slopes, where moviegoers once parked nearly a thousand cars next to posts equipped with speakers, had been converted to pedestrian lanes lined with stalls. At the front center area, people bought meals in an expanded restaurant that formerly sold popcorn, candy, soft drinks, and hot dogs. By the end of the 1980s, a new name appeared on the giant theater screen's street-side structure identi-

fying it now as SANTA FE SPRINGS DRIVE-IN THEATER. Larger
letters above the site's name now spell out SWAP MEET, and
advertise that it is open five days a week.

In early December 1995, Bruce and Harold each paid the
$1 admission fee, and spent the morning with throngs of shop-
pers strolling between endless stalls, tables, tents, and tarps
laid out on the pavement, all displaying wares and foodstuffs
of every description. A few vendors offered poster-size photos
of Hispanic heroes, including César Chávez and champion
boxer Oscar De La Hoya. Banners snapped overhead in the
cool breeze, many in the red, green, and white of the Mexican
national flag. Music floated in the air from various speakers,
from pop hits to cultural favorites, such as *"La Bamba."* Brilliant multicolored table coverings, tents, walls, umbrellas,
signs, and triple-deckered racks of clothing, mostly imported
from other countries, compensated for the overcast gray sky.
Cages of squawking tropical birds, with feathers in hues of
green, coral, and yellow, captivated shoppers, including Bruce
and his father. At an open-front art stall extending more than
thirty yards, Bruce studied paintings featuring Mona Lisa,
Marilyn Monroe, poor imitations of Michelangelo's Sistine
Chapel ceiling, and a variety of landscapes.

All of these interesting sights gave Bruce and Harold much
to talk about, but Bruce's attention focused primarily on his
gustatory interests. Considering himself an aficionado of
Mexican food, he stopped frequently at displays of various in-
gredients: chili, cumin, garlic, dried peppers, masa, jalapenos,
and other tongue-scorching spices.

His vision landed on a tarpaulin covered with rectangular
clear-glass containers of burnt-red spices. And then he caught
sight of the woman attending the display, and something happened in his brain, heart, or both. She wore a peasant blouse,
exposing considerable decolletage, and a patterned short skirt.
Her dark green eyes leveled at him, reflecting a mixture of curiosity and amusement, and her crimson-gloss lips broke into

an alluring smile, flashing perfect teeth. Dusky auburn hair spilled almost to her shoulders.

Bruce appeared to gasp for breath. He managed to stammer out a few words, trying to ask about the spices. But he really wanted to know about her, not what she had for sale. Recovering quickly, he thanked the attractive seller, and moved on with his father. Harold recognized the obvious distraction and would later speak of the woman. "She was laying some goods on a tarp for sale. I believe she was helping a friend." After Bruce and Harold stepped away, an odd thing happened.

In Harold's memory of that day, Bruce spoke words never heard before. "He says, 'Hey, I am going back and talk to that girl.' I said, 'Okay, fine.' So I walked down the lane a little ways and waited for him."

From the short distance, Harold observed his son. It seemed so out of character, and the curious father wondered just how it would turn out. "He talked with her for several minutes. Then she handed him some papers." The documents, Harold later learned, were résumés of Rebecca Salcedo's work experience. She and Bruce had discussed employment opportunities at TRW, and she asked him about job openings at the firm. Perhaps he could put in a good word for her.

As it turned out, Rebecca wanted a lot more from Bruce than a job. And the subject of their conversation may have touched on work opportunities, but actually swirled with an undercurrent of far more personal needs.

In the following days, Bruce's friends and family noticed a change in his attitude and outlook. He suddenly seemed far more jovial, positive, and happy.

Rebecca, too, expressed excitement to her friends in talking about the man she had met at the swap meet. After a couple of days at work, she couldn't wait to tell Bertha all about it. Bruce had already called her. She gushed, "Let me show you this new guy I met."

Expecting to see a photograph, Bertha couldn't believe it

when her friend handed her a credit report. Rebecca had used her job access, in credit and collections, to research everything she could about Bruce Cleland. The documents spelled out his borrowing power of up to $50,000, with no current outstanding loans or obligations. He owned several credit cards, none of which carried balances.

"This is the guy I'm going to marry," Rebecca announced.

Bertha tried to repress a laugh, but couldn't. Very little about Rebecca held any surprise these days, yet this teetered on the cliff of absurdity. Planning on marrying a man with whom she had spent no more than a few minutes? Bertha saw it as just another one of her friend's goofy shenanigans.

Adding another serving of foolishness, Rebecca said she planned to tell Bruce that she had been to bed with only one man, the father of her son. Now Bertha openly chortled. She couldn't count the number of men Rebecca had slept with, nor could Rebecca.

Apparently, Rebecca really meant her stated goal of luring him into marriage, because she even told several other people all about it. Despite a fractious relationship with her sister, Dolores, Rebecca shared with her the excitement about the new man. She admitted checking into his credit reports and said that Bruce looked like a "good catch." To Dolores, marriage to a man seemed out of character for her younger sister. Rebecca had made no secret of having a bisexual relationship with Cherie Barnes while living with her. Also, Dolores later revealed, her close friend Diana had also slept with Rebecca several times.

Rebecca revealed even more to Patricia Medina, the woman who had worked with Rebecca's mother in the medical office. She bragged that Bruce was "very well-off" and spoke of his "elderly" parents who had a lot of money. Bruce also had a very good job, she asserted, and made big bucks. And he would inherit even more when his parents passed away. Rebecca repeated to Medina her matrimonial intentions.

A few days later, Bruce followed through with his newfound

courage and called Rebecca. He finally choked out the words asking her to go out with him. They went to dinner together, and followed up with more dates.

One of their favorite restaurants, on César Chávez Boulevard in Boyle Heights, served authentic Mexican food in a setting bursting with color, gaiety, and mariachi music. They usually sat at the third table from the rear entry hall. The restaurant would play an important role in their futures.

When visiting Rebecca's tiny rental house, Bruce parked on the street. Living only a block away, Bertha saw the vehicle sitting there late into the night several times. In telephone conversations between the two women, Rebecca told Bertha that she wanted her to meet Bruce. The introduction finally took place on January 28, 1996, but not under the best of circumstances.

Although Bertha felt sick that day, her own fiancé had brought a few of his friends over to their apartment to watch Super Bowl XXX on television. Usually a gracious hostess, she remained in bed trying to cope with her illness. To make matters worse, that's exactly the time Rebecca decided to drop in by surprise and bring Bruce with her. She slipped into Bertha's bedroom and said, "I'd like you to meet him real quick. He's really nice."

Pleading her case did no good, so Bertha finally wrapped herself in a robe and came out. They shook hands, and exchanged a few pleasantries. She thought Bruce very nice, but needing to lie back down, Bertha asked her fiancé to entertain Bruce and the other guests, then retreated to her bed. While the men watched the Dallas Cowboys outplay the Pittsburgh Steelers, and Diana Ross singing at halftime, Rebecca followed Bertha into the bedroom. She couldn't resist the opportunity to demonstrate her power over the new man in her life.

"Watch," she said to Bertha, "I'm going to give him some attitude, and he'll come crawling."

"Okay, Becky, whatever," Bertha managed to whisper.

"I'm gonna be mad at him and he's gonna come running,

begging me." She disappeared into the living room for fifteen minutes, then returned to Bertha's bedside.

Moments later, a weak knock sounded on the door, and the two women could hear Bruce pleading, "Rebecca, honey . . . please." It revolted Bertha. Her good impression of Bruce slipped down several notches.

With a smirk on her face, Rebecca said, "I have him whipped. He's gonna marry me and I'll have everything." With that, she pranced out of the room like a princess on her way to the coronation.

The entire scene disgusted Bertha so much, she didn't even bother to tell Rebecca of her own imminent marriage.

The Cowboys won, 27 to 17, ending the NFL season. But Bruce Cleland's losing season had just started.

Rebecca and Bruce continued to date, but with no sexual intimacy. She persuaded him to wait by expressing fear that he only wanted her for sex. Also, she convinced Bruce of her chastity, other than that one time with her boy's father, and made sweet talk about wishing to save herself for marriage. No respectable woman of her Hispanic background, she pouted, would give herself in such a way. Meanwhile, she told him, she wasn't happy with the little backyard house she occupied. The larger residence in front was vacant and she wanted to move up there. Would Bruce help her? He readily agreed.

Of course, in the larger house, Rebecca needed more furniture. Bruce accommodated her by purchasing a leather couch and chair, a wall unit, several appliances, and a new bedroom set for her five-year-old son's room. To Bruce's family and pals, he seemed quite fond of the boy.

With the more expansive yard, Rebecca needed something to fill it up. Once at the swap meet, she and Bertha had looked at a nice outdoor spa for sale. She took Bruce to see it, and convinced him that it would be a terrific thing for them to share. Twisting her red lips into a pout, Rebecca said that sitting in the soothing bubbles would calm her "Latin nerves." Bruce bought it, figuratively and literally. The vendor delivered the bulky, crated spa to Rebecca's yard, but she just couldn't seem to get around to having it assembled and connected to a water supply. It remained in the crate, gathering dust.

When the couple went to restaurants or nightclubs, Rebecca told her friends, it embarrassed her to ride in Bruce's aging Oldsmobile. Previous lovers had provided much more luxurious transportation, even a Lamborghini. Bruce wouldn't go that far, but he did agree to an upgrade and soon bought a green 1993 Honda Accord for them to use on dates. Rebecca played at being satisfied, at least temporarily.

With another objective in mind, she batted her eyelashes seductively and persuaded him to take a little ride. They wound up at a boat show in the Pomona fairgrounds, where Rebecca pointed out something she just had to have. Bruce examined the streamlined speedboat equipped with a high-power outboard engine for waterskiing. Unable to resist her tantalizing supplication, and doing everything in his power to please her, he bought it, along with a towing trailer.

The stunning change in Bruce's spending habits left his father and his brother-in-law, Ed Brown, flabbergasted. But they said little about it to him because he seemed happier than he had ever been before. He had obviously fallen in love and wanted more than anything else to keep this woman.

Bertha watched the accumulation of material goods and shook her head. She realized early on that Bruce had been a frugal person. Recalling it, she said, "He dressed in old jeans and Hawaiian shirts, like he bought his clothes at the thrift store. I thought, 'What is this guy going to give her?' But she moved right away from the back house to the front house and got all new furniture. He bought it for her, plus a lot of other stuff. She charged all of it on his credit card. I was like, 'What a fool. What is he thinking?'"

Maybe Mark Twain was correct when he noted, "Of course, no man is entirely in his right mind at any time."

Rebecca had always managed to get what she wanted from men, but this topped anything in the past. She began dropping hints that the green Honda really didn't properly reflect their status, and they really should be seen in something a little newer and classier. Also, she suggested, it would be dangerous to tow the boat with this small car, so they needed a more powerful vehicle.

In March, Rebecca called Bertha to share news about Bruce taking her that morning to meet his parents in South Pasadena. Mrs. Cleland, she said, planned to prepare a nice luncheon for them. Ordinarily, Bertha would have shared her excitement, but on that day she felt terrible again. She had been pregnant for some time. Later describing what happened, Bertha said, "When Rebecca found out I was expecting, she reacted oddly. Some people said it was jealousy. I was at home, very sick. My husband's little brother was there with me."

As soon as Bertha told Rebecca of her sickness and that she feared something serious, Rebecca replied, "You sound weird. What's wrong with you?" She quickly added, "Oh, my gosh, I wish I could help you, but I'm on my way to go meet Bruce's parents."

Not wishing to throw any obstacles in Rebecca's path to the altar, Bertha said, "No, no. You do that, and don't worry about me." After hanging up, Bertha tried to sleep, but a loud knocking on her front door brought her out of it. Her young brother-in-law answered and invited Rebecca inside.

Rushing into the bedroom, Rebecca made sympathetic noises and handed Bertha a handful of pills. "Here," she said, "take these. They'll make you feel better."

With her head spinning, and nearly delirious, Bertha wavered between fear, suspicion, and the desire for relief. Trying to ignore her friend's advice, she shook her head in the negative. Rebecca had never learned to take no for an answer. She simply leaned forward, forced Bertha's mouth open, and pushed several pills down her throat. With a glass of water tilted through Bertha's parted lips, she made certain it was all swallowed. Turning toward the bewildered boy who had watched the whole thing, Rebecca said, "Here, give her a couple of these every hour."

Inexperienced in dealing with the problems of women, he replied, "Well, okay."

Within minutes after Rebecca left, Bertha's world spun out of control. She later described it. "I started going into convulsions. I had a seizure. My eyes rolled back. My husband's poor little brother started freaking out. He gave me the pills and they just slid out of my hand. My mother and my sister Alma walked in when I was having convulsions. They knew something was terribly wrong. They called the paramedics and I went right to the hospital. In the emergency ward, I gave premature birth to my son. He was only two pounds and fifteen ounces, and they kept him in the new infant care unit for forty-five days until I could bring him home. I was sick with severe toxemia and hospitalized, too. My family wanted to file charges. They gave the pills to the paramedics and said that Rebecca had given them to me. Assuming that she was trying to kill me, they called the police. Actually, the medicine turned out to be nothing but sugar pills. I felt bad, and knew she wasn't trying to kill me. She was actually trying to help me."

The event left Bertha with mixed emotions. "My relatives said I was just so dumb for believing Rebecca was my friend, and that she was just manipulating me. They didn't want to have anything to do with her. So I stopped talking to her for quite a while."

Rebecca may have missed having regular contact with her friend Bertha, but she simply diverted all of her energy into her goal to marry Bruce and his money. It still bothered her, though, that he wouldn't spring for a new car. When he asked what was troubling her, she admitted that the green Honda he had purchased to please her no longer met her standards of elegance. She began pressuring him to upgrade their vehicular status. As usual, he gave in to her demands. After shopping several agencies in March, close to his birthday, he bought a brand-new four-door SUV, a 1996 midnight blue Toyota 4Runner with a tan leather interior. He had a trailer hitch installed for towing the boat previously acquired to please his lady.

They used the Toyota for all social activities, and Rebecca took over the Honda for shopping or other chores. For her personal expenditures, Bruce obtained duplicates of his credit cards and allowed Rebecca uncontrolled use of them.

Bruce's romance brought new vigor and enthusiasm to his daily existence, and life seemed rosy for him, until a tragedy hit with the devastating force of a landslide.

Chapter 6

Her Pot of Gold

Ed Brown and his wife, Patricia, lived comfortably in Orange County, and celebrated family holidays with the Clelands, their child's grandparents and uncle, Bruce. Patricia worked regularly as a teacher until she began feeling ill just before the couple approached their tenth wedding anniversary. Doctors diagnosed her with a particularly dangerous form of cancer. It metastasized quickly and took a heavy toll as she underwent treatments. Every effort to save her proved futile.

Patricia died on June 22, 1996, at age forty-five. Bruce reeled in shock and emotional pain at the loss of his sister. Her bereaved husband and grieving parents arranged for burial in Rose Hills Cemetery, about ten miles from the Clelands' South Pasadena home, near the intersection of the I-605 and I-60 Freeways. Harold and Theda had long ago purchased burial plots for themselves on an upper slope of the hillside memorial park. They used the site to inter their daughter, and bought space for themselves in a lower valley. Rose Hills is aptly named for one of the most beautiful, expansive rose gardens to be found anywhere. From Patricia's tranquil grave site, those attending the services could cushion the pain by gazing over green waves of manicured lawn, checkered with glistening headstones, and appreciate its offer of soothing serenity.

A black granite headstone marks the resting place. It is etched in white with the words: *Patricia Ann Cleland Brown—A Cherished Daughter, Sister, Wife, Mother, Friend and Teacher Who Loved Her Lord. April 2, 1951–June 22, 1996.* A pair of hands, clasped in prayer, also decorates the memorial plaque.

The heartbreaking loss of their daughter prompted thoughts by Harold and Theda Cleland about Bruce's future, and theirs. They hoped to see him married and settled in a home of his own before their departure from earth. Theda would later reveal that Bruce also expressed a concern of being left all alone someday when his parents passed on.

Harold and his wife had met and accepted Rebecca, with certain misgivings. Wisdom usually comes with age and experience, and the older couple's background had taught them how to recognize sincerity versus subterfuge. They didn't voice any specific concerns about Rebecca, but they couldn't repress suspicion of her motives. Inwardly, Harold and Theda hoped Bruce might find someone else for marriage. But they kept their wishes to themselves. Bruce seemed so elated and upbeat around Rebecca, and the devoted parents didn't want to interfere with his happiness.

When the covert aspects of Bruce's job with TRW took him to other continents, Rebecca's social life didn't come to a grinding halt. She had kept in contact with stripper-dancer Dave Romero for years, and she still liked spending time with him. Even though Romero didn't have bulky muscles, he kept in good physical shape.

Rebecca, too, took measures for enhancing her body, mostly the figure and face. But rather than endure rigorous workouts, she consulted a plastic surgeon. Using Bruce's credit cards in his absence, she paid for breast enlargement surgery, a rhinoplasty to perfect her nose, and collagen injections to her lips.

Certainly, Bruce must have realized her extravagance when he paid his monthly bills, but he never complained.

In addition, Rebecca discovered the controversial product called fen-phen to help control her weight. A combination of the drugs fenfluramine and phentermine, the medication later hit headlines for allegations of causing heart problems among women who took it for dieting purposes. It worked for Rebecca's purposes, and she slimmed down again.

Bertha Awana and her sister Alma later expressed their own opinions that dietary drugs, and perhaps other things Rebecca ingested for mood enhancement, affected her behavior. Said Bertha, "Rebecca did drink quite a bit, and after meeting Bruce, she used a lot of fen-phen. I know, because she would be ballooning, then she would get real skinny. I would tell her to stop taking it and hurting herself. She wouldn't eat. Sometimes we would go to Tijuana, to those pharmacies, and Rebecca would buy that stuff. I remember that she had big breasts, but was skinny from there down."

Asked why Rebecca felt it necessary to undergo breast enhancement surgery, Bertha answered, "For the attention. She always needed that. It upset me. Why do that to your body? She hid it from me for a while, then I found out from a friend that she did it, a breast job and collagen, and then her nose. She didn't need it, but always wanted to impress people or get their attention. For Rebecca, nothing was more important than being in the spotlight, and she would do anything to achieve that. She wanted to walk in the room and for everybody to see her, and not look at anyone else. Being a good dancer helped, too. She used it to get guys' attention. She had all that going and just always wanted everyone to admire her. I don't know if it's because she didn't have that at home. Her home and family life was ridiculous. Very sad. Very lonely."

Another woman familiar with the Rebecca's life ventured a highly credible opinion about the breast enhancement surgery. "Well-endowed women, especially those who have gone through childbirth, start to sag in their late twenties. After going braless during their younger years, women can suffer the effects of gravity taking its toll. Being well-endowed, Rebecca probably used the plastic surgery to give herself the lift she needed to look perky."

When Bruce returned from one of his overseas journeys, Rebecca pouted that she had never had the good fortune of traveling. Well, that could be fixed, he promised. Immediately he arranged for a vacation in Hawaii.

Friends of the couple wondered if their trip had brought them together sexually. No, Rebecca asserted. Her closest confidante, Bertha, recalled it. "She always told me that she wasn't giving him anything, as far as sexual. She pretended to Bruce that she was saving herself for marriage. He apparently believed her." Also, Rebecca leaned on a pretext of fear that Bruce only wanted her for sex, said Bertha.

To more than one of her pals, Rebecca repeated her intent to wed Bruce, and cited the proverbial caveat: "You don't sleep with them until you are married. Why would a man buy the cow when he can get the milk for free?"

If Rebecca didn't offer Bruce personal intimacy, she perhaps made up for it with other talents. Known among her social circle as an excellent chef, Rebecca specialized in preparing spicy Mexican meals, and no other taste treat appealed more to Bruce. Said Bertha, "She was a wonderful cook. She made a lot of spicy Spanish dishes and he loved that kind of food. Also, she made Italian. She told me that when they were growing up, as kids, she and her sisters had to do a lot of the cooking. She admitted that her skill in the kitchen helped a lot in getting Bruce. He loved her cooking."

Another trip, this one to Mexico, took Rebecca and Bruce to ancient Zacatecas, located in the central highlands at an elevation of more than eight thousand feet. Once a silver-mining community, the charming city of about 120,000 residents evolved into a tourist destination featuring cobblestone streets, colonial homes, and a magnificent twin-towered cathedral dating from the mid 1700s. This time Rebecca's sisters accompanied them to attend a cousin's wedding, and Bruce paid everyone's way.

By the end of summer, Bertha had forgiven the episode of Rebecca's pills. Friendships cannot be just tossed out like yesterday's trash. Bertha recalled, "We had been estranged for some time. Finally I snuck over there and she saw my baby, and starts crying and we start hugging. She begged me to forgive her and said that she never meant to hurt me. She just wanted to help me."

The two women cautiously resumed the old pattern of companionship. Future events would take another serious toll.

Bruce's amazing transformation in spending habits after he met Rebecca baffled his family and friends. Bertha later spoke of his generosity in social situations, when she and her pals group-dated with Bruce and Rebecca. "He was a nice guy. Fun guy, very nice. They were fun together. He did drink, too. Almost every time I saw him, he was a little high. He would always take us out to eat and pay for everything. And she was *sooo* bad. She would go out to dinner, and bring her posse. She would bring me and other friends, her little entourage."

Even Uncle Arturo tagged along for food at Bruce's expense. In one restaurant, Bertha went with Rebecca to the ladies room, and again complained about her uncle's groping, but it did little good. As they returned to the table, Bertha snapped a photo of him sitting close to Bruce, waving at the camera. She recalled, "We always went as a group, because I don't think she wanted to be alone with Bruce. He was cool with it, and didn't care. The more the merrier, to him. He was very funny, too. She was always all over him. *'Oh, honey, baby, sweetheart.'* So lovey-dovey with him. She never exposed herself around him, like other times. She didn't have to. She was trying to be proper with Bruce, because she planned to marry him."

With other men, Bertha noted, Rebecca had shown an attitude of "what am I going to get from you?" And then she would dump them. But not with Bruce. Her whole pattern of behavior turned inside out. Said Bertha, "She was trying to be proper and portray someone she really wasn't. She wanted to marry him and he would be her pot of gold."

The subject of living together came up for discussion between Bruce and Rebecca, but she informed him again that respectable Hispanic women didn't do that. Their families would never allow it. Under no circumstances would she share a bedroom or even a house with him.

From that stance, the issue of marriage turned serious.

The first step, of course, would be to seal the engagement with a diamond ring. Rebecca found the perfect one, a glittery two-carat marquis stone set in gold and flanked on both sides by smaller diamonds. To friends, she revealed Bruce paid about $10,000 for it.

Taking the next step, Bruce and Rebecca discussed the possibility of buying a home, where they could share their wedded bliss. They began searching for a suitable place and located one on a prestigious elevated lot among the rolling hills of Whittier, twelve miles east of Los Angeles.

The quiet community, incorporated in 1898, had drawn Quakers among its first settlers, and is still associated in many minds with that religion. Early residents named the growing town after John Greenleaf Whittier. Even though the poet never visited the area, he wrote of it, ending an eight-line rhyme with the phrase "I leave Thee with My Name." Former U.S. president Richard Nixon played football at the local high school and at Whittier College. Academy Award–winning movie animator John Lasseter (no known relationship to the author) also attended Whittier High School. One of the most beautiful and largest cemeteries in the world is located on bucolic hills just north of the city limits, where Bruce's sister had been interred in June 1996.

The upscale house they found, with four bedrooms, three baths, swimming pool, and a breathtaking view, carried a price tag of about $350,000, a hefty sum in 1996. Bruce invited his widower brother-in-law, Ed Brown, to help him examine it. Brown had been in the construction and house painting business for nearly thirty years and Bruce valued his expert opinions. The two drove up Colima Road and turned into an ascending, curved driveway, passed a rough-stone retaining wall, and parked near a covered patio entry. They scanned a high white stack-stone chimney projecting above the one-story, L-shaped home, then entered for a walk-through of the 3,200-foot structure.

Bruce and Ed first surveyed the living room, taking notice of a fireplace and plush brown carpeting, then a family room featuring built-in light oak bookshelves covering one entire wall. A sliding glass door and ample windows provided a view of the curving, kidney-shaped swimming pool, outdoor bar, and generous lawn area containing a swing-and-slide set for children. The expansive kitchen included red-oak cabinets, laminate plank wood floor, and a built-in refrigerator. A white-tile countertop and sink jutted out, giving access from the family room as well. Both men knew that any woman would love the formal dining room with walls covered in patterned fabric and a large ceiling fan. In the master bedroom, another ceiling fan adorned with crystal lamps kept the air circulating. Light-colored walls contrasted with the darker knotty-pine surfaces of an adjacent guest bedroom.

Outside, both men scanned a magnificent, panoramic view of green rolling hills and valleys. Just below, they could see the Friendly Hills Country Club and golf course. Tropical banana trees lined one side of the yard, and several potted palm trees decorated the pool's perimeter, complementing towering palms swaying in the distant breeze. To the northeast stood Mount San Antonio, known as "Old Baldy," which would soon be capped with snow.

Neither Ed nor Bruce had any doubts about purchasing the spectacular home. With his choice made, Bruce began making plans.

Rebecca, too, granted her enthusiastic approval of the Whittier house, then gave Bruce a little frown. He asked why.

Slipping into her virtuous schoolgirl persona, she explained. If Bruce decided to buy the property, shouldn't they be married first? Wouldn't it look bad to acquire a home before tying the matrimonial knot? What would people think? It sounded reasonable to Bruce, so he agreed. But a major problem popped up. Rebecca wanted a full-blown church wedding, and that couldn't be arranged in just a few days. It would take weeks or months of planning and preparation.

Rebecca demurely suggested a solution. She could become his wife in a private civil union, and then later cement it with a formal, lavish Catholic-church wedding.

To Bruce, nothing sounded better. At last, he could make their relationship permanent and experience the connubial bliss of marriage to the woman he loved. He didn't know that his future bride had confided in her friend Bertha another reason for the civil marriage. She wanted her name on the new home's deed.

Eager and energetic, Rebecca instantly launched extravagant preparations for what she regarded as the most important events of her life. At a bridal show she attended, Rebecca saw examples of wedding pictures taken by a professional photographer named Elizabeth Lamb. Impressed with their quality, she took a business card and called Lamb in the first week of October.

Her future association with the photographer would turn out to have implications far deeper than either woman could have ever guessed.

Chapter 7

Bachelorette Party

Elizabeth "Beth" Lamb generally worked weddings in Orange County, a considerable distance from Whittier. So, when she received a call from Rebecca Salcedo in Maywood, Elizabeth listened and initially tried to think of a nice way to reject the job. But as the conversation progressed, and extended to nearly two hours, Elizabeth reconsidered. The potential client made it clear that money was no object, and that she wanted the best package available.

Another self-imposed rule against going to clients' homes, a personal-safety precaution, and to avoid expensive travel or waste of time, also fell by the wayside. Rebecca had a persuasive personality, and talked Elizabeth into driving to a neighborhood in Maywood she normally would have circumvented. They agreed on an appointment for October 14 at two-thirty. Elizabeth wouldn't be able to stay long, since she had an evening commitment for a Parent-Teacher Association (PTA) meeting.

The attractive mother of three young children, Elizabeth Lamb had studied photography as a teenager, and worked at it on a part-time basis after graduating from high school. While snapping pictures at a friend's wedding, she ran into a professional photographer who made her his assistant and taught her the finer points. Eventually she started her own business, working out of her home mostly on weekends, allowing the rest of the time for her kids. With her Mormon background, she maintained high moral values and devoted considerable time to duties as the local PTA president. The superior quality of her work kept Elizabeth busy nearly every Saturday of the year.

Arriving at Rebecca's rental house, Elizabeth wondered about her decision. Later recalling it, she said, "I drove to Maywood, not a very nice part of town. But her house inside was really, really nice, all new furniture and a beautiful stereo. I could tell right away that she was a real character, because she had blue contact lenses on, along with a perfect pedicure and manicure. The full facial facade. She proceeded to tell me all about her life. She commented that her fiancé was out of town on a business trip and left credit cards with her. She needed new furniture, so what was she to do?" Elizabeth laughed in speaking of her initial meeting with Rebecca.

During the conversation, Elizabeth noticed photographs of Rebecca and Bruce on a cruise ship. A nice-looking guy, she thought. Another snapshot showed Rebecca wearing a bathing suit. The client said it was taken in Hawaii when Bruce took her there, and hastened to add that they hadn't slept together on either trip. A surprised look on Elizabeth's face elicited much more than she wanted to hear from Rebecca. The client volunteered that she had made Bruce get separate rooms during their travels, even on the ship, and that she hadn't had sex with him.

Prattling on and on, Rebecca told Elizabeth that her own parents had passed away, and that Bruce's mother planned to help her shop for a wedding dress. She had recently resigned from her work, she said, because planning for a wedding was a full-time job.

Elizabeth noticed an ostentatious ring on Rebecca's third finger, left hand, and later offered a description of it. "She had a beautiful engagement ring. It had hundreds of diamonds, like from knuckle to knuckle. It was gorgeous." Rebecca, spilling even more personal information about her relationship, emphasized again that no sex had taken place, and repeated the old saw about men not buying the cow if they got the milk for free.

Rebecca eventually got around to selecting from the various photo packages Elizabeth offered. She picked the largest and costliest, about $2,500, then ordered extra pictures worth an additional $1,700. It amazed Elizabeth. In her experience, most clients wait until after the wedding to make supplemental orders. Rebecca wanted three full albums, one for each of her sisters and one for Bruce's parents. She said, "I don't want just one portrait, I want five big ones. I'll fill my whole house with them."

The deal would also include prewedding photo sessions in which Elizabeth would take the couple to a park or beach and pose them wearing casual clothing. These types of pictures are often displayed near the church entry on the wedding day.

After the complex transaction, which took more than three hours, Elizabeth drove back to her Orange County home and told her husband all about Rebecca, her order, and the way she had openly spoken of financial shenanigans to spend as much of her fiancé's money as possible. Listening carefully to Elizabeth's amused narrative, her husband said, "You need to call this man and tell him to run from this woman as fast as possible."

Even if Elizabeth Lamb had made such a call, it is unlikely that Bruce would have listened to the advice.

On Friday, October 25, 1996, much of the nation speculated about the next months's presidential election pitting Republican candidate Bob Dole against incumbent Bill Clinton. Others anticipated Saturday's World Series game between the New York Yankees and Atlanta Braves, or talked about the O.J. Simpson civil trial taking place in Santa Monica, California.

Oblivious to all these outside distractions, Bruce and Rebecca used that day to bond themselves together in civil nuptials.

That night, Rebecca explained to her new husband that the honeymoon would not take place until after the Catholic wedding. Disappointed, Bruce once again complied with her wishes, returned to his own place, and went to bed by himself.

A few days later, he paid a down payment on the Whittier house. During the escrow period, he and Rebecca went on a shopping spree to supplement furniture already in their new residence. He bought two new sofas, a pool table, and a beautiful four-poster bed, with a colonial-style scrolled headboard. It would be ideal for lovemaking with his new bride, after the big wedding and honeymoon.

They set a firm date for the church wedding, January 18, 1997.

As soon as escrow closed on the Whittier house in late November, Rebecca and her little son moved in. Bruce helped her transport furniture he had purchased for her in Maywood. If his parents and friends looked with a skeptical eye at the arrangement in which Rebecca could occupy the home without Bruce, they kept silent. He seemed patient enough in accepting Rebecca's request to wait for the church ceremony before sharing living quarters with her.

It made for a much longer drive for Bruce to take Rebecca home after dates, all the way to Whittier, after which he would return to his place at the beach. Sometimes, if Bruce drank a little too much, Rebecca would drive them from the Whittier house and back. When leaving the restaurant on César Chávez Boulevard, or from Uncle Arturo's house when they visited him, she always chose the same route—driving southwest on Lorena Street for access to the I-60 Freeway and an easy cruise east to the hilltop home. She consistently refused permission for Bruce to stay overnight with her.

Rebecca scheduled two more appointments for Elizabeth Lamb to visit at the Whittier house and discuss changes to the wedding photo arrangements. But she canceled both sessions, once due to Bruce's absence on a business trip, and the second time because she didn't feel good. Rebecca explained candidly to Elizabeth that she had visited a plastic surgeon to have breast enhancement surgery, for the second time, and hadn't fully recovered yet.

Lamb thought it remarkable how Rebecca called her numerous times and frankly discussed personal matters as if they had been close friends for years. She later spoke of it. "There were a couple of past brides that I became good friends with, but I usually keep it on a business level. I try to be nice and personable. You can get into trouble making clients your friends."

Not only did Rebecca refuse permission for Bruce to live in or even stay overnight at the Whittier house, but she also demanded that he call in advance before showing up, day or night. With most men, this would probably send the suspicion meter spinning out of control. Bruce, though, had zero experience in these matters, and feared losing the woman to whom he had finally given his heart. He complied with her wishes once more.

Rebecca's friend Bertha later mused about it. "I don't think he was allowed to go over there. She told me Bruce had to call in advance. When he wanted to show up, he needed to let her know in advance. I'm sure she told him, 'Oh, honey, my relatives are here and I don't want to make them leave. Just give me plenty of time to get rid of them.' After she got the house, people she hadn't paid much attention to for years, like her cousin Alvaro, suddenly wanted to be there, all of a sudden becoming her closest relatives. So she always had lots of guests there."

In addition to family, other people from Rebecca's past

came back into her life. Said Bertha, "Cherie Barnes, the woman Rebecca fell in love with and lived with for a while, started coming over a lot, even though Cherie had kicked her out. Rebecca was always in love with Cherie and always tried to get back with her. Cherie had found another woman, but kept a friendship with Rebecca."

More than a few of the guests were men. Commenting on this, Bertha said, "Bruce seemed very gullible. She would just say the man was her cousin and Bruce was okay with that. I was over there all the time. She was always having people over. Parties. Lots of drinking. Everybody having a blast. She was always very entertaining. We would call her 'the hostess with the mostess.' She was always so lively. She would have catered foods, all kinds of drinks, anything you wanted. She was an awesome hostess. Always very, very giving. And always buying it all with his money or credit cards. She wasn't working at any time during her relationship with Bruce."

Christmas and New Year's Eve passed quietly for Bruce and Rebecca in deference to the pending wedding. They celebrated the holidays with her young son and Bruce's parents.

As the big date approached, Rebecca decided that she wanted to throw one last wild bash for her female pals, and she invited about thirty of them to a bachelorette party at the Whittier house. She picked Saturday night, January 11, one week before the scheduled wedding. From a long list of women, she called Bertha, both of her sisters, Cherie Barnes, and even Elizabeth Lamb.

Asked years later if she attended, Lamb rolled her eyes skyward and replied, "Not this Mormon mom!" Rebecca, she said, tried to entice her by saying they would have plenty of margaritas, games, and even male strippers. The hostess with the mostess completely misjudged Elizabeth, who replied, "You have no idea who I am. That's not my lifestyle."

While the great majority of invitations from Rebecca went out to women, she telephoned at least one man. Dave Romero, the male stripper and promoter of his own dancing group, answered the call. Rebecca flirted briefly, chatted about their good times together, and asked if he would provide some entertainment for her party. Years later, he recalled it. "She wanted, like, three guys. So I couldn't get there to her house until eleven o'clock, maybe even midnight. But I sent one of my guys to arrive at nine-thirty and start it off. Then the other dancer and I would show up."

For additional entertainment, Rebecca invited a fortune-teller to attend the party. According to her friends, she loved hearing predictions of how her life might turn out.

Bruce came to see Rebecca that afternoon, with the understanding that he must leave before her friends showed up for a "bridal shower" party. As usual, he didn't question her demands.

Dozens of cars lined the Whittier house driveway on that Saturday night. The first few guests arrived before Bruce's departure. One of them, Jovita Garay, a coworker and friend of Rebecca's sister Dolores's, would later recall his gentlemanly demeanor. To her, he seemed like a very pleasant man and quite dedicated to Rebecca.

Soon after Bruce's departure, Rebecca led Jovita and several other guests on a tour of the house. With obvious pride, the hostess pointed out all of the things Bruce had bought for her, making it clear that she had personally picked out everything, giving him no choices in the matter.

Dolores brought another guest, a gay woman named Diana, whom she and Rebecca had known for years.

A din of female chatter soon filled the spacious family room, the area reserved for a billiard table, which hadn't yet arrived, and at poolside. The kitchen served as the hub of activity. Fountains of booze flowed into ready glasses, and enough food to feed a convention filled tables and counters. Music blared from loudspeakers. Shouts and laughter bubbled over silly games featuring lingerie and other prizes.

More arrivals swelled the crowd to at least thirty women. A shriek of delight erupted from the family room when the first male stripper arrived and went into his routine.

Bertha had also accepted an invitation, and noticed that Rebecca's mood changed in the party's midst after she consumed several drinks. She seemed suddenly depressed and started crying.

"What's wrong?" her friend asked.

Rebecca sobbed. "I don't know what I'm doing, why I got into this marriage commitment with Bruce. Maybe it wasn't the right thing to do. I'm really not in love with him."

Trying to sort things out for her friend, Bertha replied, "Well, don't marry him, then. Why are you doing it?"

In a tearful slur, Rebecca admitted her greed. "Well, look at all this. I don't want to let it all go. Look what I have already."

"So what?" Bertha asked. "You're not happy."

Rebecca shook her head. "No. I have to go through with this. The wedding invitations are out. We already have all these plans. I have to go through with it."

Resigned to Rebecca's stubborn ways, Bertha could only grimace and mutter, "Whatever."

Few of the guests noticed Rebecca's mood dip or her rapid recovery. The raucous party grew even louder with the arrival of Dave Romero and the third dancer. They stripped to throbbing music, and then embraced tipsy guests to whirl around the floor with them. Some noticed that Dave and Rebecca seemed glued to one another. One of her sisters in attendance recalled, "Becky was being flirtatious, rubbing herself all over him."

Bertha noticed that Rebecca's former female lover, Cherie Barnes, didn't show up. "If she had," Bertha later commented, "Becky wouldn't have been so close with Dave."

Years later, Bertha reminisced about the evening. "It didn't get crazy until the strippers got there, and everybody was drinking. Some of the ladies got sick. It was a typical bachelorette party. The strippers danced with the girls. A lot of fun. The guys didn't get naked, just down to their G-strings. At least while I was there. I would have left right away if it got any wilder. I had just had my son a couple of months earlier.

I really didn't even want to go. But·she made me feel bad. So I went with a friend of mine, just watching, and remained very sober through the whole thing. When you have a kid, things change. My whole outlook about a lot of things was just different. So I wasn't one of the drunk ones. I left with my girlfriend about midnight. The party probably went on the rest of the night, until morning. A lot of the ladies spent the night there. You can use your imagination about what happened after I left."

As she said her good-byes to other guests, Bertha searched for Rebecca. "I go into her bedroom looking for her and she's in there making out with Dave. All he had on was little Speedo shorts, the ones he had worn in his dance performance. After that, I don't know what they did. I didn't actually see anything except some hugging. Maybe she was just crying to him. I don't know. He seemed to be there just holding her."

Did she think they had intercourse?

"Yeah, they probably did. She could be disgusting at times."

Eventually Dave Romero would clear up any mystery about sexual contact with Rebecca. He said, "We just kinda came together at the end of the night. By the time I got there, they had already been drinking and having a good time. She was a little bit intoxicated, so she was all over me. She looked slimmer than usual . . . facial features, body. You know, she looked good."

Did they have sex?

"Yes, we did."

According to Rebecca's sister, the future bride had sex with more than one person that night. She also shared her bed with Diana, the woman Dolores had brought to the party.

Dolores had previously met Bruce's parents, and held them in high esteem. To her, they were "nice people." Her youngest sister's indiscretions with other men, and women, infuriated Dolores. She thought of telling Bruce, but she doubted that he would be able to see through his blind love. So Dolores did the next best thing, in her view. She called Bruce's mother, Theda. Later speaking of it, she said, "I told her that if she didn't believe me, she should hire a private investigator and the PI could get proof in the form of pictures, which do not lie."

Someone apparently leaked contents of the conversation between Dolores and Theda. Dolores found a "threatening" message on her answering machine. She later stated that Rebecca said in an angry voice, "You shouldn't be meddling in my business if you know what's good for you."

Chapter 8

Kick Off to a Honeymoon

When Rebecca's hangover from the bachelorette party subsided, she resumed preparations for the wedding, attending to countless last-minute details. She spent hours on the phone, checking to see if friends and relatives who hadn't responded to the mailed invitations planned to attend.

Previously she had agreed to an appointment with Elizabeth Lamb on the morning of January 13 for an "engagement sitting" in which she and Bruce would pose together. It puzzled Elizabeth when Rebecca, without stating any reason, canceled the session. Another attempt by Lamb to call Rebecca reached only the answering machine and her message in a low, throaty, erotic voice. Later laughing about it, Lamb said, "Now, let me tell you about Rebecca. When I first called her and heard her recorded answer, it was in a very sensuous voice. 'Hello, you've reached Rebecca. I'm not in . . . ,' with sexy music playing in the background. I remember telling her,

'Wow, you've really got a sexy voice.' She said, 'Oh, I know, that's what everyone tells me.' She was so full of herself."

Rebecca, determined to reach every relative she hoped would attend the nuptials, made a call to a male cousin in Texas, Robert Diaz. She thought he should be a member of the wedding party. He would later express shock about Rebecca's announcement of marriage, saying, "The last time I saw her before that, she was living with another woman."

Diaz accepted Rebecca's invitation and traveled to California a few days before January 18. In the whirl of excitement, he met Bruce, his parents, and Bruce's brother-in-law, Ed Brown. Together the men went to a tuxedo rental shop to be fitted for the stiff, formal attire. Diaz would later express great admiration for the Cleland family. Considering a move to California, Diaz asked Bruce if any job opportunities existed with his employer, TRW. Bruce suggested that Diaz prepare a résumé after which he would try to help him. Thrilled with such an opportunity, Diaz shook Bruce's hand with added warmth.

On Saturday, January 18, activities began at the Whittier house, where Elizabeth Lamb arrived early to preserve the celebration on film. Afterward, a caravan of cars headed west and drove sixteen miles to a beautiful Catholic Church in San Marino, a city of extreme wealth at the eastern border of Bruce's hometown, South Pasadena.

The eye-catching Saints Felicitas and Perpetua Church occupies three acres on the corner of San Gabriel Boulevard and Huntington Drive. Built in 1948, in an early Italian architectural style, its flat, wheat-colored exterior walls are made of reinforced concrete. Red tile caps the roof and portico, which features a triple-arched entry above a stairway leading from the sidewalk. Over the center arch is a circular stained-glass window, and to one side is a stark bell tower thrusting ten stories toward heaven.

Interior lighting hanging from dark ceiling beams casts a

golden glow on the reflective marble floor and high-backed wooden pews. Thirty-two stained-glass windows decorate the upper walls, each one representing a separate saint. A breathtaking circular window at the back filters afternoon sunlight through a depiction of Christ's resurrection.

It is a place of serene harmony and moral values. But the church's appellation relates to tragic death. It had been named for two martyred women who were led into a Roman arena, mauled by animals, and ultimately stabbed to death by gladiators.

As the wedding crowd gathered, a mariachi band arrived with violins, trumpets, guitars, and an accordion. Seven men, wearing black and silver-spangled outfits, with bolero jackets and embroidered sombreros, filled the air with traditional Mexican music.

Elizabeth Lamb mingled, pointing her cameras at everyone and repeatedly clicking the shutter. She chatted with Bruce's parents, and learned that she and Harold, who she thought was "very nice," had a mutual interest in cameras.

Lamb would recall, "At the church, the whole wedding was Rebecca's family. She was very dramatic. All the groomsmen were her cousins, except for Ed Brown. From Bruce's side, only Ed, Harold, and Teddy were there. It was one of the hardest weddings I've ever photographed. Rebecca wasn't ready. She was a total drama queen. Her uncle Arturo was in my face, too close to me, in my way, every picture. He was behind her and they acted like they were lovers. When they did the grand entrance, Arturo was right next to her. I thought it strange that Rebecca referred to him as her dad."

At last, with everyone seated inside, Felix Mendelssohn's immortal "Wedding March" reverberated throughout the interior, from entry to altar, and wall to wall. It drew muffled sobs and aching throats, as it has for 150 years. Few people know that it was originally composed for use in an 1842 production of William Shakespeare's play *A Midsummer Night's Dream.* More than one person occupying the pews hoped the event wouldn't turn out for Bruce to be a midwinter evening's nightmare.

Bruce stood at the altar beside Ed Brown, who acted as his best man, looking toward the entry in eager anticipation of sighting Rebecca.

The bride, dressed in virginal white lace, made her grand appearance and marched up the aisle, accompanied by her uncle Arturo and her bridesmaid sister, Dolores. Arturo appeared a little unsteady on his feet as he trudged forward in preparation for his role of giving Rebecca to her groom. One member of the party videotaped the processional. The images would one day appear on a television program called *Hard Copy*.

Rebecca and Bruce exchanged vows among genuflections, blessings, and a traditional ceremony. Bruce accepted the gold band from little Ryan, Rebecca's son, who acted as ring bearer. Grinning with delight, he proudly slipped a band on Rebecca's finger and she reciprocated with a ring for him. Bruce gave her the customary kiss and beamed like a man entering paradise.

Bertha observed the ceremony with mixed feelings. She later recalled, "Rebecca asked me to be her maid of honor, but I didn't, because my husband hated her. She was upset about that. I think he saw through her. I asked if it was okay for me just to be there. I watched, and thought the whole thing seemed phony. And sad." Bertha noted the wedding's price tag, about $40,000, and prayed that it wouldn't lead to grief for Bruce.

Back in their cars, some of the people drove to a nearby country club. A posh and private playground for the rich and famous, the enclave boasted a membership of mostly "old money" families who believe in tradition, and think of themselves as the upper crust. Arrangements had been made to host dozens of guests, but not all of them showed up. Fortunately, friends of the Cleland family, who had not made it to the wedding, chose to enjoy the reception.

The mariachi band made the trip from San Marino, to the pleasure of Rebecca and her uncle Arturo, who loved the nostalgic harmonies they played, such as *"Cielito Lindo"* and *"La Golondrina."* Neither of them paid much attention to a rented disk jockey's selections of pop and easy-listening tunes, but some of the other guests enjoyed his contribution.

Tables had been set with crystal, linen napkins, silver, and fresh flowers, including orchids. Expensive champagne, wine, and cocktails were unlimited. Perhaps the setting frightened off many of Rebecca's friends and families not accustomed to such affluent surroundings.

Rebecca's sister Dolores stood up and delivered a touching speech, wishing the newlyweds happiness for a long time. Neither her words nor expression betrayed a secret she held about them.

Elizabeth Lamb continued to snap pictures. Years later, in her recollection, she described a vexing problem. "When they did the toast, her uncle Arturo was right there. When they cut the cake, he was right next to her. I had a hard time photographing it without him being a part of everything. A lot of kissy-face, touchy-feely stuff. He was drunk, in my face, and touchy-feely to me, too." Lamb finally had to tell him, in no uncertain terms, to leave her alone.

Bertha spoke approvingly of the reception. " It was beautiful and lavish, just beautiful. But there were a lot of empty chairs. Most of Rebecca's family did not show up. Nearly everyone there was from his family and circle of friends. Her family was missing in action. It was just Dolores, Yvonne, Arturo, me, our friend Diana, and a couple of other people. It was all very nice, with no disruptions or crazy stuff. Everything was lovely. To me, the church wedding was pretty phony, but the reception was very nice and real, and not rowdy. She and Bruce seemed happy, laughing, contented. Everyone had a good time, with food, music, and dancing. Maybe when the booze kicked in, everybody kind of mellowed out. At church there was a lot of tension."

In the evening, Bruce and his bride left for a honeymoon in Hawaii. That's when the real disaster began.

Chapter 9

Am I Supposed to Satisfy Myself?

Photographer Elizabeth Lamb heard every sickening detail soon after the newlyweds returned to Whittier. Expecting a call from Rebecca regarding arrangements to review the wedding photo proofs, Elizabeth answered her phone one morning. The shrieking voice of Rebecca assaulted her ear. "Oh, my God, Beth," the bride complained, "You're not going to believe what happened." Their honeymoon, she said, had been a total nightmare. Bruce hadn't been able to perform his sexual duties, despite Rebecca "trying everything." She had even taken "trashy lingerie" with her to arouse him, but "nothing worked."

In shock, wondering why this client would choose to unload all of these revolting intimate details on her, Elizabeth couldn't find words to respond. Rebecca growled in disgust as she told of catching her husband masturbating. To make it worse, the furious bride offered vivid descriptions of how horrible it was.

This poor guy, thought Elizabeth. *I'm only the photographer and she's telling me all this dirt.* Rebecca continued without a pause, lamenting the discovery that Bruce had been a virgin. "Can you believe it?" Rebecca asked without expecting an answer. "I wish he had told me before the wedding, because he didn't know what he was doing. And it was the most frustrating experience I've ever had." Unrelenting, Rebecca said, "He's like a sick puppy dog following me around. He's overdue for a breast-feeding and needs to go back home to his mommy."

Over the next few days, Rebecca called Elizabeth several times, managing to discuss the photos between bouts of additional complaining about Bruce and his amatory inadequacies.

Esther Lederer, better known as advice columnist Ann Landers, wrote, *Women complain about sex more often than men. Their gripes fall into two categories: (1) Not enough. (2) Too much.*

Ed Brown, Bruce's brother-in-law, found a message from Rebecca on his answering machine. He punched the replay button and heard her crying, saying that he needed to call her. Concerned that something bad had happened to Bruce, or maybe to one of his parents, Brown responded immediately. It jolted him when Rebecca began an outpouring of complaints about the honeymoon, providing specific details about Bruce's clumsy incompetence in bed.

"Wait a minute," said Brown. "Why are you calling me about this?" Before Rebecca could rationalize it, he continued. "You should probably talk to one of your girlfriends or your sisters. Or maybe get some counseling." After hanging up, he couldn't believe what she had just told him. Brown had only seen Rebecca perhaps four or five times, and always in group situations. They had never spoken to each other, one-on-one, and had certainly never discussed anything personal. The whole incident left Brown unsettled.

Rebecca did turn to a girlfriend, her ever-loyal best pal. Instead of doing it via a telephone conversation, she spoke face-to-face with Bertha. Moaning about the "nightmarish" honeymoon, Rebecca gave Bertha details about Bruce being impotent, ignorant of sexual skills, and artless. He couldn't function, and, as a result, left his poor bride in complete frustration. "What am I going to do?" she whined, letting tears flow down her cheeks. "What am I going to do? He's not a man and has no idea how to take care of a woman. Am I supposed to satisfy myself?"

Knowing Rebecca better than anyone else ever knew her, Bertha felt a tickle of suspicion in the back of her mind. It sounded to her like groundwork for justifying a plan for continuing sexual relations with other lovers. If Rebecca's husband couldn't perform, she would have to go elsewhere, of course. Bertha even doubted the allegations about Bruce's bedroom abilities. The whole complaint sounded to her like excuses being made in advance.

Even though relations with both of her sisters had always been fractious, Rebecca contacted Dolores and repeated her complaints about Bruce. She said that Hawaii had been nice, but sleeping with him caused her to dread every night. He wasn't good in bed and she hated it. Rebecca even hinted that she might want to kick Bruce out of the Whittier house. Reacting in the same manner as Bertha had, Dolores doubted the allegations. She had liked Bruce from the first time they met, and would voice an opinion that he had married the wrong sister.

If Rebecca intended to pave the way for future affairs, it began earlier than anyone knew. Dave Romero, the stripper, would eventually reveal a telephone call from Rebecca he received *during the honeymoon.* According to Romero, Rebecca said she was thinking about him and looked forward to seeing him after she got back into town. She followed through one week after returning home.

With Bruce at work in Redondo Beach, at TRW, Rebecca made a noonday trip to a club where Romero worked. She flirted as if the wedding had never taken place, and they had lunch together. The rendezvous repeated several times over the next few weeks. Romero denied any intimate relations at that time. Those would take place later.

Elizabeth Lamb delivered the wedding photo proofs to Rebecca at the Whittier house on February 3 and briefly explained procedures for ordering prints after selecting which ones she wanted. A few weeks later, Rebecca called to place her order, but again meandered off into personal matters. She told Elizabeth of being miserable and repeated that Bruce "followed her around like a sick puppy dog." He went on a lot of business trips, she said, and she "was glad to see him go."

Bruce did work long hours and his job periodically took him overseas. If Rebecca felt relieved at his absence, she also celebrated it by entertaining friends at the Whittier house, including her stripper and sex partner, Dave Romero.

Bertha still visited her old pal, but grew increasingly uncomfortable with her. During a shopping trip to a local mall, Bertha observed Rebecca making some odd purchases and paying for them, as usual, with plastic that Bruce would pay for. Bertha knew that Bruce had arranged for Rebecca to have several credit cards in her new name, Cleland. She asked, "Who are you buying those things for?" Rebecca admitted they were gifts for Romero, including underwear and other clothing.

Indignant, Bertha asked, "What are you doing?"

In a flippant tone, Rebecca replied, "You know, he doesn't make enough money and can't make ends meet. He hasn't had any really good gigs with that strip stuff. So I'm just helping him out as a friend."

To Bertha, the expenditures reeked of betrayal. She saw irony in the fact that Rebecca had used men for her needs, and now Romero was using her in the same manner.

Evidently perceiving Bertha's aversion, Rebecca offered to buy presents for her, too. Bertha would have no part of it. The friendship had already started to crumble, and the obvious betrayal of Bruce's trust further undermined it.

Romero would later admit accepting whatever Rebecca offered. Asked what she gave him, he replied, "Groceries. Gifts. At the club, she would tip us a lot of money. She would help me out with my rent. I was having some rough times. Financially, she was helping me out a little bit." Rebecca even tried to persuade him to move from his apartment in Huntington Beach and get a place in Whittier so he could be closer to her.

Other men continued to show up at the house, even after the wedding. Bruce's apparent failure to see the warning signals mystified Bertha. "Bruce just seemed to accept it. It was terrible. I don't know if he really believed her or not. I would go over there sometimes to pick her up and go out to a club. When Bruce was there, I could see a sad look on his face, and I felt sorry for him. Rebecca would say, 'Hurry up, just go, just go. Don't even look at him.' I would ask, 'You didn't even tell him we were going?' 'No, no, just go. Come on.'"

Bruce's easygoing nature and acceptance of Rebecca's conduct did not prevent friction between them. Her restlessness increased daily and her agitated behavior overlapped to other people close to her. Dolores particularly resented the way her sister spoke to mutual friend Diana. It didn't seem to matter to Rebecca that she and Diana had previously slept together, even at the bachelorette party. Speaking later about it, Dolores said, "She was fighting with Diana and I got mad. Diana had been a true friend to her. She basically kicked me out of her house because I threw it in her face how she would take anything from her ex-girlfriend [Cherie Barnes] and she treated Diana horrible."

Bruce evidently preferred escape over confrontation. His travels for TRW seemed to increase in the weeks after the wedding and honeymoon. At least two trips to Australia kept him away from home. Harold Cleland asked his son about his domestic life, but got only vague answers in return. Speculation swirled that he tried to stay away from Whittier as much as possible, and might even have kept a motel room near his Redondo Beach workplace.

Most acquaintances of Bruce and Rebecca realized the

marriage turned rocky as soon as the vows had been spoken. It deteriorated with each passing week. Elizabeth Lamb saw early evidence of it when she drove all the way to Whittier for a March 21 appointment with Rebecca. Planning to pick up the photo proofs and firm up wedding album orders, Elizabeth found no one at home. In a subsequent telephone conversation, Rebecca complained about trouble with Bruce and asked Elizabeth to pick up the photo selections at her sister Yvonne's apartment in early April.

Despite the inconvenience, Elizabeth did as she was asked. Afterward, she called Rebecca to request some payment toward the charges of $4,000. Waffling about the amount of money, Rebecca asked if they could meet and perhaps "redo" some of the orders. Elizabeth again complied with her erratic client's wishes and said she would stand by for a time and place.

To her intimates, Rebecca started dropping hints about a possible split with Bruce. She expressed thoughts of divorce, in which she would be eligible to take half of everything Bruce owned, including his investments, salary, savings, and the house valued at $350,000. She would be set for life.

Not long after Bruce's birthday in March 1997, when he turned forty-three, Rebecca attacked. Firing a barrage of acrimonious criticisms at him, she made his life miserable. Repeatedly she told him it would be better if he just moved out and gave her some space.

Another business trip took Bruce across the Pacific to Australia. Still hopeful of salvaging his relationship with Rebecca, he telephoned frequently. But within days after his return, on April 20, just three months afer vowing "till death do us part," they argued violently. She called the police. Finally he surrendered to her demand that he move out. Bruce stuffed his clothing along with personal items into plastic trash bags and returned to his parents' home in South Pasadena. He even left behind the Honda and Toyota 4Runner, planning to drive the aging Oldsmobile again.

Ed Brown paid the Clelands a call and found Bruce "very

distraught, very upset." He had seen his brother-in-law cry only once before, at the time of Patricia's death. But now, Bruce sobbed uncontrollably. Brown tried to cheer him up, patted him on the back, and advised contact with a divorce attorney as soon as possible. He also suggested that Bruce cancel any credit cards to which Rebecca had access. Reluctantly Bruce accepted his advice, and quietly began contacting the financial institutions.

Harold Cleland saw his son's moods shift from sad to a "solemn, disgruntled attitude." The father said, "He was very quiet, didn't want to talk very much. He would come in from work, eat, then go to his bedroom and read. He would never talk. We would try, but he wouldn't answer." Neither parent had ever seen him so depressed. They, too, suggested that he consider a divorce from Rebecca.

At first, Bruce rejected the idea, and told his mom and dad that he really wanted to get back together and "make things right." As the long, miserable days crept by, though, he slowly accepted that his marriage hadn't worked, and agreed to consult an attorney.

Rebecca had openly expressed her intentions of taking everything she could from Bruce. She fully expected, in the case of divorce, to gain half of all assets. Bruce's attorney painted an entirely different picture. He explained that property acquired before marriage, by definition, is separate from community property assets. Only material wealth or treasure acquired after the marriage date, and before separation, is classified as community, under the law. Separate property, in the case of divorce, is awarded to whoever acquired it, while community assets are divided equally between the parties. This means that whatever is brought into the marriage, by the wife or the husband, may be taken out of it by that same person.

Regarding the Whittier house, even though it had been acquired after the civil marriage, and thus in joint title, Rebecca would still not be eligible for any money from it. Rule of law allows the person who puts money into the acquisition of a home to recover that amount before any other equity is divided between the divorcing couple. Bruce had funded the down payment and monthly mortgage costs, which yielded the only equity. This would go back to him, leaving nothing to divide.

A calculation of community property in the marriage of Bruce and Rebecca revealed that no more than $5,000 would be split between them in the case of divorce. Rebecca's perception of riches she would mine from Bruce melted away like the snow on Old Baldy during a hot Santa Ana wind.

If Rebecca wanted to end the marriage—but keep her affluent lifestyle—she would have to develop a new strategy.

Chapter 10

Party Time

With Bruce out of the Whittier house, Rebecca no longer made any pretense of concealing her wild social activities. Dave Romero could visit anytime he wished, and often did, frequently staying overnight. She would prepare dinner and then treat him to a bubble bath. She even invited him to move in with her, but Romero chose not to.

According to one of Rebecca's sisters, at least three other men, and one woman, slept with Rebecca during that period.

Alvaro, the good-looking young cousin, also became a big part of Rebecca's new life. He had been staying in a tiny, dilapidated camper behind a house where one of his sisters lived. Now the father of a young son, Alvaro couldn't afford to provide housing for the mother, his regular girlfriend, or even for himself.

With plenty of unoccupied bedroom space in the Whittier home, Rebecca invited Alvaro to move in. He happily accepted in late May. She granted him full use of the green Honda Bruce had bought for her, and sometimes even allowed him to borrow the new SUV. The vehicles came in handy for helping his brother Jose, who had broken his right arm and needed to wear a splint for several weeks.

Later asked if Alvaro ever shared Rebecca's charms, Bertha cast her eyes down and said, "Rebecca was always very touchy-touchy, feeling, hugging, kissing. If there was anything between them, I would never know. She was very affectionate with everybody."

Just as she had done for Dave Romero, Rebecca lavished gifts on Alvaro, including clothing and shoes. She also purchased a cell phone for him and paid the monthly bill.

That month, April 1997, Alvaro Quezada, Rebecca's good-looking cousin, wangled a job in Las Vegas, driving a limousine as part of a security team for one of the most popular fighters in the world, Oscar De La Hoya. Known as "the Golden Boy," De La Hoya had been undefeated in twenty-one previous professional matches and owned the light-welterweight championship. He arrived in Las Vegas for a scheduled bout with welterweight champ, Pernell Whitaker, to be held on April 12.

De La Hoya defeated Whitaker in the Las Vegas fight, and Alvaro had a lot to talk about after he moved in with Rebecca. She asked a myriad of questions about the ascending star, De La Hoya, and thoughts took root in her mind about targeting him as her next conquest.

Another man entered Rebecca's life through Alvaro's stay in Las Vegas. A Los Angeles Police Department officer, Robert Zavala (pseudonym), had taken some time off to work for De La Hoya, supervising the security team. In this position, he met Alvaro. The two men had a mutual friend in the LAPD, and this led to plans for future contacts. Alvaro said, "Hey, when we get back to L.A., we should all get together. Let's go party. Why don't you give me your pager number and I'll give you mine." It sounded fine to Zavala.

A different boxing event would bring them together again, in late June.

* * *

By the middle of May, Rebecca developed a case of wanderlust. She decided to take a vacation to a colorful resort on the lower tip of the Baja California peninsula, 850 miles south of the U.S. border. It features spectacular beaches among towering, rugged wind-carved cliffs, abundant fishing, and other water sports. Plenty of bar-restaurants line the colorful U-shaped marina and the adjoining town.

Still using Bruce's credit cards to fund her every whim, Rebecca invited another female cousin, Ana, to travel with her. The two women arrived on Sunday, May 25, checked into an expensive hotel, and planned to party the night away. They sampled most of the open-air bars along the marina promenade, and particularly enjoyed the atmosphere with lively crowds.

In one nightspot, Rebecca sat with Ana, laughing at a couple of other women who had possibly consumed too many margaritas, shed their inhibitions, and climbed up on a table to dance. Something else caught Rebecca's attention. She spotted a middle-aged man who sat at the bar by himself looking lonely. And wealthy. Her stare must have appeared inviting, because he rose, walked over to her table, and introduced himself.

Dr. Randy Ellison (pseudonym), age forty-four, a radiologist from Phoenix, Arizona, had made the trip to Cabo with a heavy heart. He had booked a two-bedroom condominium months earlier, planning to bring his wife for a fun-filled vacation. But she had deserted him, running away with another man. Rather than lose the nonrefundable deposit, he made the trip alone. He planned to return home the next morning, Monday, and had dropped into the bar for a few drinks on his final night. When he noticed Rebecca staring at him, he saw it as an opportunity to at least have some company.

Rebecca gave him a radiant smile, invited him to sit down, and ordered drinks for all three of them. At first, she told him to call her "Brandy," but within a short time, confessed that her name was Rebecca, or Becky. The woman with her, she said, was her "assistant," Ana. That, too, changed to "cousin" after a few rounds of drinks.

Amidst their flirtations, Ellison let Rebecca know of his profession as a doctor, that his wife had left him, and that they planned to divorce. She, in turn, said that she owned an Internet-related business associated with the entertainment industry, but she didn't want to talk about business and spoil their fun.

The drinks and laughter brought Ellison out of his doldrums. He thought Rebecca not only beautiful, but humorous and exciting. He especially enjoyed it when she somehow brought up the subject of her breasts, and referred to them as "the twins."

Ellison caught sight of her left hand, saw a diamond ring on the third finger, and asked if she was married. Rebecca nodded in the affirmative, but quickly explained that she was also in the process of a divorce and continued to wear the ring only for the purpose of keeping men away. Her husband, she said, had not been a very good sex partner. Another problem had developed, she said, and dropped a bomb that stunned both Ana and Ellison. Bruce, she said, had sexually abused her little boy.

She offered no details, and Ellison didn't ask. The conversation changed back to lighthearted banter, teasing, and laughter. Ellison would later describe his impression of Rebecca: "I'd have to say she was the most fun person I had ever met—very outgoing, the center of attention." At no time, he noted, did she seem sad, morose, or depressed.

After another round of drinks, the trio began barhopping along the waterfront walkway. When it finally came time to part company, Ellison reminded Rebecca of his reservations to fly home within a few hours. She pursed her lips in a pout, said she and Ana planned to stay for several more days, and asked if he might come back to join them. He explained commitments were waiting for him in Phoenix—a meeting with the divorce arbitrator, some family matters, and business. Still, he promised he would consider coming back to Cabo if possible. Before the flight home, Ellison said, he hoped Rebecca would have breakfast with him at a little restaurant near the beach. She accepted, and he gave the two women a ride back to their hotel in his rental Jeep.

Rebecca met Ellison soon after dawn, without Ana, and rode with him to the restaurant. They shared breakfast, and prolonged the flirtation as long as they could. After exchanging phone numbers, he dropped her at the hotel and drove to the airport.

Two hours after he arrived home in Phoenix, Ellison's phone rang. Rebecca's cheerful voice pepped him up again. She said she missed him and really hoped he could come back to Cabo right away. She repeated her wish in calls on Tuesday, Wednesday, and Thursday. Ellison finally told her he just couldn't make it due to previous commitments. He said he had booked another stay at the condo there, in October, and hoped she might be able to meet him at that time when they could spend the whole week together. Maybe, Ellison suggested, he could fly over to Los Angeles sometime soon and they could get together.

Rebecca said she would like both meetings, and looked forward to them.

During one of Bertha's visits to Rebecca after her return to Whittier, Ellison called. Rebecca giggled like a teenager during the conversation and handed the phone to Bertha. "He's a great guy. I just want you to say hi to him."

Bertha shook her head. "I don't know him, or what to say." Privately she thought he must not be too bright to fall for Rebecca's flirtations. Finally capitulating to her friend's insistence, Bertha took the handset, greeted the doctor, and listened.

Ellison gushed on and on about his good fortune in meeting Rebecca at a Cabo San Lucas bar and said, "She is so wonderful. Tell me about her."

The whole thing felt clumsy and awkward to Bertha. She tried to be courteous in her replies. In later recollections, she said, "I think he was just another target for Rebecca, someone to get some money from."

The reunion between Ellison and Rebecca did take place the next month, June. For the Father's Day weekend, he provided her with airline tickets to Las Vegas. They met at Caesars Palace hotel, where she had already checked in. He had booked a room at the Mirage hotel, and that's where they both slept. Together they gambled, dined, and talked. Rebecca mentioned that her lawyer had drawn up a legal agreement for her husband, Bruce, to sign regarding separation and division of property.

Before they returned to their respective homes, Rebecca invited Ellison to join her and a group of friends at Lake Havasu on the Fourth of July holiday. He regretfully declined, explaining that he had plans for a trip with his son to Hawaii. Maybe, she said, they could find another time to get together. She even hinted at the possibility of moving to Phoenix, just to "get away from California." Perhaps she could get a job at an exotic dance club.

Ellison finally suggested that she travel to Phoenix in early August to attend a water-volleyball party for a group of his friends, to be held in his backyard pool. She could stay at his home for a few days. Rebecca said that would be wonderful. She would drive over and bring some of her specialty— home-cooked Mexican food.

Other, more dramatic events would prevent her attendance at his party.

Shortly after Rebecca's return home in Whittier, Alvaro announced that he planned a small party of his own. He wanted to invite some friends over to Rebecca's house to watch a heavyweight championship boxing match on television. The current champ, Evander Holyfield, would take on former title holder Mike Tyson on Saturday evening, June 28.

With Rebecca's permission, Alvaro paged LAPD officer Robert Zavala and invited him to attend. The other guests would be stripper Dave Romero and one of his employees, Mark Garcia.

Romero wouldn't have far to travel, since he spent Friday night sharing Rebecca's bedroom. Early Saturday morning, raucous shouting jolted him out of a deep sleep. He heard her yelling into the telephone, "I'm not going to divorce you. It's not going to be like that." The argument lasted for what seemed like hours, while Romero covered his head with a pillow trying to drown out Rebecca's wailing voice. She bellowed, "Don't come to the house. I'll meet you somewhere."

Romero made himself a promise not to spend any more nights with this volatile woman. Wives screaming at their husbands over the phone didn't make him feel right. He did, though, accept her invitation to stay for the televised fight party that Saturday night.

Officer Zavala showed up early, as did Mark Garcia. Rebecca, now calmed down, invited them in with the charm of an experienced hostess. Alvaro, who had been out all day, returned and greeted Zavala like a long-lost buddy. He also met and shook hands with Romero, for the first time. Even though Romero had spent considerable time in the Whittier residence with Rebecca, and Alvaro had moved in, the two had somehow missed each other in coming and going. The assembled group drank beers, shot some pool, and ate snacks prepared by the supercook Rebecca. In conversation with Zavala, Alvaro mentioned that he might like to try for a job with the LAPD.

At fight time, they all gathered around a television set to watch one of the most bizarre endings ever to take place in the square ring. The bout would make controversial history when stopped by the referee at the end of the third round because Tyson bit off a piece of Holyfield's ear.

Afterward, the men chatted, and Alvaro questioned Romero extensively about the dancer-stripper profession. Rebecca stepped in and said, "Al's looking for a job. Can you take a look at him and see if he could make it, or at least try out for your group?"

"Sure," said Romero. Alvaro had been working out regularly,

buffing up his torso, legs, and biceps. Romero acknowledged that Alvaro had the looks and body that women loved, and said he would teach him the dance routines, along with the slick way of shedding special tear-away apparel.

Even though Alvaro committed to work with Romero and learn the dance business, he still maintained ambitions to join the LAPD, and arranged with Zavala to put in an application.

Before the party ended, Rebecca gave Zavala a hug and invited him to join her and a few others on a trip to Lake Havasu, in Arizona. They planned to tow her ski boat over there and celebrate the Fourth of July holiday. He said he just might go along.

The gathering finally broke up. On the night that Tyson bit off part of Holyfield's ear, something else was severed. Dave Romero kept a promise to himself by permanently ending the affair with Rebecca.

The following Monday morning, Alvaro followed up on his quest to apply with the LAPD. He paged Zavala and said he was at the YMCA on Whittier Boulevard in East L.A. Zavala volunteered to pick him up for a ride to the LAPD Hollenbeck Station, where an application form would be available.

Within a few minutes, they headed together toward Hollenbeck. When Zavala made a right turn on Soto Street, Alvaro spotted a dark-clad man striding along the sidewalk and said, "Hey, there's my brother to the right of us. Stop. I want to talk to him."

Zavala eased over to the curb, parked, and got out. By the time he reached the sidewalk, Alvaro was already in animated conversation with Jose, who wore a cast on his right arm below the elbow. He introduced him to Zavala as "Joe." They chatted for a few minutes, Alvaro gave Joe some money, and they shook hands again. The meeting took place about a mile from Fresno Street, where Jose lived with their father, Arturo.

After Alvaro picked up the application forms at Hollenbeck, Zavala took him to a nearby Denny's restaurant, where they shared lunch and conversation. Afterward, the officer returned

Alvaro to the YMCA. Before parting, they agreed to meet again for the Independence Day trip to Lake Havasu.

July 4 fell on a Friday, making for a three-day weekend. Zavala, Alvaro, Rebecca, and her cousin Ana, the Cabo San Lucas travel companion, piled into the 4Runner and drove east toward Arizona, towing her ski boat. It would take about five hours of navigating across 260 miles of stark, glaring, dry desert to reach the virtual oasis. The popular recreational resort had been headlined by news media in 1971 when an ancient London Bridge was dedicated there, after having been dismantled in England and transported, block by block, to Havasu on the Colorado River, over a three-year period. Engineers reassembled it, with certain modifications, over a narrow channel on the lake.

For three days, Rebecca and her guests partied, water-skied, drank, and dined handsomely. Zavala would later admit that he spent most of his time close to Rebecca.

They returned to Whittier on Sunday night. Zavala, scheduled to work the next day, thanked his three companions, hugged Rebecca, and left somewhat hastily. He forgot to take his ice chest and binoculars from the boat.

Not until the afternoon of Friday, July 25, did he call Rebecca to make arrangements for recovering them. It would turn out to be a pivotal day in all of their lives, and one of stunning tragedy.

Chapter 11

I Have to Play
This Charade

The shrieking threats and denials overheard by Dave Romero, from Rebecca's bed on Saturday morning, near the end of June, made it clear that the subject of divorce had been raised between Bruce and Rebecca.

Bruce had, indeed, spoken to attorney Ronald Ziff about it on June 23, five days before Romero heard the shouting match. The decision had been a tough one for Bruce. His father would later admit that he and Theda encouraged their son to divorce Rebecca. "At first, he wanted to get back together with her and make things right. But then, after a while, he saw that it wasn't to be had, so he started the divorce."

For Rebecca, the prospect of failing to walk away with half of Bruce's fortune apparently changed her attitude about divorce. She told her friend Bertha about contacting an attorney and having a separation agreement drawn up. It included requirements for Bruce to continue paying the mortgage and to give her spending money. But Bruce, she growled, had reacted angrily and refused to sign it.

Desperate, Rebecca lashed out in a whole new direction.

Wedding photographer Elizabeth Lamb received a telephone call from Rebecca about the long-delayed meeting to modify the album orders. They picked July 17 at the home of Rebecca's sister Yvonne. Before she hung up, Rebecca blurted out, "I've got a story to tell you, that you are not going to believe."

Elizabeth ignored the dramatic setup, which sounded like a network news anchor's teaser, just before a commercial, promising sensational stories to come. She drove to Yvonne's residence and opened her proof books. Elizabeth patiently explained to Rebecca and her sister all of the details regarding everyone's orders of photo packages, and asked what modifications needed to be made. Rebecca showed little interest, and interrupted with a complete change of subject. She headlined it by stating that she had kicked Bruce out because he had been molesting her son.

Aghast, Elizabeth reluctantly listened. Rebecca said she discovered the horrible facts when Bruce went on a business trip in April. She had found her little boy hiding in a closet and crying. When she tried to calm him, he refused to come out and just kept sobbing. At last, he "confessed" that Bruce had been molesting him. That's why she kicked Bruce out, Rebecca snarled.

In the middle of her dramatic revelations, Rebecca's cell phone rang. She answered and immediately hung up. Minutes later, it rang again, and she repeated the termination. "See," she told the women, "he's stalking me. He gave me this cell phone just so he could stalk me. I even caught him peeking in the windows at my house."

Mentally recoiling, Elizabeth thought, *"My house?"* Hadn't Bruce bought the lovely home, making it equally his? More important, though, could Bruce really have done the things in Rebecca's accusations? Elizabeth felt particularly sensitive to the allegations at that point in time. In her own family, a trial was under way in which a distant in-law had been charged with molesting a young female relative. Getting right to the point, she asked Rebecca, "Did you call the police?"

The response nauseated Elizabeth. Sounding incredulous, Rebecca said, "Why would I want to do that? Elizabeth, he would do me no good in jail. I'm going to get him where it hurts. When I'm through with him, he won't have a penny left to his name."

As if these revelations weren't enough, Rebecca had more to reveal about Bruce. She announced that he had made a pass at her uncle Arturo! The man she sometimes called "Dad" had been at the Whittier house one evening when Rebecca came in late. In a fit of anger, he had angrily demanded an immediate ride home. She asked him to spend the night, and Arturo had said, "I want to go home right now or I'll take a taxi." Upset, she had consented to his request. En route, he blurted out the reason for his fury. He and Bruce had been drinking, and Bruce had hinted they do something sexual.

A curtain lifted in Elizabeth's mind: "I knew right then that she was lying."

In her completely honest and ethical world, Elizabeth understood that money would be the last thing on a mother's mind when a son or daughter had been sexually molested. "When your child is hurt, you go for the jugular, not dollars." And the accusation about Bruce making a pass at Arturo dripped with insincerity.

A new sense of pity for Bruce filled Elizabeth's thoughts. Suddenly it all made sense. "I thought, 'This poor guy!' and I realized why Rebecca married him. It was all a scam. They had nothing in common. He was in love with her, obviously. She was never in love with him." Elizabeth felt the urge to get up and run, but she resisted.

Yvonne, too, appeared dubious about Rebecca's denunciation of Bruce, and her sister's greedy plan to milk the situation for money. Without warning, Yvonne vaulted from her chair and announced, "I'm leaving."

"Where are you going?" Rebecca demanded, looking puzzled. She added, "What do you mean, you're leaving? This is your house."

Glaring with disgust, Yvonne snapped, "I'm taking the kids for their swimming lessons. I'm gone. Bye."

Elizabeth understood, and felt as if Yvonne's departure confirmed her own suspicions.

None of it seemed to bother Rebecca. She shrugged and turned back to the business of ordering pictures. One particular request seemed completely incongruous to Elizabeth. Her client wanted a large poster-size print featuring Rebecca, Bruce, and the little boy sitting in Bruce's lap.

Unable to hold back any longer, Elizabeth slammed her proof book shut and asked, "What are you doing? You don't need to be ordering pictures. You're divorcing him, anyway."

"Oh, Elizabeth," Rebecca moaned. "He doesn't know it. I talked to my lawyer and Bruce doesn't know we are getting a divorce yet. The timing is not right. I have to play this charade like there's still a chance that we're going to get back together again. I've got to order these pictures."

"Look," Elizabeth replied, "It would be a waste of money for you to buy wedding pictures if the marriage isn't going to last. Tell you what. I'll credit you with two thousand dollars by taking more pictures, like you and your boy at the beach or somewhere else."

"Oh no. I have to play this charade." Rebecca spoke in a self-pitying whisper.

Elizabeth wanted to spit back a sarcastic rejoinder, but kept her thoughts to herself. *Yeah, you've been married all of six months and you probably won't be getting any money. That's why you can't let Bruce know what you are doing.*

If the whole conversation had revolted Elizabeth, Rebecca's next comment made her want to throw up. With narrowed eyes and lips drawn tight, Rebecca said, "My family is so angry at him, Elizabeth. I wouldn't be surprised if someone killed him. Maybe Arturo. And I can't be a suspect."

Speaking of it later, Elizabeth Lamb said, "My little Mormon-mom head just couldn't grasp it. The whole thing struck me as incredibly weird."

Rebecca had always shared her problems with Bertha, and something this important couldn't be kept from her friend of so many years. Driven by the urgent need to talk, she paid a visit to Bertha.

As soon as the words spilled out, Bertha felt her temperature rise and her stomach tighten. Rage boiled though her. She asked, "Exactly what did Bruce do?"

"Well," Rebecca whined, sounding reluctant, "Ryan was complaining that Bruce fondled him in his privates."

Instantly Bertha demanded, "Call the police. Report it. And get your son to a hospital for examination."

"I'm going to," Rebecca promised.

Calming down, Bertha wondered if it might have been a misunderstanding. She suggested, "Becky, maybe it was just inadvertent. Bruce never had any children and probably doesn't have much experience with little kids. Maybe the way he picks him up, he's accidentally touching him."

"No," Rebecca snorted, her eyes ablaze. "You're crazy. You don't even know what you're talking about. You haven't seen the way Bruce looks at him, and I have. I see the way he touches him."

Bertha again expressed the urgent need for police intervention and professional counseling for the boy. But Rebecca had other ideas. "Well, no, no," she resisted. "Because, you know, he's gonna pay for this. He's gonna pay for what he did to my son. I'm gonna blackmail him and he's gonna give me everything I want. I'm going to call his employer and ruin his reputation at his lovely work and with his friends."

Bertha couldn't believe the attitude. "Becky, you're the crazy one. C'mon. This is about your son, not money or reputation." Just as it had with Elizabeth Lamb, any remaining credibility about Rebecca's allegations vanished. Later explaining, Bertha said, "When she started telling me about Bruce molesting her son, I was livid, because, at first, I believed her. But as soon as she started talking about the blackmail and her plan to ruin his reputation, I didn't believe her anymore. I thought, 'No, there's no way.'"

Perhaps sensing Bertha's doubt, Rebecca poured a little more fuel on the fire. "You know," she said, "I think Bruce is gay. And he has a crush on Uncle Arturo. That's a big insult to my uncle, and I hope he doesn't try to kill Bruce. How dare he think that way about a macho man."

Chapter 12

Deadly Reconciliation

Officer Robert Zavala had been procrastinating about calling Rebecca regarding the binoculars and ice chest he had left at her home on Sunday night, July 6, when they had returned from Lake Havasu. He finally got around to it on Friday afternoon, July 25, at about two-thirty.

She answered the telephone and bubbled over with elation when Zavala spoke. She hadn't heard from him in nearly three weeks, and asked, "What happened to you?"

"I'm sorry," he replied. "I had a lot going on." They chatted about the Havasu trip for a few moments, and he said, "I left my ice chest and binoculars in your boat."

"I know you did," Rebecca chirped. "Why don't you come by and pick them up tomorrow. As a matter of fact, I'm having dinner in your area, near the Hollenbeck Station, tonight with my husband, Bruce."

"Bruce?" Zavala asked. He remembered her harsh comments about him and her boasts about kicking him out.

"Yeah," Rebecca said, "we're going to reconcile. After we talk tonight, you can meet my husband tomorrow. Stop by and pick up your stuff."

"Okay. Where are you guys going to eat?"

"At that little Mexican-food restaurant on César Chávez." She reminded Zavala that she had mentioned it before. Then, in a sudden change of subject, Rebecca asked Zavala about his job duties, exactly what area officers at Hollenbeck covered, and where he patrolled.

Zavala patiently answered her questions, a little puzzled by the specific inquiries. He reconfirmed his intention to visit her the next evening, Saturday.

Bruce's father, Harold, suffered right along with his son after the April 20 separation and during the next three months. He and Theda fully agreed with their son's decision to divorce Rebecca. That's why a telephone call from Bruce on Friday morning, July 25, amazed them.

Bruce said, "Don't fix dinner for me tonight. I'm going out with Rebecca and we're going to try to settle our differences." She had contacted him earlier, he explained, and suggested the reconciliation. They planned to share a meal at their favorite Mexican-food restaurant that Friday night, with perhaps a few drinks, and figure out a way to salvage the marriage.

Even though he agreed to the rendezvous, Bruce still came home to his parents' residence after work. According to Harold, he seemed pensive. Recalling it, the father said, "Bruce was very quiet and deep in thought. He wouldn't talk and he would hardly look at us. He was just wrapped up in his thinking."

Since there would be no family dinner that night, Harold and Theda decided to treat themselves to a restaurant meal as well. They left the house before Bruce did. He bathed, shaved, then dressed in khaki trousers, a white shirt, black socks, and leather sandals.

Shortly after summer sunset, about eight o'clock, Rebecca

arrived at the Cleland home in the 4Runner SUV. She wore a low-cut black dress, black high heels, necklace, bracelet, and her glistening diamond ring. Bruce took the passenger seat and she drove them to César Chávez Boulevard. In the cantina's crowded rear lot, Rebecca found a parking place. They climbed nine red-tile steps together, viewing signs that announced, OPEN, WELCOME, ENJOY OUR CHEF'S SECRETS FROM ALL REGIONS OF MEXICO, and COME IN.

Entering the rear doorway, they passed the kitchen, stepped through a narrow L-shaped corridor, walked by a coin telephone mounted near restroom doors, and entered the dining area. As usual, they seated themselves at the third table, next to a wall dividing the room from a second section. Bruce sat with his back to the hallway, and Rebecca faced him.

A diminutive waitress, less than five feet in stature, welcomed Bruce and Rebecca. She introduced herself as Maria Del Carmen Barron. They could call her "Carmelita." She would later tell her memories of Bruce. "He was tall, had a mustache, glasses, and dark hair, like coffee. Dark coffee color." She said they arrived about 9:30 P.M.

Instead of margaritas, both Bruce and Rebecca ordered beers. They sipped them while speaking quietly, then asked for another round. After studying the extensive menu, they gave Carmelita their food selections and continued to talk.

While they waited to be served, Rebecca excused herself and headed in the direction of the restroom. The waitress noticed, though, that she stopped at the pay telephone, made a call, and held her hand cupped over the speaker.

After the meal arrived, Bruce and Rebecca ate almost in silence. Once again, she rose, disappeared into the corridor, and made another call, this time from her cell phone.

Carmelita's normal work tour ended at ten o'clock, but on that Friday night, she stayed until at least ten-thirty, waiting for the tall man and his lady to finish eating. They ordered dessert and picked at it for a while. Finally Bruce asked the waitress to deliver a separate take-out order and put their remaining food in a carryout container. After he paid the bill, they left by the same rear door.

At the wheel again, Rebecca drove east on César Chávez Boulevard, less than a mile, turned right on Soto Street, and finally left on Fresno Street, where she parked in front of her Uncle Arturo's tiny house. They went inside, found him with a woman he called his girlfriend, and drank a few more beers with "the groper."

All seemed to be going well as they exchanged stories with Arturo and his female friend. They laughed at his risque stories and avoided bringing up recent unpleasantness. Arturo ate the dinner Rebecca had brought for him with Bruce's money. Several times during the visit, Rebecca slipped into another room to hold quiet cell phone conversations with someone, but Bruce didn't seem to notice. At about one o'clock in the morning, they said good-bye to the man Rebecca often called "Dad," and to his companion, then drove away.

Rebecca steered back to Whittier Boulevard, turned east, and passed under the I-60 Freeway. When she reached the intersection with Lorena Street, she did something strange. Ordinarily, when traveling toward Whittier, she would turn left on Lorena and drive one block to the I-60 on-ramp.

On this night, she made a right turn instead, drove five blocks, crossed over the I-5 Freeway, and suddenly turned right on Beswick Street, as if planning to enter the freeway where Beswick abutted Concord.

At the boulevard stop sign, she halted and told Bruce that a red light on the instrument panel signaled a problem. The back hatch door, she said, had apparently not locked, and it was ajar. Leaving the engine running and the headlights on, she opened the driver's door and stepped out into the shadowy night.

Bruce remained in the passenger seat, looking toward Concord and the right turn that would take them onto the freeway.

Without warning, a dark-clad figure emerged from the adjacent shrubbery, raised his right arm, leveled a handgun through the rolled-down window, and pulled the trigger twice.

An explosive pop was followed by the sound of shattering glass. A searing hunk of lead caught Bruce just above his upper lip, on the right side. It tore through the top part of his mouth and came out the other side of his head, just in front of the left ear. Of the two slugs fired, one wounded Bruce, then crashed through the driver's window, and the other embedded itself in the door's leather lining.

Shocked and spurting blood, Bruce managed to push his door open, leap out, and lurch toward the vehicle's rear. He broke into a staggering run and crossed Beswick, heading toward a driveway. The shooter followed, with less than a yard separating them, and began firing again.

Another slug ripped into Bruce's body, in the right lower back, exiting from his abdomen near the belly button. It probably would have been fatal, but the gunman evidently wanted to make sure. The third bullet blasted into the back of Bruce's head, burned through his brain, and tore out through his forehead. He collapsed onto the concrete driveway apron, mortally wounded.

His executioner delivered one more shot, a coup de grace. Bruce lay on his stomach, with his face turned toward the right. Aiming at his right temple, the killer fired a last round of ammunition. The slug went all the way through and came out the left side of Bruce's scalp.

The gunman glanced at his victim and the blood pooling around him, then sprinted toward the corner. He turned left on Concord, ran down the slight slope for a block, turned left on Garnet, and trotted across the street, vanishing into the night.

From inside her home next door to the driveway on which Bruce's life ended, Virginia Selva watched in horror. Down the slope of Concord Street, one block away, Lupe Hernandez heard shots, spotted the stalled SUV, and saw a man running down the sidewalk on the opposite side of Concord. She called 911.

Roberto Suarez, driving a black GMC pickup truck on his way home from his night shift job, stopped several yards behind the SUV. On his way to Orange County, he had planned to enter the I-5. The vehicle in front of him stood still with the passenger door wide open. And just behind the vehicle, Suarez could see the figure of a woman in a black dress, stretched out on the pavement, lying on her right side and facing the driver's-side tire. With her right arm bent and her right cheek cradled in that hand, she looked as if she had fallen asleep. Her feet, covered only in stockings, projected toward the center of the street.

While Suarez took this all in, he noticed a taxi coming around the corner from Concord. The driver slammed on his brakes and jumped out. Still seated in his pickup, Suarez conferred with the cabbie. Should they call the police? Their question needed no answer when a flashing red-and-yellow light atop an LAPD cruiser pulled up behind Suarez's truck.

Officer Jon Edson and his partner, Ben Young, had been only a couple of blocks away on Lorena Street, the route Rebecca had taken, when the dispatch call came. Edson spotted the woman lying near the rear bumper of the SUV and hurried over to check her condition. Young dashed to the man lying facedown on a driveway apron and looked for vital signs of life.

As Edson approached the woman, she groaned and sat up. She wore no shoes, and the officer noticed a pair of high heels neatly aligned, side by side, on the pavement, near a rear tire of the SUV. In recalling it, the officer said, "When I ran up to her, she was sitting down and she had her face in both of her hands. She never looked up." After he spoke, and asked about her condition, Edson studied her carefully to see if she exhibited any signs of injury or trauma. "She was not crying and she wasn't shaking and did not appear to be in shock."

Still, the woman seemed unable or unwilling to give Edson any information. Instead, she repeatedly complained, "They hit me on the head. They hit me on the head." The officer again tried to elicit information to determine what had happened. In the first few moments at a crime scene, timing is crucial for obtaining a description of the attacker and putting out an alert for the suspect. But the woman showed no interest in talking about it. Nor did she inquire about the other victim lying across the street.

Moments later, a fire truck arrived. Two firefighters, Carlos Gallegos and Johnny Green, both trained as emergency medical technicians (EMTs), made a quick decision. Of the two people who had apparently suffered injury, the prone man on the driveway took their first priority. They could see that the woman had at least sat up, and a police officer was talking to her.

Kneeling to check the male victim, Gallegos realized immediately that nothing could be done for him. Later describing it, he said, "Basically, he wasn't moving at all. My partner and I started cutting his shirt off, looking for wounds and examining his airway for any signs of life. There was quite a bit of blood. We started our survey examination and found several head wounds. . . . He was pulseless, apneic—not breathing. We could see gray matter—parts of the brain—showing."

A driver's license inside the victim's wallet would identify him as Bruce Cleland.

Gallegos turned to a captain who accompanied them and told him that the male victim was dead. The supervisor directed him and Green to check on the woman. Both men trotted approximately thirty feet over to the SUV.

Officer Edson turned the woman over to the firefighters, and began a cursory inspection of the vehicle. Looking inside, through the open passenger door, he saw broken glass and blood. Near the center console, he observed a black purse and a cell phone connected to the cigarette lighter by an electrical cord. To secure the scene of an obvious homicide, he began barricading the SUV and other sectors with yellow plastic tape. No one could miss the dramatic message: POLICE LINE, DO NOT CROSS.

Carlos Gallegos asked the woman, now standing, about any possible injuries. Still groaning, she said someone had struck her on the head. With Johnny Green aiming a flashlight beam at her scalp, Gallegos first performed a visual examination, then palpated her head, meaning use of his hands to feel for any bumps. Neither test revealed hematomas, cuts, swelling, or bleeding. The firefighters also checked her hands, elbows, knees, and face. No injury of any type showed up.

Paramedics arrived at the scene a few minutes later. Gallegos—as an EMT—would later clarify the distinction between them. "EMT training consists basically of advanced first-aid training. We're one step below paramedics. We don't administer drugs, start intravenous procedures, defibrillate (apply electrical charge to the heart), or do intubation (insert a tube into the throat to clear air passages)."

Even though Bruce showed no signs of life, the paramedics applied defibrillation procedures. It did nothing more than prove his death. They covered him with a sheet.

While Gallegos and Officer Jon Edson examined the female victim's head and limbs, they finally learned her name, Rebecca Cleland. They asked if she knew the man lying on the driveway apron. "Yes," she said. "That's my husband."

According to a later observation from Gallegos, "She basically showed no signs of any emotion considering the magnitude of the incident." Rebecca didn't cry or scream. He expected her to rush to her husband's side. Instead, she told the officer she would like to get her cell phone from the console inside the SUV and make a call to her dad. Puzzled, Gallegos offered to retrieve it for her and dial a number. In view of the horrific death of Rebecca's husband, Gallegos worried that she would be too nervous to make the call herself, or even to converse with anyone. Rebecca adamantly said she would do it without any help from him.

She leaned into the vehicle, grabbed her phone, and punched in a number. Gallegos would recall hearing her say a woman's name, then ask if *"Papí"* was there. *Papí* is Hispanic slang for father. She waited for a moment, and then said, "Something has happened. We're on Beswick. They killed him." For the first time, Gallegos thought he could see tears on her face. It also struck him and his partner, Green, as odd that she knew her husband had been killed. No one had told her, officially, that he was dead. Of course, she might possibly have overheard one of the officers or paramedics mention it.

After she exchanged a few more words, Rebecca handed the cell phone to Gallegos and asked him to speak to her dad. Arturo Quezada requested directions to the crime scene and arrived ten minutes later. As he approached the yellow plastic tape, Officer Edson asked the stranger to identify himself. Arturo said he was Rebecca's father. He wasn't allowed to see her.

While Rebecca talked on her cell phone, another police unit arrived at the location and parked around the corner, on Concord. Officer Sean Hoffman and his partner, Jerry Morales, asked her to be seated in the cruiser's backseat so they could talk to her about the incident. In Hoffman's recollection, Rebecca asked, "Can Bruce come sit with me?" He may have misunderstood, since she more than likely asked if Arturo could join her. Hoffman, unaware of what she had said in the telephone conversation about her husband being killed, gently told Rebecca that it wouldn't be possible for Bruce to be at her side.

The paramedics approached and asked Rebecca about her condition. She complained about her head hurting, so they repeated the examination performed by the two EMTs. They rechecked her head, took blood pressure and respiratory readings, and found no injury or other symptoms of trauma.

One of the uniformed officers walked down Concord Street to the Garnet intersection and knocked on the door of a corner house. He spoke briefly to Lupe Hernandez to confirm that she had heard shots, seen someone running away, and called 911. After advising her that investigators would be contacting her soon, the officer returned uphill to the crime scene.

Inside the police cruiser, Rebecca spoke to Officer Hoffman and summarized her version of what had happened.

Hoffman later recited: "She stated that she and her husband were celebrating their reunion of their wedding. They ate at a restaurant on César Chávez, then went to her parent's house on Fresno Street and had some drinks with her family. She mentioned her father specifically. After they left, she noticed a warning light on her dashboard, stopped, and got out to shut the door. She advised us that she thinks she got hit on the head or something. And whoever did it had stolen her diamond ring." Hoffman had no way of knowing that Rebecca's reference to Arturo as her parent was not true.

For some reason, Rebecca decided she needed to speak to Officer Robert Zavala, the cop who had gone to Lake Havasu with her on Independence Day. But Hoffman told Rebecca that Zavala was not on duty that night.

En route to the Hollenbeck Station and after arrival there, Rebecca continued to talk even though neither Hoffman nor his partner asked any questions. She volunteered that her husband was "pretty financially stable and very well-off." Next she told them that she no longer worked. Before her marriage, she said, she had undergone cosmetic surgery for breast enlargement and dieted to lose weight before the wedding.

In a claustrophobic cubicle of a room at the Hollenbeck Station, the officers asked Rebecca to wait for a detective who would interview her.

Veteran homicide investigator Walter Angulo, in his night shift duties, responded to major crime scenes to assure preservation of evidence, and conducted preliminary interviews of witnesses, victims, or suspects.

By the time Rebecca arrived, Angulo had already been to Beswick Street and returned. He had examined the dark-colored 4Runner facing in the westbound direction at the boulevard stop sign on Corcord with both front doors open, engine running, and the lights on. Blood had been spattered in the front seat, and shards of broken glass sparkled in the ambient light. A black purse had been left on the console. About thirty feet away, on a concrete apron, Angulo observed a white sheet shrouding the victim. After glancing around a few minutes, the detective reached inside the vehicle and switched off the ignition.

Scribbling in a notebook, Angulo made a record of his surveillance. Something he spotted at the rear of the SUV, near the driver's-side tire, seemed incongruous. A pair of black high-heel shoes looked as if they had been placed on the pavement as carefully as a woman might put them in her closet.

Satisfied about police protocol on the scene, Angulo returned to Hollenbeck. Rebecca Cleland smiled at him when he entered the interview room, where she waited. The temperature seemed comfortable to him, but Rebecca shivered and said she felt cold. From the adjacent squad room, Angulo took a coat from a hanger and gave it to her. She slipped it on and stood for him to take a couple of photos. Angulo began his interview at 4:00 A.M. by asking what had occurred that evening leading up to the death of her husband.

Rebecca spoke without hesitation. After telling her age, twenty-seven, height, five-two, weight, 118, plus her address and phone number in Whittier, she made a full statement. "Last night my husband and I went out to eat at a restaurant on César Chávez. After we ate, we ordered food to go and took it to my father's house on Fresno. My father is really my uncle, Arturo Quezada, but we are very close. After a few drinks at his house, we left to go back home. I was driving our truck and noticed an indicator was lit on my dashboard, showing that a door was not closed properly. I remembered that my cousin had put a box of pictures in the back and that the rear hatch sometimes didn't close properly. I pulled up at a stop sign just before I was going to get on the freeway and told my husband I was going to check the back door. I got out and walked to the rear of the truck, and remember closing the hatch. The next thing I remember, I was on the ground behind the truck. My head hurt and I felt light-headed. I called out for my husband and I saw a taxi. I saw a man talking on a radio at the taxi. My husband didn't come when I called. I went to my truck and telephoned my father's house. I think his girlfriend picked up the phone and told me that my father was asleep. That's the time when the police and fire department were there.

"My husband and I have had marital problems, but we were working things out. Tonight we were celebrating getting back together. I don't remember ever seeing anyone or hearing anyone around the truck when I got out. I'm missing my diamond ring from my finger."

While mentioning the loss of her ring, Rebecca glanced down at her fingers, frowned, and asked, "Where is my husband? When are you going to let me talk to him?"

Angulo had spoken to Officer Carlos Gallegos at the crime scene and heard his description of Rebecca's behavior and her insistence on using her cell phone. Gallegos had seen her key in a number and overheard her conversation, in which she told someone that "they killed him."

In view of information provided by Gallegos, Rebecca's sudden questions about her husband, and request to see him, set off a flashing yellow caution signal in Angulo's mind. Most people would probably attribute her inquiries to shock, confusion, or perhaps the result of a head injury Rebecca claimed she had suffered. As an experienced homicide investigator, though, Angulo sensed other possibilities. He asked, "Did anyone tell you what happened to your husband?"

"No."

Making a quick decision based on the probability that Rebecca already knew the facts, the detective decided not to mince words. He stated, "Your husband is dead. He was killed back there on Beswick Street."

Rebecca blinked as if surprised and contorted her face into an expression of apparent grief. She groaned, sobbed, and reached for a box of tissues on an adjacent table. Still skeptical about the veracity of her sorrow, Angulo watched as Rebecca teetered on the verge of hysteria. Before going over the edge, though, she managed to compose herself, took off the borrowed jacket, and asked if she could make a phone call.

Angulo nodded permission, then jotted down notes of his interview. He returned the coat to a hanger and gathered the information in preparation for passing everything on to another detective, who would head up the investigation.

Now in full possession of her emotions, Rebecca made the call. Within a short time, her uncle Arturo showed up and walked with her to his car outside.

Chapter 13

How's the Investigation Going?

Homicide detective Tom Herman had been with the LAPD nearly a quarter of a century when he inherited the Cleland murder case. Standing just short of six feet, with neatly trimmed grayish blond hair, blue eyes, and a muscular build, Herman knew his way around the streets of East Los Angeles. His years of experience had honed natural skills for talking to people, from executives to street thugs, and earning their trust. Prosecutors from the district attorney's (DA's) office held Herman in high regard, particularly for his ability to elicit information from criminal suspects. Said one of them, "He just has a special way of getting people to open up and talk to him, and avoid animosity between them."

A bedroom telephone ringing in the middle of the night is part of a homicide detective's regular routine, so it came as no surprise to Herman when the jangling noise snapped him out of a deep sleep at one-thirty, on Saturday morning, July 26, 1997. Instinctively, he grabbed it before the third ring, grunting a raspy "Hello." The morning-watch desk officer informed Herman of the shooting homicide on Beswick Street. "Okay, I'll be there right away," Herman said, already reaching for his pants and shirt.

Within an hour, Herman arrived at the Hollenbeck Station on East First Street in East Los Angeles's Boyle Heights section. His partner, Detective Rick Peterson, had arrived a few minutes earlier. A beefy LAPD veteran with full, dark hair and chiseled facial features that casting directors love for the role of a homicide cop, Peterson gave Herman the usual grin of anticipation. They had earned their reputation as a dynamic duo.

Following a ten-minute briefing by Walter Angulo, Herman and Peterson drove over to Beswick Street. Shortly after three o'clock, they stood next to the 4Runner SUV. Herman made a mental note about the ambient lighting. His experience told him that if any witnesses came forward to testify, it would be important to understand whether or not they could have seen very much in the middle of a dark night. The detective later said, "Basically, the lighting was excellent at the time because the incident happened right at the corner of the intersection, where there were two [street]lights, one on the southeast corner and one on the southwest corner. And there was an additional street lamp south of Beswick on Concord as you're going southbound."

Before touching the SUV or anything in it, Herman and Peterson visually examined the vehicle, its interior, and the area around it. Herman later stated, "The lights were still on and both front doors were open. I observed blood on the passenger seat, blood on the console, blood on the passenger door, and on the controls for the window and lock. I saw a black purse on the console between the two front seats. On the driver's side of the vehicle, I observed a bullet hole in the lower portion of the door panel." More bloodstains could be seen on the passenger running board and on the pavement below it.

The investigators had no trouble envisioning what had happened, simply by following the trail of blood. Congealing scarlet drops led from the open passenger door, to the rear of the SUV, and across Beswick to the concrete driveway apron, where the victim's body lay under a sheet.

After gently removing the white shroud, Herman, Peterson, and a coroner's assistant scrutinized the bullet-riddled body. Lying facedown on the cement, his knees in the gutter and legs extending into the street, he wore the remains of a white shirt that had been cut away by paramedics, khaki trousers, and dark leather sandals. The left side of his face rested in a puddle of caked blood, which had also soaked the shredded shirt and pants. As the fluid of life had drained from his body, it had formed a rivulet, which flowed several yards down the gutter.

The detectives noted that the victim wore a Seiko wristwatch and gold wedding band, with a white stone. From his right rear pocket, they extracted a billfold, which contained $25 in cash, a driver's license, and two credit cards, in the name of Bruce Allan Cleland.

Another criminalist assisted the investigators by snapping photographs of the body, the SUV, and the surrounding crime scene. His strobe flashes lit the area like miniature lightning.

As the morning sun began its lazy crawl up and over the eastern horizon, coroner's technicians at last placed Bruce's body on a gurney, wheeled it to a van, and headed toward downtown Los Angeles. At the huge county coroner's laboratory on North Mission Road, the autopsy would be conducted on Monday morning.

Meanwhile, the evidence collection process continued on Beswick Street. Detective Herman, following the blood trail from the SUV to the driveway, where Bruce's life ended, located four expended bullet casings. In addition, three live rounds lay on the pavement. Close inspection revealed markings indicating .38-caliber Super ammunition. Herman clearly understood the meaning of this information. The designation "Super" told him that the bullets were high velocity. The fact that they apparently had been automatically ejected as the shooter chased his target indicated the use of a semiautomatic pistol rather than a revolver. Most people envision revolvers as the old type of handguns carried by cowboys in Western movies, while semiautomatics, more rectangular in shape, are likely associated with detective films. Ammunition for this type of pistol is contained in clips inserted into the grip.

Herman later pointed out that in both types of weapons, semiautomatic or revolver, the projectile is launched by expanding gases, which result from the gunpowder explosion. He said, "In a revolver, the cylinder may contain as many as eight rounds, depending upon what caliber gun it is. But when that gun is fired and the projectile leaves the chamber, the casings stay in the cylinder as it revolves with each firing. They stay in there until the shooter manually ejects them. Now, in an automatic, or semiautomatic, the gas will do two things. Obviously, it causes the projectile to exit the casing, but it also actuates the slide, which comes back and causes the extractor to pull out the casing and eject it. The slide is basically the upper portion of the barrel." Live, unfired rounds, he added, may be ejected if the gun malfunctions or if the shooter is excited and works the slide manually.

In Herman's mind, he could see the killer chasing Bruce Cleland across the street, firing a semiautomatic pistol. It probably misfired at least once, and the shooter instinctively pulled the slide back to cock it again. This could have happened two or three times, in a matter of brief seconds. So it came as no surprise to the detective that he found not only the four bullet casings, but three live rounds as well.

Following time-honored and rigorous evidence collection procedures, the investigators posted numbered placards next to each casing or bullet, and photographed them. A criminalist then lifted each item, placed it in an evidence envelope, and marked it with a corresponding number.

With the help of an evidence technician, the two detectives removed the black leather purse from inside the SUV, along with a Nokia cell phone and electrical cord. Examining the purse's contents, they found a wallet containing $6 and some change, a small photo album, a container full of business cards, cosmetics, a necklace, and a bracelet. A personal address/phone book would provide the detectives with links to Rebecca's relatives, friends, and acquaintances, who might be able to shed some light on what had happened.

The wallet contained indicators of considerable buying power, including five credit cards—four issued to Rebecca Cleland and one from a famous lingerie chain store in Bruce Cleland's name. Two ATM cards and a pair of health care cards for Rebecca turned up, and one more showed the name of a child, who the detectives later learned was her young son. She also had two driver's licenses in her name and Social Security cards for herself and her boy.

One of the photos in the small album pictured Rebecca in an affectionate pose with a man Herman would later meet, Dave Romero.

The camera-wielding officer took photos of the SUV from every angle, after which a tow truck hooked it up and pulled it away to be stored at the Hollenbeck Station.

Detectives Herman and Peterson had both been awakened at one-thirty, Saturday morning, and summoned to work.

One hour after that, at 2:30 A.M., Officer Robert Zavala's phone interrupted his sleep. He couldn't believe it when Alvaro Quezada, Rebecca's cousin, spoke. He hadn't seen the husky young man since their trip to Lake Havasu. Alvaro's voice quavered, sounding nervous, despondent, and possibly drunk. Zavala asked him what the heck was going on. Alvaro said he and his girlfriend had argued, that he was really upset, and he needed a friend to talk to.

Trying to suppress his irritation, Zavala asked Alvaro where he was. The officer would later state that Alvaro, slurring his words, described a taco stand on the corner of Third

Street and Eastern Avenue. He added that Dave Romero and Mark Garcia, the two guys Zavala had met at a party in Rebecca's home, were with him.

Zavala finally said, "Hey, Al, it's really late. I talked to Rebecca yesterday afternoon, and if you want to talk about your problem, I'm going over to her house this evening and we can meet there."

Alvaro agreed. That would be great, he said, and hung up. Zavala tossed and turned for a little while before drifting off to sleep once more. At 4:20 A.M., his phone jerked him back into groggy consciousness. Alvaro sounded even worse this time, shrill and sobbing. "They killed Bruce!" he shouted.

Shocked into a state of acute awareness, Zavala asked, "Who? Who killed Bruce?"

All Alvaro could do is repeat: "They shot Bruce. They shot Bruce."

"What are you talking about? Who shot Bruce?" Zavala demanded.

"They tried to carjack Rebecca and Bruce. Someone shot him."

Zavala's police training automatically kicked in. He asked, "How did you find this out?"

In disjointed sentences, Alvaro explained that he had received a call on his cell phone from his father, Arturo, who had given only limited information. "It happened where you work, in Hollenbeck," he added.

Zavala said he was sorry to hear it and would try to find out more. He disconnected from Alvaro and called the Hollenbeck homicide desk. The officer told Zavala that Rebecca Cleland was in the interview room at that moment and said investigating officers were at the crime scene.

Now wide awake, Zavala tried to assimilate the incredible events. At 6:30 A.M., another surprising call came. Rebecca spoke to him from her Whittier house. Zavala thought she sounded "confused and couldn't recollect too much of what happened." She told him somebody had hit her on the back of the head and knocked her unconscious, but she was okay. "They" had murdered Bruce, she asserted.

The short conversation ended after Zavala offered his sympathy, and Rebecca said she would call him later.

At about ten-thirty that same Saturday morning, Elizabeth Lamb returned home from a church-sponsored girls' camp, where she had spent five days acting as a "cabin mom." Checking her answering machine for messages, she found a stunning one from Rebecca Cleland. In a hysterical screech, she sobbed, "Bruce passed away. Please call me." It jolted Elizabeth, but the next comment made her scratch her head. "Oh, and I need to order some pictures for the funeral." This woman's husband had died, and she was thinking about photographs for the funeral?

Compassionate as usual, Elizabeth thought of Bruce's elderly parents, and knew that his death must be a crushing blow to them. Before responding to Rebecca, Elizabeth asked her husband to listen to the message. He commented, "Bruce either killed himself over her allegations about molesting her little boy, or she killed him."

Elizabeth telephoned Rebecca's number at the Whittier house. Rebecca's sister Yvonne answered, apparently screening the calls. Lamb said, "This is Beth, the wedding photographer. Rebecca called me."

Yvonne replied, "Oh, just a minute."

Within a few seconds, Rebecca picked it up. Lamb, expecting a heartbroken, emotional whimper, heard instead the usual low, throaty, sensual greeting. "Helloowww."

"Rebecca, this is Beth. What happened?"

Instantly the voice changed to croaky sobbing. "Oh, Beth! It was horrible." She paused, then growled, "Just a minute. Just a minute." The next words sounded muffled, as if she covered the speaker while shouting, "Hang up the phone. I've got it." Resuming the woebegone tone, Rebecca repeated, "Oh, it was horrible. It was an attempted carjacking."

Lamb asked, "What happened? How did he die?"

As if she hadn't heard the question, Rebecca continued speaking. "I was knocked unconscious. I didn't see anything. And when I woke up, he was dead."

"Well, did anyone tell you what happened to him?" Ready to ask more questions, Elizabeth swallowed her words when Rebecca's voice changed again, this time to a harsh monotone. "My lawyer says I can't talk about it."

A realization struck Lamb like a boulder falling from the sky. Later describing it, she said, "My mouth flew open and my jaw dropped. I knew right then that she killed him. I thought, 'Your husband just died and your lawyer has already told you not to talk about it?'"

Rebecca's next comments sealed the suspicion even tighter. First she requested that Elizabeth deliver some enlarged wedding photos for display at the funeral, scheduled a week later, on Saturday, August 2. Then Rebecca asked, "Do you know a good videographer? I'm thinking about have a videotaped photo montage of our life together made for the funeral."

Elizabeth didn't vocalize the thoughts running through her mind: *You've only known him a year, and complained about every minute of your marriage, and you want a video of your life together?* Instead, she gave Rebecca a couple of names, agreed to deliver some photos on Saturday morning, and breathed a sigh of relief when the conversation ended.

Recalling the amazing exchange, Lamb said, "When I hung up the phone, I knew. I told my husband, 'Oh, my gosh, she killed him.' He told me very firmly, 'Do not do anything. Do not get involved. She could be in the Mexican Mafia.'"

The advice from Elizabeth's husband made sense. She knew that it could be dangerous to tell authorities what she believed. But Elizabeth's morality and desire to do the right thing hammered away at her conscience. She would have to think long and hard about it.

* * *

Rebecca kept her promise to call Robert Zavala at one-thirty that afternoon. A little more coherent, she expressed worry that she didn't have her house keys or car keys. Also, she declared, her purse and wallet had been stolen. She expressed fear that whoever killed Bruce would find her home address inside it and might come after her. Actually, her purse had been left in the SUV, but she didn't mention that inconvenient fact.

Zavala advised her to call the Whittier police to request an extra patrol, then volunteered to visit her that evening to see what he could do to help. He arrived at her home just before sunset. Rebecca, Alvaro Quezada, and Rebecca's sister Yvonne welcomed him. A Whittier police officer also showed up, took down some information, and left.

Alvaro explained that he had taken the evening off to protect Rebecca, in case Bruce's killer had taken her keys and came to the house. Zavala nodded, asked Rebecca how she was doing, and examined her head. He found no bumps, scratches, or any other evidence of injury.

Rebecca's answers to Zavala's questions revealed nothing more than what she had previously told him about the tragic event. She could only repeat the basics: she and Bruce had eaten, consumed a few drinks, and left the restaurant. Somebody had tried to carjack them and knocked her out.

After an hour of quiet conversational exchanges, Zavala collected his binoculars and ice chest, promised to come back on Sunday, then left with mixed feelings.

The same scenario played out when he returned the following day, with one exception. Rebecca asked, "How is the investigation going?"

"I haven't talked to any of the detectives yet," Zavala replied.

Shifting the subject, Rebecca told him of her worries about financial responsibilities, such as house payments and burial expenses. Zavala could do nothing more than express his hope that everything would work out for her. He bid her good-bye for the final time and drove away, plagued by doubts. He would later say about Rebecca, "She didn't sound like anybody mourning or someone whose husband had been shot and killed. She was very nonchalant."

In Phoenix, Dr. Randy Ellison also received a telephone call on Saturday, July 26. He had heard from Rebecca only a couple of times since June, when they had spent Father's Day together in Las Vegas. He had invited her to come to his Arizona home for a backyard volleyball party with some friends. Ellison picked up the phone and heard a woman crying hysterically. She finally managed to say, "Bruce is dead."

Ellison recognized Rebecca's voice, and made the connection as he recalled her husband's name. "I'm so sorry," he said. "Look, the party has been canceled. I feel so bad for you. Gosh, I understand if you never call me again." Rebecca made a few more comments about her grief, and the conversation ended.

Rebecca's barrage of telephone calls extended to Sunday morning. At the home of her gay friend Diana, Robert Diaz, the Texas cousin, answered. He greeted her. "Hello, Becky. What's up, cuz?"

"Let me speak to Diana," Rebecca said in a flat tone, devoid of any emotion.

"Okay," Diaz replied. At that moment, Diana came out wearing a robe, her hair still wet. "It's Becky," he said, and handed her the phone. He watched as Diana's eyes grew large and her face went pale.

Afterward, when he learned the subject of Rebecca's call, it troubled Diaz that she had treated him with such disregard by not even mentioning the death of her husband, preferring instead to tell Diana all about it. Diaz knew the two women had shared intimate relations, but he still felt hurt. After all, he had traveled a long distance to attend their wedding, and had spoken amicably to Bruce several times. Diaz had never been able to figure out his wild, wicked cousin.

Chapter 14

What Am I
Gonna Do Now?

Lupe Hernandez had heard the sounds of gunfire on the tragic night that Bruce lost his life, spotted a man running away from the scene, and called 911. Detective Tom Herman telephoned her on Monday, July 28, to ask a few questions. The short, plump woman, in her early twenties, told him that she had been in the backyard with her mother, smoking a cigarette, about an hour after midnight. "We both went back in the house. *Mi madre* fell asleep and I went to my bedroom." Through her north-facing window, she could see the intersection of Beswick and Concord, just one block away, up the gradual slope of Concord Street.

Just before she turned her bedcovers down, said Hernandez, she heard a gunshot coming from that corner. More sharp cracks followed. She estimated that about four or five shots had been fired. In the distance, she thought she could hear a woman yelling or crying.

Speaking fairly clear English, with a few pauses to search

for the right words, Hernandez told the detective, "There was a car, like a truck, kind of, like an SUV-style car, stopped at the stop sign, and there was a man running down the hill." She first spotted him as he rounded the corner from Beswick onto Concord, and sprinted down the sidewalk on the east side of the street. "It's on the opposite side from my house. He was running as fast as he could."

Spurred by curiosity, Hernandez had rushed out of the bedroom for a better angle. "I went into my kitchen area, where there's more windows, and I looked out, 'cause I could see better." From there, she had a clear view of the runner for at least "eight seconds," until he came to a point within a few yards of the intersection. "Then I lost sight of him when he came to a place where there's lots of ivy and bushes on the wall by the house across the street. The background is really dark over there." It is also under a thick canopy of trees.

While the dark-clad man remained in her line of vision, said Hernandez, she had a good look at him. She said he looked Hispanic and was probably in his early twenties. His head looked as if it had been shaved, but the black hair had grown back to about a quarter of an inch long, like "a gang member." He wore all-black, baggy clothing. She had seen his face mostly in profile, at an angle from the right side.

Hernandez commented that she didn't know whether the man was the one who did the shooting, or was running away from someone else shooting at him. After the ivy and canopy of trees obscured her vision, she assumed he turned the corner from Concord onto Garnet, across the street from her house. Hernandez moved quickly to a living-room window, but she still couldn't see him. However, she did hear a car door slam and the sound of an engine speeding away. It struck her as odd that no sound of a starting engine came to her, so the vehicle was probably waiting there with the motor running. In her perception, the car had been parked along the Garnet curb, facing east, and had driven away in that direction.

* * *

Herman, having observed ambient lighting at the scene, asked Hernandez if the streetlamps had been on that night, and had provided enough light. She unequivocally stated the light had been perfectly adequate.

The description Hernandez provided would probably fit several thousand young men in East Los Angeles, but Herman knew every little bit of information helped. He thanked Lupe Hernandez for her cooperation and pulled out his checklist of things to do. It included talking to Rebecca Cleland and a male stripper named Dave Romero.

Before Herman could leave the office, Officer Robert Zavala paid him a visit. He volunteered information about his connections to Rebecca Cleland, including the recent visits to her home after Bruce had been killed. In addition, Zavala detailed his attendance at a party held in Rebecca's home to watch a televised championship boxing match, and the trip to Lake Havasu. Zavala gave Herman a few names of people linked to Rebecca, including her cousin Alvaro Quezada, his brother Jose, and a couple of strippers named Dave Romero and Mark Garcia. Alvaro, he said, had called him twice in the early morning of July 26. The first call had been to bemoan problems with his girlfriend, and the second one to announce that Bruce had been killed. Alvaro had stated that his own father, Arturo Quezada, had informed him by telephone.

Herman knew that Rebecca had asked to see Zavala while still at the crime scene, but the meeting had not taken place. Before the meeting ended, Herman expressed his appreciation for the fellow officer's willing cooperation. Zavala said he would help in any way he could.

Dr. Irwin L. Golden reported to his workplace at North Mission Road on Monday morning, ready to dissect, probe, and analyze Bruce Cleland's body. It would be one of more than nine thousand autopsies conducted in the facility during 1997—1,301 of which were homicide victims. Well-qualified for the task, Dr. Golden had been employed by the county coroner since 1989, during which time he had performed thousands of autopsies.

Training and licensing for Dr. Golden's specialty is no minor process. After earning medical degrees, he had spent an additional five years of postgraduate residency to qualify himself as a board-certified forensic pathologist. Defining his job, Golden said, "Pathology is a diagnostic field of medicine where tissues and substances from the body, including blood, are analyzed. A pathologist is the laboratory doctor who performs and supervises the tests, including the surgical specimens. A forensic pathologist is a doctor that deals with applied medical knowledge to legal matters. In the coroner's office, the forensic pathologist performs autopsies to determine the cause and manner of death, and provides reports on his findings."

When a homicide is taken to trial, the autopsy can often make a profound difference in the outcome.

For the layperson, medical examination of a deceased person is a gruesome process, and it certainly denies the body any last vestige of dignity. Typically, the process involves weighing the remains, then making a large Y-shaped incision from both shoulders to the sternum, and down to the pubic bone. After ribs and protective chest bones are separated with an electrical saw, the internal organs are removed, weighed, and examined. Another special electrical tool, called a Stryker saw, is utilized to cut through the skull for access to the brain.

In his work on Bruce Cleland's body, Dr. Golden thoroughly inspected the bullet wounds, looking for entrances and exits, the angles taken by the slugs, damage to vital organs, and how each one influenced his death. Golden later commented on one of the related problems: "Sometimes a bullet in passing through breaks up or fragments. And even though the main part of the bullet may pass through the body, pieces can be broken off or shaved off, and these fragments may remain in the body."

Two small bullet fragments had lodged in Bruce's head.

Dr. Golden's meticulous examination found that Bruce Cleland had sustained a total of four gunshot wounds, all of which had passed completely through him and were potentially life-threatening. With no scientific method for determining the order of the gunshots, Dr. Golden could not unequivocally number them in sequence. That would be up to the police investigator, using logic and an understanding of evidence at the crime scene.

According to Dr. Golden, two of the projectiles would have been immediately fatal, since they had smashed through the skull and perforated the brain. Another had entered through his lower back, about seven inches to the right of his spine, and exited through the lower intestine, making it also potentially life-threatening. The fourth slug, which had entered above the upper lip and exited near the left ear, could have eventually caused death through internal and external hemorrhaging.

As a requirement of future legal needs, Dr. Golden had rods inserted in each bullet wound, through entrance and exit holes, to demonstrate the respective bullet paths. An assistant snapped multiple photographs.

Just as important for forensic purposes, Dr. Golden documented clearly visible stippling on the skin around the victim's head wounds. Stippling refers to tiny "peppering marks" left by the discharge of a firearm in proximity to the victim. Particles of gunpowder, both burned and unburned, strike the flesh around the bullet hole, leaving small red and black marks. It is sometimes referred to as "tattooing." For detectives, the information is crucial in determining approximate distance between the shooter and the victim.

In discussing this, Dr. Golden pointed out that stippling is generally noticed when the weapon's muzzle is between six inches and two feet from the victim's skin. "There's no way the pathologist can know the exact range of fire without the actual weapon and ammunition used. It has to be test-fired to determine the exact range. But in broad limits, if the weapon is within two feet, it will leave the marks."

In addition to the injuries caused by bullets, Dr. Golden noted multiple scrapes and abrasions on the face and forehead, and on the victim's hands, consistent with someone who might have been running and had fallen to the pavement.

After Dr. Golden concluded his work, he used notes along with observations to prepare a formal report, and gave it to Tom Herman. The detective reviewed the autopsy findings and clenched his jaw. This particularly brutal slaying demanded justice for the victim and punishment to the perpetrator. So far, though, no evidence pointed to a possible suspect. Lupe Hernandez had seen someone running from the crime scene, but no one knew if he was the shooter or a frightened bystander trying to avoid being shot himself. From what Herman had heard about Rebecca Cleland, her behavior seemed odd, but it might be written off to nerves, confusion, or traumatic shock. The carjacker claim didn't sound at all plausible. Thugs planning to forcibly take a vehicle from the driver don't shoot the victim, then run away leaving the vehicle engine running and a purse on the console. Also, Rebecca's comfortable position on the pavement with her hands pillowing her head looked strange. So did the meticulous placement of her shoes, upright and side by side. Still, in any case, it did not appear that she could have been the shooter. A mountain of work lay in front of Herman and his partner, Rick Peterson.

Bertha had spent the weekend of July 26 to 27 in Las Vegas. She returned early Monday morning and went right to work. At her desk, she received a call from Diana, who said, "You are not going to believe this."

"What?" Bertha absentmindedly asked while concentrating on business documents.

"Bruce is dead."

Bertha nearly fell out of her chair. "Dead? What? She got rid of him? He's gone?" Later discussing it, Bertha said she had interpreted the surprising announcement as meaning that Rebecca had purged him from her life, or perhaps agreed to a divorce.

Diana yelled, "No! Dead! Killed."

"What do you mean?" Bertha shot back. "What are you taking about?" Big red letters flashed through her mind spelling out a name. *Becky!* She asked, "Diana, did Becky have anything to do with Bruce's death?"

"I don't know. But she's been acting crazy. I've been trying to talk to her, and she doesn't want me to come over. She doesn't want to tell me what happened. Only that someone hit her over the head."

Bertha left work and drove straight to Rebecca's house in Whittier. In her recollection, she said, "I walked in there and she didn't seem to know what to do or say. I asked, what happened? She started crying, but, like, with fake tears. More like scared tears. She was nervous."

Rebecca looked directly into Bertha's eyes and stated, "I don't want to talk about it."

Unwilling to accept her diversionary tactics, Bertha insisted, "No, talk about it. What happened? Are you okay? Diana said you got hit over the head. Let me see."

Rebecca refused to let Bertha touch her. "No, no. I'm okay."

"No, you're not okay. I thought they knocked you unconscious."

"No, no, I'm fine. I already went to the doctor."

Bertha had long since learned to recognize when Rebecca shaded the truth. She knew the claim of seeing a doctor sounded completely phony. "Well, what's going on? Tell me what happened."

They both sat down, Rebecca on a light tan recliner and Bertha on a matching couch, with a coffee table between them. At last, Rebecca opened up, but her story only confused Bertha. "Well, we were at my uncle's house. I don't know. These guys came out of nowhere and they knocked me out and they killed Bruce." She started sobbing.

As Rebecca spoke, Bertha noticed a newspaper clipping lying on the coffee table. Glancing down at it, she realized it contained a story from the Monday-morning edition about Bruce's death. She asked, "Why did you cut this out? Are you keeping it as a souvenir?"

"Oh, I need to send it to the insurance company," said Rebecca.

Each new facet of the story grated on Bertha's nerves. "What? What do you mean? Why do you need to send it to the insurance company?"

Rebecca changed her tone to the high pitch of a pleading young girl. "Well, who's going to take care of me? What am I going to do now? I have to take care of this right away, because I need them to pay me. How am I going to live here? I gotta survive. Bruce is dead and I have no money. The sooner I send this in, the better. I can get the money and survive. Otherwise, what are me and my son gonna do?"

At first, the reasoning left Bertha speechless. It seemed so cold and calculating. But, as she thought it over, it began to make a certain amount of sense. Later explaining, she said, "I'm thinking, 'Well, yeah, okay. He got killed, and maybe this is logical for her to be worried about what's going to happen next.' Even though I thought it kind of weird, you should be thinking about your husband. Not about money. But then, again, this was Rebecca."

The rationalization had just started to satisfy Bertha, when the arrival of someone else sent her skepticism to the boiling point again. Rebecca's attorney walked into the room. Bertha didn't know if he had been lurking out of sight and listening, or had just arrived. She knew that Lucy, Rebecca's late mother, had once dated the lawyer, and Bertha suspected that Rebecca had already made a place for him in her bedroom.

He barked, "Rebecca, I need to talk to you. Alone." They went into another room, leaving Bertha sitting by herself. After twenty minutes, with her patience exhausted, and even more doubtful about Rebecca's behavior, Bertha could take no more. The whole situation smelled of guilt. She interrupted the private conference, said good-bye, and slammed the door on her way out.

Chapter 15

Mystery of the Missing Ring

Detective Herman began Tuesday, July 29, with an interview of Dave Romero at the Hollenbeck Station. With his special knack for setting people at ease, Herman soon had the male stripper chatting with him like an old friend.

Romero admitted that he had performed for Rebecca's guests at a bachelorette party in January, and he had slept with Rebecca both before her marriage to Bruce and several times afterward. "She wasn't happy with him," Romero said, "and wanted to see more of me." The detective needed a few more details, and the exotic dancer readily provided them. "She even called me while she was on her Hawaii honeymoon. Later she told me that she hated her husband, that she wasn't happy, and married him only for his money." Even though Rebecca had lavished Romero with gifts, given him bubble baths at her house, and helped him out with his rent, he said he didn't respect her.

"One time," Romero recalled, "she wanted me to come live with her in Whittier."

"Why did you stop seeing her?"

"Because she was an evil person, and I didn't like the way she treated Bruce. So we went our separate ways."

"Do you know a man named Mark Garcia?"

"Yes. He's an old friend of mine, and was one of the guys who worked for me at entertainment gigs."

"Stripping at parties?"

"Yeah." Romero added that Alvaro Quezada, Rebecca's cousin, had recently joined his stable of dancers.

Herman focused his next few questions on Romero's activities for Friday night, July 25.

"Did you work that night?"

Yes, the dancer replied, he had entertained until quite late at a club in El Monte, about fifteen miles east of downtown Los Angeles. He couldn't remember exactly what time he went home.

Thanking Romero for his aid, Herman said he would be in touch.

After making out a report of the interview, Herman walked to the adjacent impound yard to have another look at the SUV Rebecca had been driving. He and another officer examined every inch of the interior in search of something that Herman had not been able to locate at the crime scene. Bullet casings for every round that struck Bruce after he had jumped out of the SUV had been picked up from the pavement, but the casing for the initial shot, which struck him in the lip, had eluded them. Herman located it wedged between the windshield and the dashboard on the driver's side, near the vehicle identification number (VIN) plate. The .38-caliber Super shell exactly matched the others.

To make certain that no detail could be overlooked, Detective Herman conducted interviews with four of the men who initially responded to the scene shortly after someone shot Bruce Cleland to death. He started with firefighter Carlos

Gallegos. The fifteen-year veteran, who had been trained as an emergency medical technician, described his arrival, along with his partner, Johnny Green, and their immediate examination of the male victim.

"Did you see the female, Rebecca Cleland?"

"Yes. She was behind the SUV, near the bumper's left side, lying down at first. She got up into a crouched position right away." Gallegos said he found several gunshot wounds on the prone man, who was "definitely deceased." After verification of the death, he notified the captain and then followed his instruction to check on the woman. "She said the she had been struck on the head. It was pretty dark, so Johnny held a flashlight while I palpated her head, checking for any hematomas or cuts."

"Did you find any type of injury?"

"None. There were no bumps or bruises and no sign of blood. We also checked for any injuries to her arms, hands, knees, elbows, and her face, with the same results." Gallegos told Herman about offering to assist Rebecca with the cell phone, her refusal to accept help, and the call to her *Papí,* or father. During the whole time, he stated, she showed very little interest in her dead husband across the street. Gallegos had also noticed the high-heel shoes neatly placed near a rear tire of the SUV. Herman took notes, and asked Gallegos to review them and sign his concurrence of accuracy; then he thanked him for his cooperation.

Paramedic Martin Enriquez described examination of both the deceased victim and the female. His account matched Gallegos's, with one small exception. "While we were checking her pulse," he said, "I noticed a tiny bit of blood on one of her fingers. I don't remember which hand, but it ended up on the white glove I wore, and that's what brought it to my attention." But his examination of her head and limbs never revealed the blood's source. "It did not come from her head, because I found no injury to her face, scalp, or neck."

Two more interviews of technicians who worked the scene revealed nothing new.

Harold and Theda Cleland arranged for their deceased son to be buried next to his sister in the beautiful Rose Hills Cemetery. Patricia had preceded him in death by thirteen months.

The funeral, scheduled for Saturday, August 2, involved a special two-tiered viewing to take place on Friday.

Bertha Awana later spoke of the uncomfortable situation. "They had a viewing at Rose Hills. The family requested that Becky not be there. So they had a special viewing for Becky and her family, which is only six of us. It was me, my friend Diana, Alvaro Quezada, another male cousin, plus Rebecca and her attorney! I wondered what the heck he was doing there. It was an open casket, and they had fixed Bruce up pretty well, but you could tell where the gunshot wound was in his face. He looked okay. Dark blue suit. Music playing, lovely flowers. We were in there about forty-five minutes."

At one point, Rebecca turned to Bertha and started talking about her attorney. In a high, whiny voice, she said, "Oh, doesn't he look handsome in that blue suit?"

Bertha whispered back to her, "We're at your husband's viewing, so why is your lawyer here?" In recalling it, Bertha registered disgust. "She was all over him. I mean, she was sitting next to him, holding his arm, sighing, and sobbing. I was in disbelief, thinking how sad it was. This was about six o'clock in the evening, on a Friday. As we were leaving, his family is arriving. We had to be there an hour before Bruce's family, and were supposed to leave before they got there. That was part of the agreement explained to us. Rebecca said she believed the parents thought she had something to do with Bruce's death. So they wanted nothing to do with her. And they didn't want to be anywhere near her. Bruce's mother stared daggers at Rebecca, like if looks would kill, she would be dead. We crossed paths, down the hallway. And, of course, the person in charge wanted to make sure we were out. Rebecca said, 'This is ridiculous. This is my husband and they are asking me to leave.' She was making a scene."

Elizabeth Lamb had committed to deliver enlarged photos to Rebecca in Whittier on Saturday morning before the funeral services. Concerned about her own safety, she took a Spanish-speaking female friend with her. She later explained, "If they were talking in Spanish, I wanted to know what they were saying, because I was a little bit afraid."

A small gathering of Rebecca's relatives and friends stood outside when Elizabeth arrived. She recognized Alvaro, saw Jose for the first time, and thought they looked like bodyguards. Elizabeth noticed Rebecca's hands and whispered to her friend, "Look, she's wearing her wedding ring again, as a grieving widow. Playing it to the hilt." After delivering the photos, Elizabeth and her companion left, declining an invitation to attend the funeral.

About thirty-six people gathered on a warm, picturesque hillside late Saturday morning and seated themselves in folding chairs. The clear sky and serene landscape offered sanctuary from the world of violence and pain. Still, a certain amount of tension hung in the air. Rebecca, Bertha, Alvaro, his girlfriend, and one more of Rebecca's relatives occupied chairs at one side. On the other side, Bruce's parents and Ed Brown were joined by a coterie of relatives, friends, and business associates. A noticeable number of empty chairs formed a cold wall of conflict between the polarized groups.

Bertha recalled, "At least, Rebecca's lawyer didn't attend. She just sat there in a daze, and all of his people were giving her and me dirty looks. I felt terrible. Bruce's mourners would stop near Mrs. Cleland, then turn toward Rebecca, glaring, like they believed she had caused his death."

After the services and eulogies, each group went its separate way.

* * *

On Sunday after the funeral, Rebecca made another call to Dr. Randy Ellison, the man she had met in Cabo San Lucas. She told him all about the services at Rose Hills Cemetery and how Bruce's people had been so rude. She thought they were pointing the finger at her as being responsible for his death. The subject made Ellison uncomfortable, and he kept the conversation short.

Even though doubts plagued Bertha, she still felt sorry for her old friend and kept in touch with her over the next few days. Bertha knew that Alvaro lived in the Whittier house with Rebecca, and she hoped he would assist her through the difficult times. When Bertha later spoke of how Alvaro helped, she rolled her eyes upward, trying not to be harsh. "Of course, she kept giving me her sob story how she was hurting and couldn't sleep. How Al would console her and lie on the bed with her for comfort, because she was so upset and sad about what had happened to Bruce. She said she was so lucky that Al was staying there with her. That's when I started thinking they were having a thing. I don't know. I never actually saw it. He was always very flirtatious with women. And Becky was always very affectionate with everybody. So I don't really know." Bertha's expression made it clear what she believed, though.

Alvaro himself would eventually add fuel to Bertha's suspicion. He revealed that he and Rebecca had no inhibitions about nudity in each other's presence, and sometimes they slept in the same bed. According to Alvaro, it was no "big deal," since Rebecca had grown up with him and his sisters. He remained silent about the issue of having sex with her.

By the following Wednesday, Elizabeth Lamb's acute sense of right and wrong demanded some relief. She had been struggling with a decision; to tell the police what she knew or play it safe and keep her mouth shut. A new piece of news helped her decide. Word came to Elizabeth that Rebecca had claimed the "carjacker" stole her diamond ring. Elizabeth recoiled in shock. The ring had clearly been on Rebecca's finger when Elizabeth delivered photos for the funeral. She had even pointed out the gaudy diamond to her companion. If any doubts existed in Elizabeth's mind about Rebecca's honesty, they evaporated instantly.

Elizabeth had known a police officer in Orange County for several years. She called him for advice. In careful, sequential detail, she told the cop what had happened, including Rebecca's comment expressing the possibility that one of her relatives might kill Bruce, and if that happened, Rebecca didn't want to be a suspect. The officer said, "Beth, you need to call Los Angeles Police Department right away and tell them you have some information about a murder that happened. They'll get you in touch with a detective, and probably just talk to you on the phone. It sounds like mostly hearsay, which can probably never be used in a court of law. And she will never know that you are talking to them."

He added, "A homicide investigation is like a puzzle, and you have one piece of that puzzle. If Rebecca is not a suspect, they'll throw it away. But if she is a suspect, they need to hear what you have to say. It's really important that you do this. Don't worry. She will never know."

Taking a deep breath, and organizing her thoughts, Elizabeth called the LAPD. They connected her to Detective Tom Herman at the Hollenbeck Station. After about two hours on the phone with him, he asked her to come in for a personal interview.

Later describing it, Elizabeth said, "I went to East L.A. to the station. It was pretty funny, nothing like the television show *Law and Order*. I was in this tiny room, like a hole-in-the-wall. It was a trailer, you know, with papers everywhere. They put me in a room, where there were handcuffs by the table and obvious tape-recording equipment. They told me Rebecca was a suspect and I was one of the only witnesses that she was still talking to. She wasn't even talking to her sister Dolores anymore. They wanted me to talk to her as much as I could and call them every time."

In her recollection of it, Elizabeth laughed at herself with self-deprecating good humor, making fun of her speaking skills. She said she had read a transcript of the interview. "I didn't realize how much I talk like a hillbilly until I read my own words. I don't finish sentences. I say 'uh' a lot. And I jump from topic to topic."

People who know Elizabeth disagree, and have nothing but complimentary observations about her ability to express herself intelligently and clearly. In the interview, she provided details of everything she knew about Rebecca, from the very first contact and all of the ensuing events.

Willing to help with the investigation, despite possibly endangering herself, Elizabeth agreed to keep in contact with Rebecca and report back to Herman. She called Rebecca several times and even made a few visits to the Whittier home. Elizabeth found it interesting that Rebecca never again mentioned the alleged molestation, and instead spoke mostly of her own tribulations as a grieving widow. Rebecca repeatedly emphasized how she just couldn't live without her husband, and said she had sought professional counseling in an effort to rid herself of ongoing nightmares.

Elizabeth didn't have to find excuses for visiting. Rebecca asked her to come over to discuss revisions in the orders for albums and wedding pictures. Now she wanted to convert them into a tribute to her dear departed Bruce and present a customized album to his mother. Elizabeth asked Rebecca how many albums and photos she wanted for herself. The answer didn't make sense. Rebecca snapped, "Oh, I don't care, just give his mother all the proofs and albums."

The two women agreed to meet the following week at the Whittier house. With unsettled nerves, Elizabeth contacted Detective Herman and told him of the appointment. He had a special favor to ask. Herman delivered a voice-activated tape recorder for Elizabeth to carry in her purse.

When Elizabeth arrived at Rebecca's home, two men sat in the living room with her. Elizabeth recognized Alvaro, but not the other person, who was introduced as "a cousin." Speaking of it later, Elizabeth said, "She and Alvaro acted like they were lovers. They had matching tongue piercings."

Despite her best efforts to prime the pump of Rebecca's mouth, and fill the tape recorder with information needed by Herman, nothing useful developed from the visit. Elizabeth later said, "They didn't get anything out of it. I tried to get her to talk about the murder, but Alvaro wouldn't let her. She would go dramatic, complain about not being able to sleep, and then she would talk about how much fun she was having."

While monitoring Elizabeth Lamb's efforts to uncover new facts, Detective Herman continued his agenda. In the middle of August, he knocked on doors close to the crime scene and spoke with Virginia Selva. The teacher's aide readily told him about being awakened by gunshots and seeing Bruce Cleland trying to run away from a man firing shots. She had also heard what sounded like a man and a woman arguing, but attributed it possibly to a neighbor girl and her boyfriend. Selva had spotted a woman lying behind the SUV and watched the dark-clad man running toward Concord Street, where he disappeared. She dutifully reported to Herman everything she could remember. He thanked her, returned to his office, prepared a report of the conversation, and added it to his growing "murder book."

In Herman's mind, he tried to link some of the puzzle pieces. Virginia Selva had heard shrill, arguing voices. Paramedic Martin Enriquez had seen a tiny bit of blood on Rebecca's finger, but no visible wounds on her. Perhaps it came from gory smears of fresh blood inside the SUV. Yet, if Rebecca had been knocked out while standing behind the vehicle, how could she have been anywhere near the vehicle's interior? On the other hand, if her story about being slugged from behind and collapsing on the pavement turned out to be untrue, then the entire scenario needed to be reexamined. Perhaps she had accidentally touched some of Bruce's blood, and then had a loud verbal exchange with the shooter, which would account for the strident voices heard by Virginia Selva and Lupe Hernandez. Rebecca's credibility about the events had certainly been undermined by her actions and her mouth. She had lied to Robert Zavala and to Elizabeth Lamb about her purse, wallet, and ring being stolen. Moreover, the way she had pillowed her head with her hands as she lay on the pavement, and the careful placement of her high heels behind the vehicle, could be on a satirical television show about dumb criminals.

None of this, Herman realized, would support arresting Rebecca. But it certainly deserved additional probing. If proof could be found of her involvement in Bruce's murder, a link had to exist between her and the shooter. Herman's investigation would focus on finding that link, if it existed.

Chapter 16

Photograph
Number Four

By keeping tabs on key players in the Cleland drama, Tom
Herman heard that Alvaro Quezada had succeeded in his new
career of dancing and stripping with Dave Romero's stable of
entertainers in the late summer of 1997. They worked together
at bachelorette parties and special nightclub gigs.

Bertha Awana observed two major changes in Alvaro during
the time he buffed up his physique to become a stripper. Not
only had his body been altered, but so had his personality. At-
tributing his bulging muscles to the heavy use of steroids,
which she figured had started the year before, Bertha said the
happy-go-lucky kid she had known no longer existed. The
drugs, in her opinion, had released much darker urges hidden
inside Alvaro.

In late September, Tom Herman had another chat with Officer Robert Zavala. The helpful cop had previously mentioned
some contacts with Alvaro Quezada, and Herman wanted to

know more about the two strange phone calls on the night Bruce was killed.

Zavala searched his memory and went over the details to the best of his recollection. One call had interrupted his sleep at two-thirty Saturday morning, and the second came at four-twenty. In the first call, Alvaro had wanted to talk to someone about domestic problems with his girlfriend. More important, the second call reported that Bruce had been shot.

Herman made a mental timeline, noting that call number one came slightly over one hour after Bruce's death, and number two took in excess of three hours after the brutal slaying. During the first call, Alvaro had given Zavala his location, saying he stood near a taco stand at Third Street and Eastern Avenue. Checking a map, Herman calculated the distance as a little more than two miles from the crime scene. Two men were with him, Alvaro had said. Herman wrote down the names, Dave Romero and Mark Garcia.

The next day, Herman sat once again with Dave Romero. The cooperative dancer recapitulated his accounts of Rebecca's mistreatment of Bruce, and her unfaithfulness. "She kicked him out of his own house," Romero said. "She told me that she hated her husband and could never have been happy with him. That's the main reason I stopped seeing her."

"Why do you think she married him?"

"Rebecca had only one thing in mind. She wanted his money."

Herman subtly changed the subject to Alvaro, and asked how he was doing as a dancer. Romero gave him a good appraisal.

"Do you guys ever socialize together?"

"Not really. We used to go to work in a car pool sometimes. We'd have shows in Victorville or Palm Springs, so I would carpool with everybody. That way we could talk about the jobs. The only time I saw him socially was at Rebecca's house. One time we were all together for a televised fight between Tyson and Holyfield, and we kinda partied that night."

"Do you keep a schedule and records of when your guys work, and where?"

"Yes. Every Monday night we have rehearsals, and that's when I make the schedule, who's working and where."

"Did Alvaro work on Friday night, July twenty-fifth?"

Romero made a check of his records, and answered, "He wasn't on the schedule, so he didn't work that night."

"Did you see him that night at all?"

"No, I didn't."

Herman jotted down Romero's answers, and wondered why Alvaro had made the call to Zavala in the first place, and why he had apparently lied about Romero being with him. It sounded like a clumsy attempt to establish an alibi.

It didn't take Herman long to round up the other stripper, Mark Garcia, and pop the same questions. "Did you ever go out or socialize with your colleague Dave Romero?"

"Occasionally," Garcia replied.

"Do you ever go out drinking in the evening with Al Quezada?"

"No" was the unequivocal answer.

"Let me ask you, more specifically, were you with Al Quezada at any time on Friday night, July twenty-fifth, of this year?"

"No, I wasn't."

Garcia volunteered that he had no real connection with Quezada other than working with him as a dancer/stripper. Also, Garcia said, he had tried to sign up for cell phone service, but his poor credit record made it impossible. So Al had acquired one and let him use it regularly. Garcia gave Herman the cell number.

Tom Herman added another page to his expanding book. Experienced homicide investigators seem to have a sixth sense telling them when they're on the right track, and Herman sensed a pending breakthrough to something important.

It would take a great deal of pavement pounding, endless hours of telephone calls, and exploring blind alleys, but he felt confident the mystery of Bruce Cleland's murder would be solved.

Elizabeth Lamb's collaboration had kept the spotlight on Rebecca as a suspect. The helpful Mormon Mom had exposed Rebecca's lies about the diamond ring and laid bare her contempt for Bruce. Now Tom Herman looked to another woman who might be able to come up with some information. He knew that Rebecca and her sister Dolores were no longer on speaking terms. He hoped the anger between them might inspire Dolores to open up and reveal facts she had kept secret. A previous talk with Dolores had been unproductive, but Herman figured he needed to give it another try.

On October 17, he met with Dolores, and found her much more talkative this time. She spoke about the bachelorette party and accused Rebecca of having sex with both Dave Romero and Diana Harris in the same night. Rebecca didn't love Bruce, Dolores said. She wanted him dead.

Herman tried not to show any excitement as he devoured each word. Dolores, on a roll, said that after Rebecca married Bruce in a civil wedding, but before the church wedding, she talked about getting his money if he died. "Rebecca and I were at a bar in Whittier, on a Friday night before the bachelorette party, and she said some bad things."

Once again calling upon his skills for getting people to talk, Herman urged Dolores to continue. She gave him an eye-opening statement, confiding that Rebecca wasn't happy and had sought her help to get rid of Bruce.

Herman asked, point-blank, "Did your sister say specifically that she wanted Bruce killed?"

"Well, basically, yes."

"What did you say to her?"

"I couldn't believe what I was hearing, and I told her that I didn't know anybody like that. I didn't even want to think about it. And then I asked her how she knew that I wouldn't go right to the cops and tell them what she asked me to do. She goes, 'I'll just tell them that it was all your planning, that you were having an affair with Bruce, and it was all your doing.'"

Perhaps fearful of Rebecca's threat to shift the blame to her, Dolores had not reported her sister's devious scheme to the police. At the wedding reception, Dolores had shelved everything in the back of her thoughts while delivering a speech wishing Rebecca and Bruce a lifetime of happiness. For the nine months since Dolores had heard the ominous words, they had festered in her mind.

Herman asked Dolores if she had told anyone else about this.

"Yes," she said. "I told my coworker on the next Monday at work, and I also told my cousin Robert Diaz."

"What is your coworker's name?"

"Jovita Garay."

As soon as Detective Herman obtained information from Dolores to contact Jovita Garay, he made arrangements for his partner, Rick Peterson, to interview her. The woman, who had been at Rebecca's bachelorette party, agreed to speak with him. Peterson asked if she had talked to Dolores a few days before the party.

"Yes, I did," said Garay.

"What did she tell you?"

"Well, Dolores was taking me home that day. And she said she had something to tell me, but she was very scared. I asked her what it was. She told me that Rebecca had asked her for help to hire someone to kill Bruce." Garay corroborated Dolores's account about Rebecca's threat to accuse her sister of having an affair with Bruce, and to blame the idea for killing Bruce on Dolores.

* * *

Herman understood loyalty among family members and friends and how it can impede criminal investigations. Their reluctance to inform on one another when laws are broken is not unusual. Fear of reprisals can also seal the lips of witnesses. Still, when a brutal murder takes place, it is difficult to suppress frustration at anyone who hides important information.

According to Dolores, she had told one other person of Rebecca's insidious plan. Robert Diaz, her cousin from Texas, had attended the church wedding. Beforehand, he had exchanged friendly conversations with Bruce and his parents while the men were being fitted for tuxedos.

Detective Herman met with Diaz to ask him a few questions. He learned that Diaz had moved to California in April 1997 and had stayed temporarily with Dolores. At that time, she had confided Rebecca's lethal proposal, along with the follow-up threat to blame Dolores. Diaz said he had thought the whole thing was a stupid joke.

Answering Herman's questions, Diaz said he and Dolores had been at Rosarito, several miles south of Tijuana, on the weekend of Bruce's murder. They had returned early Sunday morning and Dolores had dropped him off to visit their friend Diana. Later that morning, he had answered Diana's phone while she was in the shower, and he had spoken to Rebecca. She sounded "normal, not distraught or anything like that," and asked for Diana. When he learned the subject of Rebecca's call, to announce the death of her husband, it had puzzled Diaz that Rebecca hadn't bothered to tell him, but had wanted only to speak with Diana.

Even though Diaz characterized Rebecca's scheme as a joke, Tom Herman retrospectively wished that Dolores, Jovita Garay, and Robert Diaz had at least given law enforcement an opportunity to investigate the threat. Such action might conceivably have saved Bruce's life.

Tom Herman and Rick Peterson could now concentrate their search on evidence of Rebecca's involvement in the murder plot, and to identify exactly who might have helped her carry it out.

As the weeks rolled by after Bruce's death, Rebecca's demeanor as a grieving widow rapidly changed. Reverting back to the party girl mode, she entertained in and out of the Whittier house. Bertha watched the change develop, and later described it. "Rebecca really started living it up. She was having a blast. Having people over to the house all the time. She had yet another stripper, and she would say, 'Oh, look at him. Isn't he cute?'" She even tried to hook me up with him. They were smoking marijuana and she offered it to me. I said, 'I don't want that stuff, and I don't want anything to do with him.'"

Another "hookup" by Rebecca astonished Bertha. A muscular youth, Jimmy Fontana (pseudonym), delivered pizza to the Whittier house one night. Rebecca invited him in and turned on her coquettish act. Her flirtation soon led to an intimate relationship. Not long afterward, Bertha and her husband visited Rebecca. They couldn't believe it when they saw Jimmy sitting in the living room. Bertha's husband had known him for a long time, as his mother's neighbor. Surprised, he uttered, "What the hell is Jimmy doing up here?"

They learned that Rebecca and Jimmy had been "partying" for several weeks and had discussed the possibility of him moving in with her. Rebecca even divulged plans they had made for a trip to Jamaica together, scheduled for the following spring.

Looking back at that time, Bertha said, "He was a cute young guy. Rebecca told him the whole sob story and he believed her. Always before, she had used men to get something from them, but with Jimmy, she didn't need to do that. She thought she was going to have a lot of money, so now she just wanted him because he was young and good-looking."

Other friends and relatives of Rebecca heard her loftier goals for "hooking up" with a man. According to one of her confidantes, the world-famous boxing champion Oscar De La Hoya was the bull's-eye in the dead center of Rebecca's target. The stripper and the pizza delivery guy, Jimmy, were nothing but temporary diversions for fun and sex. Rebecca really wanted to hit the big time by luring De La Hoya into her web. Never mind that he could attract virtually any woman he wanted. The Golden Boy had won two more championship fights since Bruce's death, and had another scheduled for December. Rebecca's self-confidence suffered no limits.

Even though Rebecca told Bertha that she expected to gain a substantial amount of money from Bruce's insurance, she complained about being financially strapped in the interim. Sympathetic as always, Bertha and her friend Diana went shopping. They brought back groceries, cleaning supplies, bathroom necessities, and even some clothing for Rebecca's son.

The generous efforts didn't satisfy Rebecca. She asked Bertha for a loan of $5,000. Bertha replied, "I can't do it. My husband and I are in the process of buying a house. We need all of our savings for a down payment."

As if she hadn't heard the reasoning, Rebecca kept begging. "Please. I need that money. Please let me borrow it, 'cause I'm broke."

Once more, Bertha tried to explain. "Becky, I can't lend you the money. It belongs equally to my husband, and it's for our house."

"Well, what am I going to do?"

"I don't know, but I can't help you."

Bertha would eventually discover something that made her glad she rejected Rebecca's pleas.

Although Rebecca may have had a celebrity boxer on her mind, she still tried to keep her fences mended with other men. She hadn't talked to Dr. Randy Ellison since the day after Bruce's funeral; she gave him a call. Ellison listened as she rambled on about her financial problems. They would be solved soon, she said. As the beneficiary of several insurance policies on Bruce, she could receive a payoff close to a million dollars.

Ellison, somewhat relieved that she didn't ask him for a loan to tide her over, expressed his sympathy again for Bruce's death and his hope that the money would give her some comfort. Rebecca changed the subject and invited him to her home to help celebrate Christmas, only a month away. Ellison said he thought that would be fun and agreed to make the trip. A couple of days later, he even bought airline tickets to Los Angeles. He told a close friend about his plans, expecting the usual approving backslap. Instead, his buddy warned, "I don't think that's a good idea. Why don't you just let it all get sorted out before you make a trip over there."

Thinking it over, Ellison could see the wisdom in his friend's advice. Maybe he had been blinded by Rebecca's flirtations and ego-stroking compliments. And perhaps, even though the possibility seemed slim, she might have been involved in her husband's sudden death. Ellison made a decision. He would never socialize with Rebecca Cleland again.

In late November, Detective Tom Herman continued his quest for leads to Bruce's killer. Alvaro Quezada had gone to some trouble to establish an alibi with his calls to Officer Robert Zavala. To an experienced detective, this type of behavior usually raises a red flag signaling that the individual has something serious to hide. Also, in Herman's opinion, Alvaro seemed to have good reason for wanting Bruce Cleland dead. He had moved in with Rebecca and appeared to be enjoying the fruits of Bruce's wealth. If Rebecca had reconciled with her husband, Alvaro would probably be out on the street. Herman began assembling the paperwork to subpoena Alvaro's cell phone records.

Meanwhile, in reconstructing the events of that Friday night when Rebecca and Bruce had gone to dinner, Herman contacted the waitress who served Bruce and Rebecca at their favorite Mexican restaurant. Carmelita Barron clearly remembered the couple because she had worked beyond the end of her shift for them. She thought it odd that the woman had gone into the narrow corridor to use the pay phone for a short time, then later stepped back there again to make a call from her cell phone. Herman thanked her and jotted down the pay telephone number.

With a warrant, Herman obtained telephone company records to see what numbers had been called from the restaurant pay phone on the evening of July 25. Only one showed up. It belonged to a woman named Ilma Lopes. Herman contacted her and asked if she remembered receiving a call that night. Yes, she said. A woman had spoken to her in Spanish and asked for someone named Jose.

"Do you remember the last name of the person she asked for?"

"No, I'm sorry, but I can't recall it."

"Could the last name have been Quezada?"

"Yes, that was it. Jose Quezada."

"What happened then?"

"I told her that I didn't know anyone by that name. And she hung up."

Evidently, Rebecca had tried to call her cousin Jose that night, but had punched in the wrong number. Several similarities could be seen between Ilma Lopes's and Arturo Quezada's telephone numbers.

Still concentrating on the final night of Bruce's life, Herman wondered why Rebecca had taken him to her uncle Arturo's house on Fresno Street, where they lingered at least two hours. If they really intended to discuss a reconciliation and talk about salvaging the marriage, it seemed odd to spend that amount of time with Arturo and his girlfriend. And why had she tried to call Jose just a short time earlier?

From arrest records, Herman knew that Jose had not always been a law-abiding citizen. Based on the erroneous call made to Ilma Lopes, Herman decided to try something. He obtained a photo of Jose from previous arrest files and assembled a six-pack, a photographic lineup to show witnesses.

On Wednesday, December 3, Herman drove to Lupe Hernandez's workplace. He escorted her into a private area and talked briefly about her recollections of seeing a man dressed in dark clothing running down Concord Street on the night someone shot Bruce Cleland to death. Then he read aloud to her from a standard form: *"In a moment I'm going to show you a group of photographs. This group of photographs may or may not contain a picture of the person who committed the crime now being investigated. Keep in mind that hairstyles, beards and mustaches may be easily changed. Also, photographs may not always depict the true complexion of the person. It may be lighter or darker than shown in the photo. Pay no attention to any markings or numbers that appear on the photos or any other differences in the type or style of the photographs. When you've looked at all the photos, tell me whether or not you see the person who committed the crime. Do not tell other witnesses that you have or have not identified anyone."*

Herman asked Lupe if she understood, and she acknowledged that she did. He handed a square section of poster board on which photographs of different men, numbered from one to six, had been imprinted. Lupe studied it for a couple of minutes. She finally pointed to photo number four, and said it was the man she saw running down the sidewalk on that night.

Photograph number four was a clear shot of Alvaro's brother, Jose Quezada.

Chapter 17

Cell Phones
and Cell Doors

Murder is frequently related to money. Homicide detectives know this and nearly always look for the connection. With the help of representatives and investigators from several insurance companies, Tom Herman and Rick Peterson tracked down what appeared to be a solid lead linking Bruce Cleland's death to financial gain.

Policies had been issued by three insurers to pay off in the case of Bruce's accidental death. The operative word here, Herman knew, was "accidental," which would include being shot to death. The beneficiary would stand to receive $517,000, $200,000, and $44,000. Two of the policies had been purchased in June 1997 by Rebecca Cleland. In addition, she would be eligible to receive $196,829 from his TRW employee's stock savings plan. Other minor sums would also be paid, making Bruce's death potentially worth $986,688 to Rebecca.

It especially interested Herman that policies had been

purchased for *accidental* death. They require no physical examination, so Bruce may not have even known about them.

Based on mounting suspicion against Rebecca, and lies she told about her ring being stolen—as discovered by Elizabeth Lamb—Herman acquired a warrant to search the Whittier house. He, Rick Peterson, and a team of officers made a surprise visit eight days before Christmas.

Wearing an all-white cotton sweat suit and white socks, Rebecca opened the front door. Her face went slack and darkened, as if the looming forms of two detectives had blocked out the sunshine. Her multicolored hair made it obvious that several weeks had passed since the last red dye job. It looked like she had just walked through a violent updraft, exposing dark roots. Her green eyes widened at the sight of uniformed officers and two civilian-clothed investigators. Like a little girl caught raiding the cookie jar, she kept her hands behind her back.

Alvaro joined her at the door and listened as Herman presented the search warrant. Neither Alvaro nor Rebecca showed any signs of resistance.

Later, describing events of that day and Rebecca's behavior, Peterson said, "I escorted her to the living-room area after we rendered her safe and searched for weapons. She seated herself in a chair in the living room." Peterson noticed Rebecca's odd posture. "She had a pillow and she was kind of taking her hands and putting them on the sides of her legs. It gave me the impression she was trying to conceal her hands."

"I approached her and said I would like to see her hands." Looking subdued, Rebecca complied. She withdrew both hands from their hiding place and held them out for Peterson to examine. On the third finger of her left hand, she wore a gaudy diamond ring. It matched a photograph Elizabeth had snapped at the wedding and later supplied to the detectives. The "carjackers" had not stolen it, as Rebecca had insisted many times.

One of the officers snapped multiple photographs of Rebecca sitting in the chair with her hands visible, then took even more close-ups to show details of the jewelry.

Peterson asked Rebecca to remove rings from both hands. She meekly complied and handed them to him. The detective placed the jewelry in evidence collection envelopes and followed the required procedure of documenting it. Her lies about losing her diamond ring had resulted in it coming true.

A closer glance at her hand told Peterson something else. Tan lines had formed, leaving a band of lighter-colored flesh where the ring had been. Rebecca had obviously been wearing it most of the time since that deadly night.

Herman's team departed, hoping they could soon find enough evidence to support arrests.

The investigation advanced another big step toward the week's end, when, with another warrant, Detectives Herman and Peterson obtained a stack of records from telephone companies for landlines and cellular service. The investigators wanted to know what other calls Rebecca had made on the night she and Bruce went to dinner for "reconciliation" talks.

Two surprises came with examination of cell phone service in Bruce and Rebecca Cleland's names.

First, on the afternoon of July 26, just before two-thirty, Rebecca had called the cellular provider and canceled Bruce's service. Her husband had been dead a little more than twelve hours. Such hasty action didn't fit the usual behavior of a grieving widow.

Second, about three hours later, she had called again. She had suspended service on the cell phone in her name. According to a fraud investigator for the company, this type of request is normally made in the case of a lost or stolen cell phone. The instrument is rendered unusable and the customer is no longer charged, but can still retain possession of the assigned number for future use. In Rebecca's request, she didn't mention the reason. That came on a third call, August 12, in the early evening, when she reported that her cell phone had been stolen. She even provided a police report number, which is required by the phone company when customers say they have lost the instrument due to theft.

To Detective Herman, it appeared that Rebecca had anticipated that her cell phone records might reveal something bad, so she had worked out a way to mislead the police. She apparently thought if investigators discovered who it was that she called that night, she could claim her cell phone had been stolen, but being grief-stricken, she had waited a couple of weeks to report it. Or, maybe by suspending the service, the detectives wouldn't be able to access her records. Herman smiled. *Wrong on both counts.*

Rebecca's and Alvaro's cell phone records revealed a remarkable spate of activity on Friday night, July 25.

She began at 4:37 P.M. with a call to her uncle Arturo.

At 5:36 P.M., she connected to Alvaro Quezada's cell phone.

At 9:30 P.M., she reached Alvaro's number again.

At 10:01 P.M., another call went to Alvaro.

At 10:03 P.M., Ilma Lopes, a stranger to Rebecca, received a call originated at the restaurant pay phone, in which a female voice asked for Jose Quezada.

At 10:24 P.M., Alvaro called Rebecca's cell phone.

At 10:52 P.M., another call came from Alvaro.

At 11:13 P.M., Rebecca called Alvaro.

At 11:56 P.M., Alvaro called Rebecca.

At 11:57 P.M., Alvaro connected with Rebecca again.

At 1:01 A.M., less than ten minutes before someone shot Bruce, Rebecca called Alvaro.

Alvaro also made several calls to his father's house during the time period Rebecca and Bruce stopped over.

Tom Herman marveled at the incredible number of times Rebecca and Alvaro needed to communicate in the few hours before Bruce died. It seemed especially amazing, in view of another fact. An examination of records for the previous four weeks indicated that Rebecca had called Alvaro a few times, but Alvaro had never called her cell phone.

Now, for Herman, a new problem surfaced. Would it be possible to trace the locations of cell phone users at the time they placed or received calls? The detective made a few inquiries and learned that a brand-new technology might be exactly what he needed.

An engineering director named Saiful Huq, with Pacific Bell Wireless, which would eventually become Cingular, provided expert information. He explained that when a cell phone user dialed a number and hit the send button, the signal went to the nearest cell tower, known as a cell site. The tower would relay it to one of many centralized computers. The computer would seek out the cell site of the number being called and transmit the signal through a switching system to a tower within proximity of the targeted cell phone.

In 1997, each centralized computer in that system serviced from fifty to 150 cell sites.

Herman wanted to know if the same process worked to interconnect calls made from one cell phone service provider, such as Verizon, to another, such as Pacific Bell Wireless. Huq said it did. He pointed out that each cell site tower was equipped with at least three vertical antennae, which gave it 360-degree coverage of the area. In some cases, four or five antennae were required to compensate for obstacles, such as nearby buildings. And each antenna would cover a specific sector, thus dividing the 360-degree circle into three areas, like a pie cut into three roughly equal pieces. In East Los Angeles, he said, a cell site would cover an area of about a mile or two. In rural areas, the range might extend sixteen miles.

"If I have a cell phone, and someone is trying to call me," the detective asked, "how does the computer know which cell site to send the call to?"

Huq explained that when a user's cell phone was switched on, in the "idle mode," it constantly sent scanning signals in search of the antenna, thus registering its location through a cell site and into the computer. But if the cell phone was turned off, then the system would not be able to locate it.

The next part of Huq's explanation provided exactly what the detectives hoped to hear. The expert asserted that the computer kept records of every call made through the cell sites, right down to the sector antenna. It tracked the route through which calls originated, and the sites at which calls were received. The records included telephone numbers, dates, and times.

Of the numerous calls exchanged by Rebecca and Alvaro during those crucial hours, several of them went through a cell site located on Boyle Avenue, between Seventh and Eigth Streets. Tom Herman located it on a map and measured the distance from the cell site to the murder scene. It was barely over one mile. Another cell site had processed other calls. It stood only two blocks from the spot where Bruce died.

A picture that had been in soft focus up until now suddenly turned razor sharp. Phone company records of cell phone contacts with Rebecca placed Alvaro Quezada at or near the crime scene. His brother, Jose, had been identified by witness Lupe Hernandez as the man running away from the spot where Bruce had died. She had heard a car's engine start and accelerate shortly after the runner disappeared into the darkness. Herman theorized that Alvaro had been waiting for his brother, in the driver's seat. As soon as he leaped into the getaway car, Alvaro sped away.

If the mounting evidence against Rebecca worried her, she didn't show it. On the contrary, she went on a spending spree. In retrospect, Bertha talked about it. "She had asked me for money, but after [that], she started spending like crazy and running around all over the place. She booked the Jamaica trip for herself and Jimmy, and had parties at her house catered. She paid for Alvaro's cell phone, shoes, clothing, and gave him plenty of cash."

The relationship with Alvaro, Bertha said, began to develop some cracks. "I asked her why she was being so generous with him. She said he wasn't making any money and really needed her." But that changed, and in telephone conversations between the two women, Rebecca complained bitterly about Alvaro. She called him a loser who contributed nothing to his own support. She griped about him living for free and not even trying to work.

"Why don't you kick him out?" asked Bertha.

"Well, no, he keeps me company and I'm scared to be here by myself." Perhaps her fear came from something else she and Alvaro secretly shared.

Alvaro appeared to be buckling, perhaps from pressure of the ongoing murder investigation. Bertha recalled visiting the Whittier house several times after Bruce died, and couldn't understand why Alvaro would lose his temper about her showing up there. She said, "Once, Rebecca sold me her son's bed for my little boy and gave me a key to pick it up. I went over there, and Alvaro arrived at the same time. He was furious! He yelled, 'What the hell are you doing over here? Who do you think you are? This is not your house. You can't just walk in here.'"

Bertha responded with her own anger. "Who the hell do you think you are? I have permission to be here. You're the one who has no business here."

"Yes, I do," Alvaro growled, and stomped around in a tantrum.

"He went off on a rampage," Bertha recalled. "The way he acted around that house was like she owed him something. Like he had entitlement. I always knew something was fishy there. This guy is a jerk. He would get mad at Rebecca for talking to me and would drag her away. I think he was afraid that she might say something to me."

Rebecca did tell Bertha that Alvaro had increased his use

of steroids. Bertha could see it, and his behavior reconfirmed her opinion that the drugs changed his personality. "When he was younger, he was cheerful, fun, and happy-go-lucky. But he got very moody after Bruce moved out."

As usual, Rebecca filled her life with self-imposed conflicts. And Bertha could see other symptoms of a fractured existence. "She was taking phen-fen and all these pills. That girl was always popping pills and always boozing. Every time I saw her, she was drinking wine or other stuff."

As the investigation grew more intense, Bertha wondered if the police would want to question her. "Sure enough," she later said, "the cops went looking for me. And something happened that really made me look bad."

Bertha had bought a brand-new Nissan Maxima and Rebecca took a liking to it. Looking back, Bertha said, "She told me that she needed a car but said it was too emotionally difficult to drive Bruce's SUV anymore. And stupid me, dummy me, I don't know what the heck I was thinking. I was being the good friend. She asked, 'Can I borrow your car? I can't drive the 4Runner because Bruce was shot in there. I know he wasn't killed in it, he was shot in it, and it's too sad for me to drive it. Can we swap cars for a while?' So I traded cars with her for a week. I thought my husband was going to kill me. I felt terrible about it."

Detectives Herman and Peterson chose that time frame to seek out Bertha for an interview. She happened to be out shopping with her mother. Bertha's husband called on the mother's cell phone and said, "The detectives are here. You need to talk to them."

In Bertha's view, she felt she knew nothing to help move the investigation forward. She replied, "I wonder what they could possibly want from me?"

"Well, it's regarding Bruce, and they are parked outside, waiting for you."

Later describing it, Bertha's face turned red as she laughed about her arrival. "And guess who drives up in the 4Runner—they must have thought I had something to do with his murder so I could have the SUV."

She emerged from the vehicle, contorted her face into an exaggerated, submissive grimace, and said, "You don't need to take me in. I'm volunteering."

At the Hollenbeck Station, Bertha talked freely, divulging anything she thought might help. She had been fond of Bruce, and sincerely wanted the killer, or killers, to be caught.

Detective Herman revealed to her that Rebecca had taken out accidental-death policies on Bruce.

Bertha squealed, "No way. Why would she do that?"

"Well, she did. And she forged his signature on them."

Neither Herman nor Peterson tried to hide their powerful suspicion of Rebecca's complicity in Bruce's death. Gradually, Bertha began to see it as well.

The next time she visited Rebecca, Bertha described the encounter at the police station, and showed her Detective Peterson's business card. She said, "He told me to give it to Alvaro and tell Al that Detective Peterson wanted to speak to him." Alvaro came in at that moment, and Bertha followed through with the detective's request.

Alvaro's face assumed a mask of impassiveness. He muttered, "I don't care." Bertha shrugged and went outside with Rebecca to bask in the winter sun on the patio. Alvaro followed and asked exactly what Peterson wanted.

"I have no idea," Bertha said. "Why don't you call him."

Alvaro maintained his aloof stance and repeated his comment. "Oh, whatever. I don't care." He didn't sound very convincing to Bertha. Within a few seconds, Rebecca and Alvaro went back inside together, and Bertha could see them in an animated, arm-waving discussion.

In her recollection of those days, discussing the suspicious cloud around Rebecca, Bertha said, "She was getting ready to leave on a trip to Jamaica with Jimmy Fontana. And I thought maybe it would be a good thing. The detectives thought she was going to flee the country to avoid being implicated in the murder. At first, I wanted to defend her. You know, there's no way, and I believed her."

Detectives Herman and Peterson didn't believe her. On February 17, 1998, backed up by uniformed officers, they arrested Rebecca Cleland and Jose Quezada.

Chapter 18

We Have a Hit to Do

Elizabeth Lamb had been cooperating with the detectives, trying to get Rebecca to make incriminating statements, but without much luck. In early February, Detective Herman called her and said they appreciated her help, but now she could back off. "We have enough evidence and are in the process of getting an arrest warrant. We're going to get her."

Relieved, Elizabeth replied, "Okay, I just finished her album, and want to get it to her. I don't want it anymore."

Herman said, "You're going to make an appointment with her? Hang on just a minute." After a long pause, he returned to the phone and said, "Beth, we need your help again. Make the appointment for February seventeenth, about ten o'clock in the morning. We don't want to go to the house unless we know she's there. Because if she sees police approaching the house, she's going to run. She'll head right to Mexico. We know it. Can you please make the appointment for ten o'clock, and we'll come in right after you leave?"

With her pulse racing, Elizabeth replied, "You know what, I'll make the appointment, but come in right *before* I get there. I don't want her to have any idea that I was any part of this."

"Okay," Herman agreed.

In her recollection, Beth admitted a certain amount of fear. "I was very nervous. Not afraid that she was going to hurt me, but I just didn't know what to expect. I was willing because I just wanted justice. I knew she was involved and didn't want her to get away with it. Bruce was such a nice guy and his parents were great. My heart broke for them. Both of their children had died."

On Tuesday morning, February 17, Herman telephoned Lamb. "Call Rebecca right now to confirm that she's home. Rick Peterson and some uniforms are waiting outside of her house."

Elizabeth followed his instructions, and confirmed to Herman that Rebecca was in the house. Years-later she didn't try to cover a self-satisfied smile. "I played it to the hilt," she recounted, beaming.

After arresting Rebecca, Rick Peterson seated her in the back of his vehicle and drove ten miles to a parking lot near the I-605 Freeway. There he met Tom Herman, who had already taken Jose into custody at his East Los Angeles residence. Tom Herman escorted Jose from his vehicle, led him over to Peterson's car, and assisted him into the backseat next to Rebecca.

The two cousins glanced at one another, but the only words came from Jose. He muttered, "How are you doing?" After that, neither of them said anything. Herman and Peterson observed carefully and made note of the odd way they ignored one another, as if they had never met. On a prearranged excuse, the two cops walked a few yards away from the vehicle, but they kept it in sight. The detectives hoped that a hidden recorder would pick up incriminating comments from either

Rebecca or Jose whispering to each other. But the suspects held their silence. Streetwise and angry, Jose may have recognized the setup. Rebecca, perhaps, picked up on his unspoken signals and kept her mouth shut, too.

About an hour later, Elizabeth Lamb called Rebecca's number again and left a message. "Hey, I came by your house and you weren't there. Give me a call. I didn't leave the album on the porch 'cause it looks like it's going to rain. Call me so we can reschedule." She hoped the ploy would erase any hint of her complicity in the arrest.

At the downtown Los Angeles County Sheriff's Department and jail, both suspects went through the process of being searched, photographed, booked, and led to cells in separate sections of the custody area. Herman asked Jose if he knew the woman with whom he had ridden in the backseat. "I've never seen her before," Jose asserted.

A few minutes later, Herman asked Rebecca if she knew the man. She admitted, "He's my cousin Jose."

Both detectives knew they didn't have enough evidence to hold Jose Quezada more than a day or two, but they needed him in custody for another purpose. In Rebecca's case, she had filed a false police report regarding theft of the ring. This would hold her in jail until more evidence could be collected to support murder charges.

Witness Lupe Hernandez had already arrived at the jailhouse and waited in the front row of a small auditorium. Jose's arrest had been for the primary purpose of lining him up with five other men on the stage to see if Lupe could pick him out as the man she had seen on July 26, 1997. An officer briefed her on the procedure and gave her a form to enter her selection. He had told her that suspects involved in the crime may or may not be in the lineup, and she was not obligated to select any of the men. The purpose, he emphasized, was to eliminate any innocent person, as well as to identify someone who might be responsible. Lupe was instructed not to talk to anyone during the lineup. If she had any questions, she should raise her hand, and an officer would respond. A prosecuting attorney, Deputy District Attorney (DDA) Eleanor Hunter, would be present, he advised, and might wish to ask her some questions. Also, defense attorneys might be in the auditorium, but Lupe was under no obligation to speak with them.

The arresting officers, Herman and Peterson, left the auditorium after the briefing, and waited in an anteroom for it to be completed.

Lupe watched through one-way glass as six men entered from a side door, lined up on the stage elevated about thirty inches above the auditorium floor, and stood there, facing her. They could not see anyone in the audience. Each man wore a numbered placard, from one to six, hanging from his neck. They stood at a corresponding number on the stage. An officer conducting the lineup directed them, one at a time, to step forward a couple of paces, stand for a few seconds, then make various turns to present themselves in profile and from a rear view. Finally each man returned to his designated position.

After a few minutes, Lupe raised her hand. Would it be permissible to get up on the stage for a closer look at the men? she asked. The officer allowed her to do so. She would still be on the side of the one-way glass where she could see the men, but they could not see her. Lupe rose, walked up the steps, and studied one man more than the others. She returned to her seat and entered her selection on the provided form, picking the man who wore number six.

Afterward, she met Detective Peterson in the anteroom and walked out to the parking lot with him. Herman and DDA Eleanor Hunter remained inside to collect photocopies of the documents. Outside, Lupe said to Peterson, "I'm ninety-eight percent positive that number six was the man I saw that night."

She had picked out Jose Quezada.

The DA's office felt that a little more evidence would be

required before Jose could be taken to trial. So, two days later, he walked out of the jail facility.

Rebecca remained behind bars. She telephoned her most reliable friend, Bertha, and asked her to pack up some of her personal possessions inside the Whittier house and put them in storage. Rebecca even offered to give Bertha the pool table in exchange for her help. Rebecca hinted that she would like for Bertha to personally store some of the more valuable items, and keep them until this whole business concluded. Her attitude reflected confident expectation to be exonerated and released soon.

Bertha turned down the offer of compensation, agreeing to help her old pal. She drove to the Whittier house and began collecting the things Rebecca had itemized. Fortunately, Alvaro had business elsewhere.

While sorting through Rebecca's desk and files, Bertha found Rebecca's checkbook. She glanced through it and felt a surge of anger. It showed a deposit of more than $100,000 from Bruce's TRW savings plan.

Later discussing it, Bertha said, "She got it immediately after he died. This meant she was lying to me, to Diana, and whoever else she thought she could fool. She had written checks totaling about ten thousand dollars to her attorney, and given money to other people, including her uncle Arturo. Cousin Alvaro had received five hundred dollars from her, in one check."

Disappointed again in Rebecca, Bertha set aside the mixed feelings and fulfilled her promise to put some things in storage. A few days later, she drove to the jail for a personal visit. She brought up Detective Peterson's allegation about Rebecca purchasing accidental-death policies on Bruce and forging his signature.

"Oh, my God," Rebecca whined. "That's not true."

"Becky, why are they saying that? Did you do it?"

"No. Don't believe them. It's not true. Why would you even believe that?"

"Well, why would they tell me that?"

"They are just trying to turn you against me. You are my only friend and they are trying to make it seem like I did this. And I didn't do anything. You have to believe me."

"I want to believe you, but it's hard, Becky."

On a subsequent visit, Bertha took Jimmy Fontana with her to visit Rebecca. En route, he asked her a barrage of questions. Bertha replied, "You know what? I'm not going to say anything. You decide for yourself."

Indignant, Jimmy replied, "Well, I believe her and I think she's innocent. Why did they arrest her? She had nothing to do with it."

Years later, Bertha said, "He was totally convinced by her that she wasn't involved in Bruce's death. Eventually I think someone convinced him and he backed away."

In a final visit to Rebecca, Bertha did her best to avoid a confrontation. The conversation stayed light. Bertha told Rebecca that the murder investigation was all over the news. "Oh, my gosh, you're popular. It's everywhere. They are saying it's a high-profile case, because Bruce was a software engineer, had money, was from South Pasadena. Gosh, Becky, you're gonna be famous."

Rebecca's eyes lit up, like in the old days. She laughed, saying, "Maybe they'll make a movie out of this after it's over. Carmen Electra could play me, and Pamela Anderson could play you, Bertha."

Later reminiscing about it, Bertha said, "We were kinda joking about it. We both were treating it with humor, and saying that she was going to be found innocent and would make a lot of money out of it when she got out."

Little by little, though, Bertha finally had to accept that her childhood friend had probably arranged Bruce's death. "I started learning more, and the detectives shared more facts with me about the evidence they had. I had a hard time, but finally thought, 'That's it. I want nothing to do with her. I don't ever want to see her again. I will do whatever I have to do to make sure they convict her, if she really had something to do with killing Bruce.'"

Even though Bertha ended her jailhouse visits to Rebecca, other people continued to make the trip. Alvaro came to see her one Sunday, April 12, 1998, for a whispered conversation. His father, Rebecca's uncle Arturo, dropped by a few times. And one sister, Yvonne, kept lines of communication open. A gulf between Rebecca and the other sister, Dolores, grew even wider.

Alvaro's visits to his cousin came to a sudden halt on April 16, for a very good reason. Detective Rick Peterson arrested him for conspiracy to commit murder. While standing up for the booking photograph, Alvaro removed his white YMCA warm-up jacket, slung it over his left shoulder, and posed in a black tank top, revealing part of his muscular chest. He flashed a broad, toothy smile, as if to show the absence of any concern.

On that same day, Tom Herman took Jose Quezada into custody again, charging him with murder. It struck Herman's sense of irony that Jose's clothing included a black leather jacket and dark trousers, perhaps the same outfit he had worn nine months earlier on a deadly Saturday morning. In contrast to his brother's devil-may-care expression, Jose appeared stern, tough, and sinister.

The additional evidence needed to charge Jose came through a serendipitous route. Detective Herman, working simultaneously on other murder cases, made a concentrated search for a man named Charlie Lebec (pseudonym), who had allegedly witnessed a killing. Underground word came to the detective that Lebec's brother, Pierre (pseudonym), had been seen hanging out in Boyle Heights. Herman found Pierre and asked if he knew the location of his brother. Pierre, whose rap sheets would fill a file drawer, hemmed and hawed. Finally he mumbled something about a house on Fresno Street. That name rang a loud bell in Herman's brain, and he immediately connected it. The groper—Arturo Quezada—still lived on Fresno Street, where he had raised two sons, who now faced murder charges. Once more utilizing his remarkable skill for persuading street people to talk, Herman asked Lebec if he knew Jose and Alvaro Quezada.

"Yeah, I know 'em," Pierre Lebec snarled. "Grew up with them."

"Have you seen them lately?"

"It's been quite a while. I remember Jose coming up to me and asking where he could get a handgun. And he said he needed a driver, too." Lebec admitted his reputation for running guns and selling drugs, which netted about $1,000 a month for him, but he claimed that he had given up such illegal activities.

"Do you remember when this conversation with Jose took place? Was it in 1997?"

Mumbling and pausing frequently, Pierre appeared to struggle with the answer. Herman, realizing the need to give him some time to rationalize telling these things to a cop, offered a little slack. Both men agreed to talk again in a few days.

In the second meeting, Herman repeated his questions. Lebec said he couldn't recall exactly when Jose had brought up the subject of obtaining a gun. "But we talked about it twice. I totally believe that those two conversations took place in the same year."

"Well, how long before the murder of Bruce Cleland, did he ask you about getting a gun?"

"I'm not sure, but probably about three or four months. The second time he came around, he said he still wanted a gun, but didn't need a driver anymore."

"Did he ever say what he wanted the gun for?"

"Yeah," said Pierre. "He said he and his brother Al had a job to take care of. He told me, 'We have a hit to do.'"

Herman realized that even if he could get Lebec to repeat this information in front of a jury, defense attorneys would swarm all over the man's shady history. Yet, such powerful evidence could not be ignored.

Another issue needed patching up before the suspects could be brought to court for preliminary hearings. Jose had denied knowing or ever associating with Rebecca. Even if evidence proved their familial relationship, it didn't mean that they ever socialized. Detective Herman called again on a person whose honesty and morality would win over any jury. He telephoned Elizabeth Lamb and asked her to attend a live lineup.

Motivated by her desire to help bring about justice, Elizabeth agreed to do it. She sat in the same small auditorium where Lupe Hernandez had identified Jose. She watched six different men, all wearing numbers, parade on the other side of one-way glass. She easily picked out the man she had seen at Rebecca's house in January 1997, a few hours prior to Bruce's funeral. Jose Quezada's pretense of not associating with his cousin Rebecca came apart like wet newspaper.

PART 2

Chapter 19

Greedy Wives

The case against Rebecca Cleland, Jose Quezada, and Alvaro Quezada bristled with challenges for the district attorney's office. Ron Bowers, creator of the Trial Support Division, recognized the minefield littered with potential disasters. To aid deputies in forthcoming courtroom battles, he examined not only evidence, but collateral issues and obstacles as well. In his four decades on the job, Bowers had seen literally thousands of homicide cases. He understood the tilted scale between male and female defendants.

Men, of course, heavily dominate the ranks of violent, cold-blooded killers. Women usually solve problems with more oblique, sometimes backhanded tactics. Images in criminal lore, such as Kate "Ma" Barker and Bonnie Parker (of Bonnie and Clyde fame), may be iconic gun molls; however, they were probably more legend than reality. Other recent exceptions to the man-woman imbalance, such as serial killer Aileen Wuornos, executed in 2002, or Patricia Krenwinkel and Susan Atkins, members of Charles Manson's "Family," may be regarded as anomalies.

Probing the charges against Rebecca Cleland, Bowers wondered about the evolutionary process that leads women into the unnatural role of murderess. Is there a discernible pattern in all these cases? What factors make a woman want to take someone's life? Who are their ususal victims? How successful are they? What is their undoing?

Crime statistics reveal several remarkable facts about wives killing their husbands and the problems encountered in prosecuting these crimes. In 1988, for example, an analysis of 540 victims in marital homicides committed in the nation's largest counties (318 wives slain and 222 husbands) concluded that wives charged with murder were less likely to be convicted. Slightly more than half of these women pleaded guilty in return for shorter prison sentences, an average of about six years behind bars. One hundred of them faced trials, and of these, 31 percent were acquitted! Husbands received harsher treatment from judges and juries—with no more than a 6 percent acquittal rate.

Searching for more facts and trends, Bowers dug into files of Los Angeles County trials involving female defendants. Some of them could be classified as "burning bed" women, wives or girlfriends who could no longer endure years of physical or mental torture and decided to kill the abusive partner.

Those cases shed negligible light on Cleland, though, so Bowers scanned convictions in which the motives did not suggest revenge or escape from mistreatment. He began to see a pattern developing in the untimely demise of husbands. It brought to his mind the profound advice offered by "Deep Throat" to reporter Bob Woodward during the unveiling of President Nixon's Watergate crimes. The shadowy informant had whispered, "Follow the money." Bowers used this tip and hit a bull's-eye. *Insurance money!* Greedy wives wanted their husbands dead in order to collect enrichment as beneficiaries.

The most intriguing aspect, he noted, showed that these women seldom tried to do the killing themselves. Most women have a horror of blood and gore, so they nearly always hired assassins, or hit men, to carry out the nasty aspects of the execution.

In virtually all of these cases, the predatory wives had obtained large insurance policies, often for accidental death rather than for term life. They bought policies only on their husbands, not on themselves. And many of the transactions involved forging of the doomed mate's signature. A simple equation came into focus for Bowers. These husbands were worth more dead than alive. The proceeds from the victims' insurance policies could buy widows a life much more exciting and pleasurable than the humdrum existence of a dull marriage.

A few of the cases under Bower's magnifying glass offered insights for proceeding in the prosecution of Rebecca Cleland.

One of the highly publicized trials, *The People* v. *Mary Ellen Samuels,* resonated with sex, greed, hedonism, and multiple layers of murder. The press had dubbed Samuels the "Green Widow" in reference to published photos of her lying nude on a bed covered only with $20,000 in $100 bills. In 1988, Samuels solicited several people to kill her husband, Robert. These attempts ended in failure. Then, in December, she tried a different approach, similar to the concocted story employed by Rebecca Cleland. In order to motivate someone to assist in getting rid of her husband, Samuels sought out her adult daughter's boyfriend. She told him that his girlfriend had been sexually molested by her father. The enraged young man agreed to enlist the help of a hit man to kill Robert Samuels.

A short time later, Robert died from a shotgun blast to the head. Mary Ellen convincingly played the role of grieving widow and collected $240,000 in life insurance. She also received an inheritance, plus proceeds from his business and home, for a total of close to $500,000. She bought a condo in

Cancun, a Porsche, fur coats, and custom outfits from a trendy store called Trashy Lingerie. Her new lifestyle consisted of snorting cocaine, rubbing elbows with male strippers, and posing for mother-daughter cheesecake photos.

In the meantime, her daughter and the boyfriend married. Unfortunately, a dispute erupted between the new husband and his mother-in-law as to whether Mary Ellen had fully paid him for his involvement in the hit. She began to worry that he might contact the police. Unwilling to face such a risk, Mary Ellen decided that her daughter's husband, too, had to be killed. Six months after the death of Robert Samuels, the son-in-law's body turned up in a remote site, where he had been left to rot after being beaten and strangled to death.

Someone blew the whistle on Mary Ellen, and she ended up charged with both murders. After a long trial, a jury returned guilty verdicts on each count and sentenced her to death. The accomplices were tried and convicted separately. This grandmother's present address is on death row at the Central California Women's Facility, near Chowchilla.

As Mary Ellen's case wove its way through the court system in 1990, another woman committed a similar crime. Catherine Thompson's husband of ten years, Melvin Thompson, owned and operated an auto transmission shop on Santa Monica Boulevard. Catherine claimed that on the evening of June 14, around seven o'clock, she came by to pick him up. She told police of hearing what sounded like backfire from a car, then seeing someone running from the shop. Catherine called 911. Police arrived, and upon entering the building, they observed a male slumped against the bathroom wall. Gunshot wounds riddled Melvin Thompson's head, mouth, and chest. The victim was fully clothed, and nothing had been taken from his wallet.

Outside, the officers found Catherine to be mildly upset, claiming that she had noticed a black man walking in the alley. She related that her husband kept large sums of cash in his office and had an expensive watch in a desk drawer, all of which were missing. The police originally suspected the killer to be a thief known as the "Rolex Robber," who had been targeting victims in the Beverly Hills area.

Soon afterward, Catherine attempted to collect on Melvin's $500,000 life insurance policy.

Investigators later determined that she had hired a shady business partner to do the hit for a measly $1,500. The murder plan might have been successful, except for the vigilance of a neighbor next door to Melvin's place. On the day of the murder, he had seen a man emerge from a stopped car, glance around suspiciously, and slip down the alley while the car raced to a side street, out of sight. The alert witness scribbled down the license number. When police responded to Catherine's 911 call, the neighbor handed over the license number. By midnight the investigators had traced it to a rental car. Detectives went to the address listed on the contract and found the vehicle parked in front. They knocked on the door, received permission from the resident's wife to enter, and spotted a burly man seated on a sofa. He turned out to be the hit man hired by Catherine.

The Catherine Thompson crime resembled the Rebecca Cleland case in several ways. Both wives were present when the shooters killed their husbands. Both feigned a robbery— one claiming the loss of a Rolex watch, the other alleging theft of her expensive wedding ring.

An exhaustive investigation of the Thompson case, followed by a meticulous prosecution, resulted in Catherine being convicted and joining Mary Ellen Samuels on death row.

In 2000, Bowers worked on the prosecution of Wanda Warden (pseudonym), which varied somewhat, but had many of the same characteristics as the other cases. The defendant, a longtime social worker, had fallen for a South Central L.A.

liquor store manager, Flavio Sanchez. They rented a place together, but Wanda longed for a home of their own. With their combined incomes, they qualified for a loan and eventually bought a quaint cottage in the bedroom community of Norwalk.

If anything happened to Flavio, Wanda reasoned, she needed a life insurance policy on him to avoid losing the home. He agreed. This provided a level of comfort that nothing unforeseen, such as Flavio's untimely death, would scuttle her fantasy of having her own house.

As is often the case, other forces came into play that dissolved Wanda and Flavio's union. Flavio fell madly in love with a new sports car, which he couldn't live without. A high-interest loan consumed all of his money, and he let the mortgage payments lapse. After Flavio moved out, Wanda learned of his financial shenanigans. Her income couldn't cover the deficit, nor could she continue to make both the payments.

Two years after they had moved in, the house went into foreclosure. She lost not only her dream home, but all of the equity as well, and faced bankruptcy. Wanda never recovered from this devastating financial blow, nor the personal humiliation in which she saw everything evaporate like a desert mirage. Unable to accept Flavio's desertion, she felt her disappointment turn to anger. She wanted vengeance for all the heartache and misery he had caused. Wanda asked a female coworker if she knew of anyone who could beat up Flavio and teach him a lesson. Yes, the woman said, and gave Wanda the telephone number of an ex-con, Avance Smith. Wanda negotiated a deal with Smith for the sum of $300 down and $200 upon completion.

Of course, Wanda realized, she needed an alibi to prevent anyone from linking her with the hit. She arranged for a group of women to congregate for a card party at a friend's house. While Wanda and her cronies indulged in games, Avance Smith lurked outside the liquor store. After 2:00 A.M., Flavio locked up, strolled over to his nice new car, got in, and drove off. Within a few blocks, he came to Main Street

Rebecca "Becky" Salcedo's friends described her as beautiful, fun, sexy, outrageous, generous, and affectionate. Some, though, saw darker aspects in this complex woman. *(Courtesy of Bertha Awana)*

Rebecca *(far left)* lived periodically with her best friend Bertha *(center)* and didn't mind showing off her body. *(Courtesy of Bertha Awana)*

More like sisters, Rebecca *(left)* and Bertha *(center)* met in their early teens and shared adventures for more than ten years. *(Courtesy of Bertha Awana)*

Despite their joyous expressions, tensions developed between Rebecca *(left)* and Bertha *(right)* after Bruce Cleland came into their lives. *(Courtesy of Bertha Awana)*

Bruce Cleland in senior year at South Pasadena High School. Self conscious, shy, and frugal, he avoided asking girls for dates and concentrated instead on education. *(Yearbook photo)*

Bertha Araiza Awana, a successful businesswoman, spoke openly in 2008 about Rebecca's wild and crazy lifestyle. *(Author photo)*

Bruce grew up in this upper-middle-class South Pasadena home with his older sister and parents. *(Author photo)*

As a senior at prestigious Harvey Mudd College, Bruce carried a beer keg to a party, but still feared asking women out. He later earned a master's degree at Stanford University. *(Yearbook photo)*

Bruce met Rebecca at a swap meet on the grounds of this old drive-in theater. Author Don Lasseter stands in the foreground. *(Author photo)*

Rebecca sold bottled spices from a stall on a gaudy vendor lane like this one. She flirted with Bruce, and gave him her phone number. *(Author photo)*

On dates with Rebecca, Bruce (in striped shirt) wound up paying the tab for an entourage that included her uncle, Arturo Quezada (waving), who had a reputation for drinking and fondling young women. *(Courtesy of Bertha Awana)*

Overcoming his extreme frugality, Bruce bought Rebecca countless gifts including a spa, a boat, a car, furniture, and this luxurious hilltop home in Whittier. *(Author photo)*

At his church marriage to Rebecca, Bruce thought he had reached the pinnacle of happiness, but his euphoria would soon crash. *(Courtesy of Beth Lamb)*

The Catholic church in San Marino where Rebecca and Bruce exchanged vows. *(Author photo)*

Wedding photographer and "Mormon mom" Beth Lamb heard shocking descriptions from Rebecca about a honeymoon gone wrong and allegations of repulsive behavior. *(Author photo)*

Happy smiles on the faces of Rebecca and Bruce shortly after their marriage mask anger, hurt, and a tragic future. *(Courtesy of Bertha Awana)*

After kicking Bruce out of the Whittier house, Bertha and a female
cousin partied in a bar on this Cabo San Lucas promenade.
She met a doctor and targeted him for her next conquest.
(Author photo)

Alvaro "Al" Quezada, son of Rebecca's Uncle Alvaro, moved in to
the Whittier house with her and became a dancer-stripper.
(Courtesy of Bertha Awana)

Author Ron Bowers sits in the same spot occupied by Bruce on the last night of his life, when he and Rebecca went to dinner at their favorite Mexican restaurant. *(Author photo)*

Bruce and Rebecca left by the rear door of the restaurant, climbed into their SUV, and headed toward a fateful destination. *(Author photo)*

Rebecca drove the SUV and stopped to close the rear hatch. Someone stepped out of the dark brush and opened fire. Bruce, hit once, jumped out and ran across the street. *(Courtesy of Los Angeles Superior Court)*

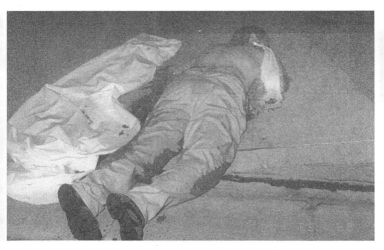

The gunman chased Bruce and fired several more shots, killing him. He died on a driveway apron, thirty paces from the vehicle he left. *(Courtesy of Los Angeles Superior Court)*

An aerial photo of the crime scene. The X near the top shows the location of the SUV. Arrows indicate the path taken by the killer as he followed Bruce across the street, killed him, and then went around a corner to the bottom of the photo where a car and driver waited for him near another site circled X. *(Courtesy of Los Angeles Superior Court)*

The gunman's path took him under a canopy of trees, next to an ivy-covered slope, in the dark of night. A witness saw him and called 911. *(Author photo)*

Months after the murder, detectives executed a surprise search warrant of the Whittier house. Rebecca tried to hide her hands but obeyed the order to show them to officers. *(Courtesy of Los Angeles Superior Court)*

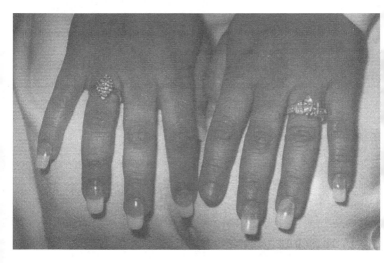

Rebecca claimed that the carjackers knocked her unconscious before shooting Bruce and then stole her diamond ring. But the search showed that she wore the ring.
(Courtesy of Los Angeles Superior Court)

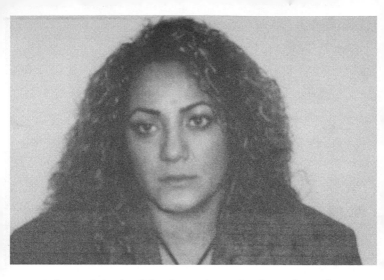

Rebecca Salcedo Cleland was charged with murdering her husband for financial gain. *(Courtesy of Los Angeles Superior Court)*

Al Quesada was accused of driving the getaway car and faced trial for complicity in the murder. *(Courtesy of Los Angeles Superior Court)*

Jose "Joe" Quesada, Al's older brother. Charged with shooting Bruce, he stood trial three times. *(Courtesy of Los Angeles Superior Court)*

Deputy D.A. Craig Hum endured the rigorous challenge of three trials while prosecuting Rebecca, Alvaro, and Jose. *(Author photo)*

The gravesites of the entire Cleland family; Bruce, his sister Patricia, his father Harold, and his mother Theda. They rest in one of the world's largest and most beautiful cemeteries, Rose Hills near Whittier. *(Author photo)*

and stopped at a red signal. He probably never noticed the vehicle following him.

Avance slowed, then halted next to Flavio on the driver's side. Without warning, he raised his gun and pulled the trigger. After six shots, Flavio's lifeless body collapsed onto the steering wheel. His prized sports car, as if in slow motion, rolled through the intersection and crunched into a parked vehicle on the opposite curb.

Wanda had a habit of confiding in her friends. This time she told too many people that she wanted Flavio harmed, if not killed. After interviewing a few of her acquaintances, detectives regarded her as a prime suspect in Flavio's death. The life insurance policy amounted to $104,600.

Anna Phillips, a highly skilled deputy DA, inherited the Warden and Smith prosecutions. Ron Bowers, collaborating with Phillips, admired her enthusiasm, persistence, and ability to build her cases, stone by stone. For Flavio's murder, Phillips prepared for two separate trials, since she wanted to introduce Wanda's statements for the purpose of implicating Avance. She encountered all sorts of witness problems, along with frustrating logistical and legal issues.

Phillips's vigorous presentation in each trial appeared solid to Bowers, but both juries failed to agree on verdicts. Refusing to capitulate, Phillips readied herself for another round. For Avance Smith, the prospect of facing yet another jury evidently broke his will. He entered a plea of guilty to voluntary manslaughter in exchange for a sentence of twenty-two years in prison.

Wanda Warden decided to fight and the matter was set for a second trial. Bowers worked with Anna to make the facts more understandable for jurors. Together they developed visual aids to convey Wanda's involvement in the conspiracy to murder Flavio Sanchez. The graphics seemed to help jurors focus on the facts and deliver a verdict of voluntary manslaughter. They evidently believed that she didn't intend for the hit man to kill Flavio, but merely to beat him up. Legally, said Bowers, she still should have been found guilty of murder under the theory of "natural and probable consequences." However, for sympathetic reasons or other moral compunctions, the jury gave her a break.

As a result of this reduced finding, Wanda received a sentence of only twelve years in state prison. Said Bowers, "This was a perfect example of jury nullification, a concept that the criminal justice system likes to ignore, but does, in fact, exist. Undoubtedly, the jurors didn't like Flavio, who caused Wanda to lose the house she loved. Perhaps they sympathized with her, since she had toiled all her life as a social worker and maintained that she never wanted Flavio killed, but simply taught a lesson. Only the jurors know their reasoning."

Trials of wives who hire hit men can be the most arduous in a prosecutor's career. According to Bowers, jurors have an inherent mind-set that women—especially housewives—by their very nature, can't be murderers. "A higher threshold of proof is required to convict a woman rather than a man. What makes prosecution problematic is the fact that the wife has spent months, if not years, planning every detail of the killing. The wife knows the importance of having an unshakable alibi or story." In these husband-death cases, the police may suspect the wives, but hard evidence seldom materializes. In fact, many new widows undoubtedly get away with murder simply by restraining themselves from telling friends too much, or from being too greedy.

Bowers added, "After considering these types of murder cases, I see an evolving pattern in which the same set of facts are all too common. For whatever reason, the women become disenchanted with the marriage and want a divorce. But after they find out how little they would receive in a settlement, they realize their husband is worth more in death. Life insurance or accidental-death policies tilt the scales. At this point, fantasies about collecting big money evolve into plans for having the husband killed. However, it is extremely rare for any of them to actually do the murder. This may be attributable to women's reluctance to try physical force, or a lack of familiarity with using guns. Both issues create a major obstacle for the women since they generally don't run in circles conducive to finding hit men. So women generally turn to friends, relatives, or acquaintances who might have access to the unsavory element of society."

Shopping for someone willing to carry out a murder carries multiple risks. First the prospective assassins could turn informant. Also, women soliciting murder need to know how much money the killer will charge and about his competency to do the job. She doesn't want to end up with a critically injured husband needing even more of her time and energy as a nurse. The hit man must be reliable and clever enough to avoid being caught. And finally she must be able to trust the killer not to blackmail her in the future, long after she has paid him off.

Life insurance benefits are the catalyst. They make the greedy wife think all the problems are worth the effort. However, overeagerness in collecting the payoff can be the equivalent to waving a gigantic red flag, attracting attention by homicide detectives. Many of the wives have grandiose plans of how they want to spend the insurance proceeds and can't wait to start a new life with different partners.

To Bowers, the Rebecca Cleland case fit the common mold of other wife-killing-husband cases. She had planned to stay with Bruce only long enough to pave the way for profit. When Rebecca learned the divorce settlement would not yield the expected wealth, she came to the same realization as other wives before her: her husband was worth more dead than alive. Next she had to find a hit man. For her, this presented no problem, since her cousins appeared ready, willing, and able.

Other similarities showed up in the Cleland murder. Rebecca

used the child molestation allegation against Bruce to encourage her cousins to help her. This mirrored false accusations by Mary Ellen Samuels in claiming molestation of her daughter by the husband.

Bruce died in the early morning hours of July 26, 1997, shot to death on a dark residential street. Rebecca's arrest didn't take place until April 17, 1998, nine months later. The persistence of Detectives Rick Peterson and Tom Herman, along with the willingness of civilian witnesses to come forward, finally led to the arrest of all three suspects.

Now would it be possible to convince a jury that this trio had conspired to kill Bruce, and one of them had pulled the trigger that ended his life?

DA Craig Hum faced a battery of staggering obstacles in the pending trial.

Chapter 20

Preparing
for Battle

For the prosecution, the trial of Rebecca Cleland, Jose Quezada, and Alvaro Quezada encompassed all the traps and perplexity of a sophisticated video game or a treacherous obstacle course. The DA's team had little to rely on except circumstantial evidence and the statements of two witnesses who saw a shadowy dark figure running away from the crime scene. Observers and analysts considered it a defense attorney's paradise.

In June 2000, with Americans across the nation beginning to argue about the forthcoming presidential election showdown between George Bush and Al Gore, a group of lawyers, officers, reporters, and prospective jurors assembled for a different battle. On the ninth floor of the downtown Los Angeles Criminal Courts Building (CCB), they all filed into Department 109, Judge Jacqueline Connor's courtroom.

The nineteen-story building had been the site of numerous, dramatic legal-contest battles since its opening in 1971, providing endless fodder for books and movies. O.J. Simpson had been acquitted of murder in Judge Lance Ito's Department 110, next door to Jacqueline Connor's domain. Down the hall, "Night Stalker" Richard Ramirez, who had sprinted along sidewalks a few paces from the Cleland murder scene, had been found guilty of thirteen savage killings.

With collar-length streaked-blond hair, attractive photogenic features, and statuesque height, Jacqueline "Jackie" Connor could have been mistaken for an entertainment celebrity. However, lawyers who underestimated her professionalism, intelligence, or dedication to the law found themselves in a world of hurt.

For Ron Bowers, a long-standing knowledge of Judge Connor brought back both pleasant and embarrassing memories, particularly in connection with DDA Craig Hum, the prosecutor assigned to the Cleland-Quezada case.

Long before Connor or Hum's appearance on the legal horizon, Bowers had established a DA's branch office in the City of Alhambra, several miles northeast of the L.A. Civic Center. His wife, Rosemarie, worked there as a courtroom clerk.

In 1977, fresh out of the University of Southern California Law School, Jacqueline Connor launched her legal career as a neophyte DDA in Alhambra. By that time, Bowers had been reassigned, but his wife, Rosemarie, remained working at the courthouse. Recalling it, Bowers said, "Within several months of Jackie's arrival, my wife told me how impressed the judges and jurors were with her skills in the courtroom. She didn't suffer the usual pitfalls and seemed a notch above the rest. When Jackie moved on, my wife made a point to inform me that administrators in the DA's office should take note of this young lady because she had real potential. I made a mental note and later used it in support of Jackie. Within a couple of years, she was assigned to create a sexual assault unit downtown. Over the years, I had the opportunity to be in contact with Jackie on special cases and became keenly aware of her organizational skills and decisiveness."

As an operations administrator, Bowers needed to fill an

important vacancy in the problem-riddled Inglewood office. He persuaded officials to assign Connor as deputy-in-charge. "She was a master at planning and implementing improvements." By 1986, these attributes were noticed and it wasn't long before she was appointed as a municipal court judge, and two years later, she advanced to the Los Angeles County Superior Court bench. Her friend and colleague Lance Ito donned a black robe and followed her progression.

It didn't take "Judge Jackie" long to establish a no-nonsense reputation in running her trials. She placed a high priority on expeditious, efficient use of time, and had no patience with requests for delays. This brought about a sharp sting for Ron Bowers.

Loren Naiman, his assistant, had been shepherding a complex case through the court system involving notorious members of a criminal gang. It landed in Judge Jacqueline Connor's court, but Naiman fell seriously ill and needed a postponement. Said Bowers, "Loren called me up from his sickbed to ask if I would go to Judge Connor's court and request a two-week delay. I agreed, and with supreme confidence, I went to Department 109. With defense counsel present, I stood in front of Jackie requesting a short continuance to allow my assistant to recover. Jackie gave me a stern look and said she was not about to grant a continuance, since she had previously warned both sides that no delays would be tolerated. I pleaded that this wasn't a convenience continuance but was based on the prosecutor's serious illness.

"She responded that all prosecutors are fungible and can be replaced. I explained the complexity of the case, which involved a confidential informant issue. It would be physically impossible for another deputy to get up to speed in the next couple of days. Jackie gave me the coldest stare, freezing me in my tracks. In a firm voice devoid of any emotion, she instructed me to get prepared because the case would be starting in her court on Monday morning. Her intractable stance stunned me. I couldn't believe that she would act so callous in such a situation, especially in view of the support I had given her for so many years.

"Completely dismayed, I hightailed it to the seventeenth floor, marched into the Hardcore Gang Division, and talked to the head deputy, whom I had known for years. I told him that I needed to immediately find a prosecutor with incredibly fast learning skills who could grasp this case over the weekend. To his questions about the sudden dire circumstances, I described the confrontation with Judge Jackie. The mention of her name brought an understanding smile to his face. Without hesitation, he said he had a very promising deputy who was up to the task.

"The next day, I met Craig Hum for the first time. In his thirties, tall at six-one and slim, impeccably dressed, he moved with athletic grace. Craig wore his thick jet black hair in a full style, partly covering the tops of his ears. His penetrating dark brown eyes fixated on the person to whom he spoke, yet flickered with mirth. I realized that jurors would like his appearance and his boyish voice."

A Los Angeles native, Hum's tanned face made it appear that he had spent his life on the beach. In fact, he had worked two jobs while attending undergraduate school. Next he enrolled at Stanford University, Bruce Cleland's alma mater. At first, Hum entertained the idea of becoming a forest ranger, then considered studying political science. But, he said, "there isn't a huge job market for ps grads, so I decided to pursue a career in law." Perhaps, he thought, it would allow him to help less fortunate people in society.

Explaining his background, Hum said, "I thought I would be interested in being a public defender. That was originally my goal. But between my second and third years of law school, I wanted to do an internship. I found out the public defender's office didn't have a comprehensive summer internship program. They didn't give you courtroom experience, just a lot of legal research and writing. With the DA's office, you could actually go into a courtroom. I spent half of that summer clerking for a civil law firm, earning good money, but never got anywhere near a courtroom. In the second half, I went to one of the DA branch offices in Whittier and met everyone out there. They introduced me around one day, took me down to the courtroom, walked me to the counsel table, and sat me down next to the deputy who was in a preliminary hearing. The head of the office said, 'Give Craig a file, he's going to do a prelim today.' I'm like, *what?* Influenced by that experience, I decided that's what I wanted to do.

"I clerked for the DA's office for a semester, and in my third year. As soon as I got out, I worked a summer as a senior law clerk, then took the bar. The day I passed it, they said, 'Well, you've been a senior law clerk, Craig, do you want to be a DA?' I said sure. And I was hired. Got sworn in September 1986."

In the meeting to discuss taking over a gang case on which the judge would grant no delay, Hum's demeanor impressed Ron Bowers. "He listened to my spiel about his need to quickly assimilate the facts. After just a few questions, Craig gave me a reassuring expression. He advised me not to worry, and said that he would handle the situation. Relieved at his willingness to step up to the plate, I still wondered if I had adequately communicated the serious urgency and depth of work necessary to prepare himself for trial so soon.

"Monday came, with the usual avalanche of hiring and training requests. It wasn't until Tuesday I had a moment to think about the gang case in Jackie's court. I called Craig's office to leave a message, assuming he would be in court. But, to my surprise, he answered the phone. I asked him if he had picked a jury and started trial. In his laid-back style, Craig responded, 'Oh no. I told the judge that I wasn't prepared and I would need a couple of weeks to get ready for trial.'

"His complacent manner left me speechless. Amazing! Craig went on to explain that Jackie tried to pressure him, but he refused to say the magic words 'Ready, for the people.' He told me that he knew that there was no way she was going to dismiss such a big case.

"I thought to myself, 'How did this relatively new deputy call Jackie's bluff?' All my support and praise of her over the years proved to be worthless when I had asked for a continuance. She was so concerned with keeping her trial schedule on track. After hearing how Craig had stood up to Jackie's demand, I knew he had the right stuff for prosecuting in any judge's courtroom."

After that early contact with Craig Hum, Bowers had the opportunity to see him in action several times and to learn more about him. Besides being a cutting-edge trial attorney, Hum's years at Stanford Law School had prepared him to be a true legal scholar. His tenure with the Hardcore Gang Division gained recognition for him as an expert in the law involving multiple defendants. Prosecutors prefer to try defendants jointly whenever possible, because it is faster and more convenient for the witnesses. Even though this method is fraught with problems, Hum mastered the solutions.

As a gifted public speaker, he became the top legal instructor for the California District Attorneys Association. His success in courtrooms didn't go unnoticed and resulted in an elevation to the exclusive DA's Major Crimes Division.

While handling some of the most difficult cases in the DA's office, Hum earned a reputation not only as a tough prosecutor but also a skilled student of the law. He won praise for handling a high-profile murder case in which three Asian gang members robbed and killed Dr. Haing S. Ngor, famous for his Academy Award–winning role in *The Killing Fields*.

Ngor, a former physician and army officer in Cambodia, had been captured, imprisoned, and tortured by the Khmer Rouge while resisting that government's despotic regime in the 1970s. After immigrating to the United States in 1980, he had settled in Los Angeles's Chinatown section. Without any acting experience, he was selected to portray Dith Pran in the 1984 film. Pran had worked as a photographer alongside a *New York Times* journalist covering the Cambodian civil war.

In February 1996, three members of a street gang accosted Ngor in his carport, snatched his Rolex watch, and ordered him to turn over a locket. Because it contained a photo of his late wife, Ngor refused, and the thugs shot him to death. He is buried at the Rose Hills Cemetery, not far from Bruce Cleland and his sister, Patricia.

Craig Hum prosecuted the trio of defendants in a single trial featuring three separate juries. Two of the killers were sentenced to prison for twenty-six years to life and fifty-six years to life, respectively, while the third man received life without the possibility of parole.

In June 2000, Hum readied himself to prosecute three people accused of killing Bruce Cleland, this time with a single jury.

When a prosecutor states the words in open court, "The people are ready for trial," that's the equivalent of saying, "It's showtime." Those words trigger the opening curtain and set into motion a legal system shrouded in tradition and cloaked with arcane rules. What gallery observers and news watchers don't see are the arduous months of preliminary work before the prosecutor can announce his or her readiness. The Cleland case required an inordinate amount of advance labor, coping with factual and legal challenges. Research and planning can make or break a case. The intense efforts are anything but glamorous, but a seasoned litigator knows it is the foundation upon which rests success or failure.

In the Cleland case, Craig Hum faced the problems of trying three defendants simultaneously. It couldn't have been much more onerous, since different types of evidence would be required in each phase. Rebecca's case was based completely on *circumstantial* evidence, while *direct* evidence of eyewitness testimony would be the primary ammunition against Jose. For Alvaro, the verdict would rest for the most part on *scientific* evidence in the form of telephone records.

It is difficult enough for a prosecutor to lodge a convincing case against one defendant, and the complications increase exponentially when multiplied by three. Craig Hum understood the need to avoid serious consequences by confusing twelve laypeople arbitrarily picked from the community and appointed as "triers of fact."

To help keep the facts sorted out in jurors' minds, Craig consulted with the DA's Trial Support Division, headed up by Ron Bowers. Together they examined numerous photos snapped by investigators, including various angles of the crime scene, the SUV Rebecca drove that night, Bruce Cleland's body lying on the concrete driveway, cell tower locations, plus interior and exterior shots of the house in Whittier. Experimenting, Hum and Bowers tried a variety of groupings and sequences before settling on a graphic depiction of the story they wanted to tell.

Bowers recalled, "The cell tower locations were crucial as to showing Alvaro's involvement. Craig wanted to clarify exactly how telephone connections between Alvaro and Rebecca not only placed him close to the shooting, but implicated her as well. Craig also asked us to enlarge each defendant's booking photo and mount them on poster boards, with names at the bottom, to show exactly what they looked like at the time of arrest." This could help counteract the usual defense tactic of bringing out their clean-cut, well-dressed clients, creating the image of upscale, law-abiding citizens.

With Alvaro Quezada's enlarged photo, an interesting development took place among Bowers's staff, particularly with female employees. In describing it, Bowers had difficulty suppressing laughter. "I noticed some commotion among my people while they prepared individual photo boards of the defendants. There seemed to be an inordinate amount of attention being paid to Alvaro's picture. I remember several of the ladies asking me if there could be a mistake. When I asked why, they responded that he didn't look like a murderer. Admiring his 'buff' look, and his handsome, chiseled face, a few said they would like to meet him. None of the women showed any interest in Jose or sympathy for Rebecca. The consensus seemed to be that it would be a terrible waste, and certainly a loss for womanhood, if Alvaro had to spend the rest of his life in prison. The next time Craig came by, these women besieged him with more questions about Alvaro's background. With a coy smile, Craig revealed that Alvaro had been a male stripper. That information seemed to unsettle a few of them, who, I guessed, reflected on the times they had seen male strippers. Could they have seen Alvaro at some prior performance? Could he be one of the dancers they had honored by stuffing twenty-dollar bills into his spangled jockstrap?"

Both Bowers and Hum wondered if female jurors might have the same reaction.

Chapter 21

Opening Statements

The opening statement is often the most crucial part of a prosecutor's case. It gives jurors a chance to hear what the trial is all about and how witness testimony interlocks with other evidence to make a complete picture. The opening can best be described as a road map to help jurors understand the journey ahead, and who they will see along the way. Essentially, prosecutors and defenders alike are supposed to use this as an opportunity to explain what they believe the evidence will show.

Many attorneys believe the final argument, at the trial's end, is equally or even more important. Some lawyers risk angering the judge by attempting to squeeze argument into the opening statement. To disguise such efforts, and stave off objections, they have learned to start nearly every sentence by saying, "The evidence will show . . ."

Ron Bowers has spent years trying to convince prosecutors that old-fashioned oration—the staple of legendary litigators, such as Clarence Darrow and Los Angeles's immortal

J. Miller Leavy—no longer works. Jurors today live in the age of high-tech entertainment. They need powerful graphics to supplement speeches. "Surprisingly," says Bowers, "few trial attorneys master the art of the opening statement. It takes the skills of a great storyteller to capture the jurors' imaginations and maintain their interest span. Using visual aids or a slide show presentation can expand the jurors' interest in the message and cement images in their minds. Because of scheduling problems, a prosecutor knows that many of the witnesses will be called out of the logical sequence. The opening is the time for enabling the jury to grasp exactly how names, places, and events fit together within specific time spans."

Defense attorneys sometimes choose to delay opening statements until after the prosecution has presented the evidence in its case. By waiting, the defender knows exactly the strength and weakness of the people's case, which allows adjustments in strategy. Decisions on major questions are easier to make. For example, will the defendant testify? What expert witnesses will be necessary?

In early June 2000, on a morning of typical gloomy overcast spring weather in Los Angeles, the twelve triers of fact filled Department 109's jury box at the right side of the room. They settled into faux-wood swivel chairs with royal blue padding. In the gallery, observers crowded four rows of high-back benches under the watchful eye of a bailiff. The uniformed officer sat on the left side separated from spectators by a pair of seven-foot glass panels and within a few steps of the three defendants.

Rebecca Cleland, dressed in an expensive, fashionable black suit with a red blouse, and wearing glasses, sat next to her attorney. She had gained considerable weight, and had lost her famous charm. Prosecutor Craig Hum noted, "The way Rebecca looked in court was nothing like she usually appeared when attracting men." Jose Quezada and his brother,

Alvaro, had also altered their images, shedding the old street garb. They had both undergone makeovers, giving them the appearance of neat, law-abiding average citizens.

Diffused lighting from the high ceiling softened the atmosphere and allowed a feeling of space in the modern black-walnut–paneled chamber. On the other side of the yard-high divider between the gallery and the court, lawyers worked at end-to-end counsel tables. Light blue carpet silenced their footsteps.

From her elevated, semicircular desk, under a five-foot wooden replica of California's great seal, Judge Jacqueline Connor commanded a view of the entire space. Much of the time, she focused on a computer screen mounted to her left, on which rapidly scrolling words entered by court reporters appeared.

Shortly after the lunch break, Judge Connor asked Deputy District Attorney Craig Hum if the people were ready to present opening statements. "Yes, Your Honor," he replied, his voice vibrant with confidence.

Standing at a lectern, Hum scanned the jurors' faces, smiled, and gave them the salutary "Good afternoon, ladies and gentlemen." After they responded in unison, he said, "This case is about the murder of Bruce Cleland, a forty-three-year-old computer software designer from TRW, who was killed for his money by his wife, defendant Rebecca Cleland, and her two cousins, defendant Alvaro Quezada and defendant Jose Quezada."

Hum had learned not to waste time with unnecessary rhetoric. He agreed with an analogy often expressed by Bowers about receptiveness among those twelve attentive people. "It's like a majestic, wide-open window in which the jurors' minds are hypersensitive, absorbing every word you utter. But as the minutes tick by, the window starts to lower, until it is only partway open." This early eagerness to learn the details must be exploited and treated with the greatest of care.

Stepping away from the lectern, Hum said, "This is what happened. Bruce Cleland met twenty-six-year-old Rebecca Salcedo at a swap meet in late November of 1995. Bruce was a rather shy, introverted man who had no prior experience with women, and he was immediately taken by the outgoing Rebecca. They struck up a conversation, and shortly after that, they began dating. Bruce thought that he had found the love of his life, and the more they saw of each other, the happier Bruce became."

Scrutinizing jurors' expressions for any sign of confusion or inattention, Hum paused momentarily. He wanted to present Bruce as a naive victim, but not a fool. By no means did he wish to portray a fellow Stanford University graduate in a negative light or devoid of common sense.

On the other hand, Hum intended to describe Rebecca's sociopathic intentions, not only as a greedy opportunist, but as someone insensitive to the damage she would inflict on Bruce and his family. "Unfortunately for Bruce, Rebecca was only interested in one thing, and that was Bruce's money. From the beginning, Rebecca's scheme was simple. She told several people that she planned to marry Bruce, get pregnant, divorce him, and then sue him for lifetime child and spousal support. She mistakenly thought that if she married Bruce, she would be entitled to half of his money, including a substantial inheritance Bruce would receive upon the death of his parents."

Hum chose his words carefully to portray the manipulative con game Rebecca used in persuading Bruce to spend money on her. "Almost immediately after they began dating, Rebecca convinced Bruce to start buying her expensive gifts. These gifts came to include a car, furniture for her rental house, a new boat, and a huge diamond ring. Bruce took her on a cruise, flew her to Hawaii. He also paid for extensive cosmetic surgery on her breasts, on her lips, on her nose."

The mention of the breast enlargement surgery raised a few

eyebrows among jurors, and some frowns. Hum knew this tit-illating detail would lodge in their memories, even though it carried little significance to the case. But it paved the way to a revelation of a considerably more important gift from Bruce to Rebecca—the purchase of a hilltop home in Whittier. Her insistence on a civil marriage preceding the religious Catholic wedding, as leverage to buy the home, would demonstrate Rebecca's complex scheme for getting anything she wanted from Bruce.

"They began to discuss marriage, and they actually made plans for a church wedding on January 18, 1997. Basically, everything was going exactly according to Rebecca's plans. Prior to the church marriage, Bruce and Rebecca started looking for a house in the Whittier Hills, where Rebecca wanted to live. They found one that she liked, in October of 1996, for about three hundred fifty thousand dollars."

Hum waited a moment for jurors to fully appreciate that sum. In the 1997 infancy of a skyrocketing real estate boom, $350,000 represented a huge investment for a house. By the time of the trial's opening, the Whittier property had sur-passed $1 million in value.

"Before buying the house, however, Rebecca insisted that they get married immediately, believing that if she was mar-ried to Bruce at the time they bought the house, and her name was on the deed, she'd get half of it. Bruce, always eager to please her, agreed to this, and so on October 25, 1996, Bruce and Rebecca were married in a civil ceremony at a courthouse. Shortly thereafter, Bruce purchased the house in Whittier."

Hum realized the next part of the story might strike some jurors as incredible, while others would see it as perfectly log-ical. Certainly, the men in the jury would believe that any red-blooded male who buys a house would expect to live in it. Rebecca's opposition to sharing living quarters with Bruce, and his capitulation to her adamant conditions, stood a good chance of dividing jurors into two camps. Hum gingerly spoke of it. "Rebecca immediately moved into that house, but she refused to let Bruce move in before the wedding, claiming that it just wouldn't look right. In reality, the reason Rebecca didn't want Bruce living in that house is because she was continuing to see other men, and she didn't want Bruce to find out."

Women on the jury, particularly conservatives, probably would sympathize with Rebecca's rationale that a couple shouldn't live together until they are married in a church wedding. And just "seeing" a few male acquaintances might be okay if nothing else took place. So Hum clarified the arrangement, and the subsequent pain inflicted on her new husband. "Bruce and Rebecca got married in a church ceremony on January 18, 1997. Almost immediately after the wedding, Rebecca starts to complain about Bruce to anybody who will listen. In April of 1997, after living together for less than three months, Rebecca throws Bruce out of his own house. She's not working. She continues to use Bruce's credit cards to pay her living expenses, to buy gifts for herself and her boyfriends, and to take various trips and vacations with her friends. Bruce, still very much in love with his wife, continues to pay the bills. Rebecca consults an attorney, who drafts a separation agreement for Bruce to sign requiring him to continue to pay the mortgage on the house, allow her to continue living there, and requiring Bruce to pay spousal support. At this point, Bruce refused to sign the agreement and starts canceling her credit cards. And that's when Rebecca starts plotting to kill him."

As a general rule, jurors' impassive faces reveal very little about their receptiveness to a lawyer's words. Body language, such as crossed arms or staring into the distance, may give the speaker slight hints. Craig Hum hoped that he had hit some nerves by showing Rebecca's true colors. He figured that no one would envision her with angel's wings, but he had no way of knowing if he had yet implanted the image of her as a killer. Now he needed to shift gears and discuss the allegations of her conspiracy with Jose and Alvaro Quezada. "What she does is decide to enlist the aid of her cousins Al and Jose to help kill her husband. They decide the best way to get away with this is to make it look like an attempted carjacking."

Launching into dramatic opening statements after lunch is problematical for prosecutors. If the jurors have overindulged in heavy food, they might feel the onset of drowsiness. Hum observed closely to see if any of them seemed to be dozing off. To his relief, every person in the box sat upright, or leaned forward in a posture of alert attention. Using his best spellbinding techniques, Hum segued into the murder plan. "On Friday July 25, 1997, Rebecca calls Bruce and arranges a dinner date, supposedly to discuss a reconciliation. In reality, this is a ploy to lure Bruce to East Los Angeles, where her cousins Al and Jose can kill him. So Bruce and Rebecca go to dinner that evening at a small restaurant in East Los Angeles. They eat dinner. They each have a couple of beers, and they leave. Later on that night, they go to the house of Arturo, who is the uncle of Rebecca and the father of Al and Jose. At the house, Rebecca continues to feed Bruce alcohol, until at about one in the morning, on July 26, 1997."

A good storyteller knows the value of a hook to pull listeners in. Realizing he had snagged the jury, Hum sought to erase any doubts about Rebecca targeting her husband to die. Step-by-step, he laid out the trio's implementation of their deadly plan. "Bruce and Rebecca leave Arturo's house, supposedly heading back to Whittier. Rebecca is driving Bruce's dark blue Toyota 4Runner, and Bruce is in the front passenger seat. Rebecca doesn't take her normal route home. Instead of getting on the 60 Freeway at the usual on-ramp that she uses, Rebecca heads for the on-ramp to the southbound Santa Ana Freeway. That entry is located in a secluded residential area."

Now Hum had the jurors in the palm of his hand and could sense a certain morbid curiosity. From this point on, he knew he must provide sufficient details but not get bogged down in minutiae. "Just before getting on the freeway, Rebecca stops the car and gets out. At that moment, Jose, who had been hiding nearby, approaches the passenger side of the 4Runner, where

Bruce is seated, and Jose reaches through the open passenger window, aims a .38-caliber handgun at Bruce's head, and pulls the trigger. The gun fires and Jose's first shot hits Bruce in the upper lip area. That bullet travels through Bruce's lip, through his mouth, and it comes out the other side of his head near his left ear. The wound, however, isn't immediately fatal. So Bruce, bleeding profusely from his head, manages to get out of the car, and he starts to run. Jose chases him. And as Bruce crosses the street running for his life, Jose fires again. This bullet hits Bruce in the lower back. It passes completely through his abdomen [and] comes out his stomach."

Since the jury knew the defendants had been charged with murder, Hum didn't need to state the obvious, that Bruce had died from these gunshot wounds. Still, the prosecutor wanted each of the twelve people to grasp the perpetrator's savagery. He intended to pluck their heartstrings, and raise visceral emotions about the brutal killing of a helpless, unarmed man, who had no way of resisting.

Energizing each word, Hum said, "At this point, Bruce starts to stagger and falls to the ground. But Jose is not finished, because he has to make sure that Bruce is dead. So Jose walks up to Bruce and pumps two more bullets directly into the victim's head. One bullet strikes Bruce in the back of the head, tears completely through his brain, and it comes out his forehead. The other bullet Jose fires right into Bruce's right temple. That bullet, too, goes completely through Bruce's brain and comes out the other side. After he finished murdering Bruce, Jose runs down the street to a waiting getaway car, That car is driven by his brother, Alvaro, and they speed off. The police and the paramedics arrived on scene almost immediately, but there's nothing they can do for Bruce Cleland, forty-three years old, who dies in a driveway on Beswick Street, murdered by his wife and her two cousins."

Craig Hum thanked the jury for their attention. His compelling presentation had consumed nearly an hour, and had riveted observers in the gallery. None of the jurors showed signs of diminished attention.

After a brief break, the attorney for Jose Quezada accepted the judge's invitation to present his opening and took command of the lectern. Jeff Kelley enjoyed a reputation of balancing pleasant, personable characteristics with outstanding legal skills as a public defender. The short, bespectacled African-American spoke in a clear, deep, booming voice, understandable to jurors, as well as spectators in the gallery's last row.

Following the time-honored pattern of courteously greeting jurors in a pleasant manner, Kelley chose the right words to ingratiate himself and his client in their minds. Speaking gently, he said, "I never had the opportunity to meet Bruce Cleland, but from all accounts, he was a very sweet man. I've also had a chance, just from speaking to them in court the few times they've been here, to know his family a very little bit, just from exchanging greetings, and they seem like very nice people, too. And they certainly did not deserve what happened to them."

It's a tight line for defenders to walk. They can't risk an appearance of condescension and must avoid the slightest hint of smarmy, obsequious behavior. Most important, they need to establish credibility with the jury.

If Kelley believed he could convince enough of them that witness identification of Jose as the darkly clad man fleeing the crime scene had been erroneous, he first needed to earn the jury's trust.

Kelley began his statement by verbally undermining allegations of previous association between Jose and Rebecca. Yes, they were cousins, said the defender, but his client and Rebecca had not been close, and had spent very little time together. Jose's own sister, said Kelley, would testify that Jose hadn't even been invited to Rebecca's wedding. Also, Jose's association with his own brother, Alvaro, had been unusually sparse.

They had few friends in common and seldom socialized with the same crowd.

The prosecution had announced plans to link both Rebecca and Alvaro to Jose by the use of cell phone records. Kelley refuted the inference that this tied his client to the alleged conspiracy. He promised to show, from stacks of documentation, that neither Rebecca nor Alvaro had made one single call to Jose's phone number.

Furthermore, he stated, the prosecution would be unable to prove the brothers had seen each other more than one time in a period of weeks prior to the crime. It happened when Officer Robert Zavala took Alvaro to obtain an LAPD job application, and they sighted Jose walking in the neighborhood of the Hollenbeck Police Station. In other words, Kelley asserted, these brothers hadn't been close enough to form a murder conspiracy.

If the defender could, indeed, present evidence supporting these claims, doubt about Jose's complicity in the crime might easily lodge in jurors' minds.

Pressing forward, Kelley opened an attack on the credibility of a key eyewitness for the prosecution. Guadalupe Hernandez, who lived a block south of the shooting site, had told investigators she could identify Jose as the man she saw running down the sidewalk, across Concord Street from her home. Kelley chose not to quarrel with the witness having seen someone, but berated her ability to positively state the shadowy figure had been Jose.

First, he said, Hernandez's view had lasted only a few seconds and had taken place under poor lighting conditions. How could she possibly discern the facial features of this person, dressed in dark clothing, in the middle of the night, and flashing past in an instant? When she called 911, Kelley said, the witness hadn't even been able to tell the man's race. And, the following day, in describing the individual to detectives, Hernandez had guessed his age as eighteen to twenty, his height as about five-five, and his weight as between 150 and 160 pounds. Observers and jurors couldn't resist stealing a glance at Jose, dressed nicely and seated at the defense table, to see if he fit the description Hernandez had given.

With incredulity straining his voice, Kelley emphasized that Ms. Hernandez had admitted the inability to see the runner's face! Driving home the point, Kelley reiterated his contention. "Now, over four months later, and mind you she had a mere few seconds to make her observations, she is shown a photographic six-pack. . . . It's basically a group of head shots, six supposedly similar-looking individuals. She views this six-pack . . . and obviously one of those pictured was Jose Quezada. And this is what she wrote after viewing it. *Of the six . . . , photo four is the closest to the person I saw running down Concord after the shooting.* These were her words." To Kelley, *"the closest"* did not mean a positive identification.

He didn't bother to tell jurors whether the identification had been accurate—whether photo number four had actually portrayed Jose Quezada. Observers wondered, too, and hoped the prosecutor would settle the matter by introducing the six-pack into evidence.

Kelley added that witness Hernandez had later attended a live lineup and used similar wording when she picked out one of the men. In neither case, he complained, had she unequivocally identified the picture, or the live person, as the man she saw running that night.

Maybe the mystery would be cleared up if Craig Hum decided to seat Ms. Hernandez in the witness chair.

If jurors and court watchers thought Kelley had nearly exhausted his ammunition supply, he surprised them with another volley. He said the evidence would show that Jose probably could not even fire a gun! The defendant had been in an automobile accident a few weeks before the crime, resulting in a broken right wrist. A cast had immobilized his arm, from elbow to knuckles, until just a few days before Bruce died, and had left Jose with a weak grip. Medical testimony regarding a civil suit, Kelley offered, would show how the injury had left his client seriously incapacitated, unable to grip anything, like a handgun.

Concluding his opening statement, Kelley said, "The bottom line is I don't believe the evidence will support a finding that Jose Quezada was in any way involved in this heinous crime. And after you hear from all of the witnesses that testify, I'm sure you will return a verdict of not guilty."

As soon as Kelley seated himself at the crowded defense table, Judge Connor turned toward Richard P. Lasting, Alvaro's attorney, and invited him to present an opening statement. In his late fifties, with a full thatch of gray hair and faded blue eyes, Lasting stood a little shorter than Craig Hum's six-one height. A private attorney, Lasting had been appointed by the court to represent Alvaro Quezada. The defender thanked Judge Connor and began by characterizing the crime as extremely brutal. He called it a "very chilling murder, a cold-blooded killing." With that acknowledgment on record, Lasting immediately turned the jury's attention to his client and announced that Al had absolutely nothing to do with it. "I would submit that you will find the truth of this case. You will find the truth. Al Quezada is not guilty of conspiracy to commit murder. He's not guilty of participating in the murder. He was not present in the area where Bruce Cleland was shot down in cold blood. He wasn't sitting in a car . . . waiting for the shooter to come running and spirit him away from the crime scene."

Alvaro's defender understood the necessity of erasing an important image left by the prosecutor. Cell phone records, Craig Hum had said, would place Al near the crime scene at the time of the shooting. Court watchers wondered if Lasting would suggest that Alvaro's cell phone had been stolen, or that someone had borrowed it. The defense decided, instead, to cast doubt on the credibility of scientific evidence. Technology related to tracing the location of users, according to Lasting, hadn't been around long enough to support a murder conviction. The system, he snorted, ". . . was in its infancy." Metaphorically tossing the investigative data into a trash bin, Lasting said the methodology had been operational for no more than two months prior to the report's preparation.

Just in case the jury failed to accept this tactic, Lasting also declared the evidence would show that his client had been elsewhere on the night in question. Testimony from Alvaro's former girlfriend, the defender said, would reveal his state of mind resulted from hearing this woman say she wanted to break up with him. The devastating news plunged Alvaro into deep depression and created a need to have some drinks with his buddy. During those early-morning hours when Bruce was shot to death, Alvaro and the friend went to a night club in El Monte, ten miles from the murder scene. Afterward, they drove to a second tavern, where the mother of Alvaro's son tended bar.

If these two witnesses, the buddy and the bartender, offered convincing testimony, it could be tough for the jury to convict Alvaro. The execution of Bruce had taken place shortly after one o'clock in the morning, and the defendant could not have been in both places at once.

For good measure, his attorney promised to call character witnesses, who would vouch for Al. For example, Lasting said, Alvaro was the type of guy who would stop and help a motorist stranded by a flat tire on the freeway. Generous acts like this are not consistent with the behavior of a savage killer.

Scholars of human nature know that image often plays an important role in how people are judged. Clean-cut good looks versus the stereotypical appearance of a thug should have no impact in a jury trial, but the potential of being swayed by good looks certainly exists. Between the two brothers, Al had been blessed with handsome features, charm, a dazzling smile, and a twinkle in his eyes. Would that have any influence on jurors, especially the women? As he sat at counsel table, Alvaro still radiated the good-guy image, and his attorney wanted to capitalize on it. Lasting ended by saying, "You are going to learn that evidence of good character . . . can raise a reasonable doubt as to whether someone is involved in a murder. And when all the evidence is presented and you have heard everything, I would submit to you that with regard to Al Quezada, you will find the truth. And the truth is he is not guilty of these charges."

At last, Rebecca's attorney rose to address the jury. When Joseph B. Orr stood, he couldn't be missed, towering at six feet six inches, topped by curly gray hair. Ron Bowers had worked with Orr previously and knew him pretty well. A former deputy sheriff, Orr had started his legal career in the district attorney's office and eventually changed to the defense side.

Orr faced the unenviable task of following powerful declamation from three strong orators. Keeping the jury's attention presented a challenge. Orr knew he needed to keep his opening short, and to the point. After reciting the old maxim of two sides to every story, in a deep, gruff voice, Orr offered several examples, including Rebecca's choice of driving routes to Whittier on that night. The prosecutor had planted a theory that the alternate route she drove, to the I-5 entrance rather than the usual I-60, supported allegations of the murder being planned in advance. Orr said simply that the I-5 Freeway was also a reasonable path to Whittier.

Another issue cited by the defender caught observers off guard. He said the evidence would show that one of the paramedics who conducted an examination of Rebecca saw a spot of blood on the tips of her fingers. Perhaps it came from an injury to his client's head.

Keeping his presentation concise, Orr emphasized the absence of any evidence to prove that a conspiracy existed between Rebecca, Jose, and Al to commit this murder. He repeatedly asked the jurors to keep an open mind about the facts of the case. His brevity may have made points with weary listeners.

When Orr sat down, the marathon session of oratory had come to an end. Judge Connor ordered a short recess, after which the first witness would be called by the prosecution.

Chapter 22

Witness for the Prosecution

If the opening statements could be compared to the hundred-meter dash in a track meet, the trial's next phase resembled a cross-country marathon. Craig Hum stretched and took a deep breath to ready himself for the grueling task ahead.

A neatly dressed, elderly man made his way forward and followed instructions to raise his right hand. He listened to the familiar words known nationwide: "Do you solemnly state that the testimony you may give in the case now pending before this court shall be the truth, the whole truth, and nothing but the truth, so help you God?"

Harold Cleland spoke a simple "yes" and settled into the blue-padded witness chair. The victim's father carried himself with grace and dignity. Born in 1919, he had entered his eightieth year the previous September.

Unsure of Mr. Cleland's ability to endure the pressures of testifying, Hum began with basic, easy questions intended to endear jurors to the victim's gentle parents and to educate them about Bruce's background. Hum asked about the elderly man's marital status. Cleland smiled at his wife, Theda, sitting in the gallery's first row and said he had been married fifty-eight years.

"Did you have any children?"

Sadness creased Cleland's face and his voice cracked in saying, "I had two."

"Was one a son and one a daughter?"

"Yes." Answers by Bruce's father touched the hearts of observers, and probably jurors as well. He told them that his only other child, Patricia Ann Brown, Bruce's older sister, had died of cancer at age forty-five. Her death had preceded Bruce's by only eleven months. This tragedy had spurred Mr. and Mrs. Cleland's desire to see Bruce get married and settle down. Maybe, he said, they had been a little selfish in hoping that Bruce, with a wife, could look after them in their twilight years. Listeners thought they could detect a tinge of guilt in Cleland's voice, perhaps in the belief that all this might not have happened if they hadn't been pushing him to the altar.

Pride could be seen in the octogenarian's face as he spoke of his son's high grades and a master's degree from prestigious Stanford University. Bruce had worked at TRW, Cleland said, and earned more than $100,000 a year.

"Were you close with your son, Mr Cleland?" Yes, the father said, and agreed that they had been best friends. Hum also brought out Bruce's shy, quiet personality. When the prosecutor inquired into Bruce's level of sophistication with women, his father leaned back in the chair, sighed, and lamented that Bruce didn't seem to know much about meeting women or talking to them.

Hum asked how Bruce had met Rebecca. Cleland described how he and his son occasionally visited a swap meet at an old drive-in theater in Santa Fe Springs. Late in 1995, they had spent the morning there, strolling along endless aisles and browsing through a huge variety of goods for sale.

"All of a sudden," he said, Bruce stopped and announced he was going to go back and talk to "that girl."

"What do you mean by 'that girl'?" Cleland glanced toward the three defendants, raised his hand in their direction, and mouthed the name "Rebecca," as if it pained him to even say her name. Wanting this moment to be indelibly engraved in the minds of the jurors, Hum asked, "When you say 'Rebecca,' you kind of gestured with your hand. Do you see the person, the one Bruce started talking with, here in the courtroom today?"

Tilting his head toward Rebecca, Cleland answered, "Yes, she's sitting over there."

Judge Connor interceded to ask, "Can you tell me what she's wearing today so we all know who you're talking about?"

The witness, apparently reluctant to spend time or effort discussing someone who had brought so much pain into his life, replied simply, "A black suit."

Connor stated, "Ms. Cleland, for the record."

Hum asked, "While Bruce was talking with the defendant, Rebecca Cleland, did she give him anything?"

"Yes. She handed him several papers that I later found out to be résumés of her work. She wanted him to see if he could help her get employment at TRW."

Craig Hum's next few questions focused on how the relationship between Bruce and Rebecca flourished.

Transitioning to another subject, Hum brought up Bruce's frugal ways and how Rebecca changed him into a more generous individual. The father remarked that Bruce seemed happy buying a boat, cars, and even the large house in Whittier for Rebecca.

To Hum, it appeared that the strain of testifying might be taking a toll on the elderly witness. He offered a recess to allow Cleland a brief break, giving him the opportunity to compose himself if needed. The father thanked him but said he was all right.

Posing his questions as gently as possible, Hum inquired about the last night Cleland saw his son. In the father's recollection, Bruce had told his parents about plans to have dinner with Rebecca to see if they could work out their differences and possibly reconcile. Bruce, he said, had seemed melancholy and distracted, as if he had been deep in thought.

Craig ended his questioning. With such a sympathetic witness, defense attorneys appeared reluctant to attack. Their cross-examination, a series of slow pitches, avoided offending jurors with heavy-handed inquisitions, and they kept it diplomatically short before announcing, "No more questions."

A palpable sense of admiration filled the room as the elderly gentleman rose and made his way toward the exit. Cleland looked weary, but his quiet courage and resilience in the face of tragedy garnered respect, especially from sympathetic parents among the crowd.

Ed Brown, Bruce's brother-in-law, next took the oath. He had been not only a relative by marriage, but also a good friend to Bruce. The prosecution needed Brown's testimony to fill in blank spots about the victim's background and his whirlwind romance with Rebecca. Answering Hum's questions, Brown characterized Bruce as a studious young man who had done well in college, at both Harvey Mudd and Stanford. Emphasizing a shy and introverted personality, Brown told jurors that Bruce made virtually no effort to find dates until the fateful swap meet encounter. Bruce's transition from extreme monetary caution to remarkable generosity had amazed the brother-in-law.

Regarding the purchase of an expensive home in Whittier, said Brown, Bruce had asked him for advice and sought approval. In serving as best man at the wedding, Brown observed giddy happiness in the groom. But the euphoria vanished soon after Bruce returned home from his honeymoon.

Craig Hum asked the witness to clarify that observation. Brown leaned back as if to brace himself and took a deep breath. Groping for the right words, he explained that Rebecca had complained to him about Bruce's "performance in bed." By April, he said, the marriage had started to unravel, so Brown felt obligated to step in and provide Bruce with some guidance as he seemed to be drowning in a sea of despair. He advised Bruce to see a lawyer, examine his options, and consider the advantages or consequences of a divorce.

Ed Brown fit the last few puzzle pieces into place with his narrative of Bruce's life; then after a short cross-examination, he stepped down.

To follow up on Bruce's inquiries about dissolution of the marriage, Craig Hum summoned attorney Ron Ziff to the witness chair. Bruce had consulted him about the possibility of a divorce and financial settlement matters. Ziff's testimony gave the jury a minicourse in community property law. He explained that "community property is only that which is acquired after the marriage, up to the date of the separation." The marriage hadn't lasted six months. So Rebecca would be entitled to virtually nothing. It would be no more than half of Bruce's earnings during that six-month period, *after* deduction of living expenses. The lawyer testified that, according to his calculations, Rebecca would receive about $2,500 or less in a divorce settlement.

She would have had no claim, said Ziff, to any share of the Whittier house. Since Bruce had used his own separate assets for the down payment, he could recover that value upon sale of the home. Rebecca had miscalculated in her effort to grab joint equity by entering into a civil marriage before purchase of the house. Attorney Ziff informed jurors that people often have a misunderstanding about such a transaction. He said that Rebecca was entitled to only half of any appreciation of the Whittier house that may have occurred over that six-month period. Since there had been negligible appreciation in the house's value, Rebecca would receive nothing in a divorce settlement. Yes, said Ziff, he had explained all of this to Bruce and made him understand that he would suffer no financial setback by divorcing her.

This evidence supported Hum's assertion, in opening statements, that Rebecca had mistakenly believed her husband to be worth more dead than alive.

Hum now brought forth witnesses to give jurors a clear image of Rebecca's greedy and lethal intentions. He began with Bertha Awana. Jurors soon learned that she had met Rebecca during their early teens while attending continuation school, and how the close friendship had lasted for about fifteen years. Rebecca, Bertha said, had dated many men during that period, but she had only one serious relationship.

Hum asked, "And what was that person's name?"

"Bruce Cleland."

Answering a string of short inquiries from the prosecutor, Bertha spelled out how Rebecca and Bruce had met at the swap meet and of Rebecca's extreme interest in his credit report. In considerable detail, she told the jury that Rebecca, using employment credit records accessed through her job, had immediately searched out reports on Bruce and found that he had high credit limits with zero balances. The prosecutor walked Bertha through each gift Bruce had lavished on Rebecca, from a backyard spa at the Maywood house, a Honda, boat, an expensive ring, the Toyota 4Runner, and finally to the purchase and furnishing of the Whittier home.

The witness described Rebecca's unappreciative responses, insatiable desire for more gifts, and plans to wring every last dollar from Bruce. Bertha said that Rebecca, using deceit, paid for breast enlargement with Bruce's credit cards without his knowledge.

"At the time, did defendant Cleland have a child?"

"Yes. The little boy was four years old when [she and Bruce] met."

"Now," asked Hum, "back in January 1996, did you have a Super Bowl party at your residence?"

"Yes," Bertha said, answering in crisp, clear terms with a well-modulated voice. "That's the day I met Bruce. She had already told me she was going to marry him and that he was a good guy who had lots of money."

The prosecutor wanted the jury to begin understanding how Rebecca treated Bruce, even that early in the relationship. "Did you witness an incident at the Super Bowl party with regard to how defendant Cleland and Bruce interacted?"

Bertha had committed to hold nothing back, but she still softened her description of what happened. "Well, she left him in the front room with my husband and his friends and she came in the bedroom with me and was just ignoring him. Then she got into a little spat with him. She said to me, 'Watch, he'll come back. He'll come knocking at the door and calling for me.' Which he did."

"Now, in October of 1996, did defendant Rebecca Cleland tell you that she and Bruce had secretly gotten married?"

"Yes. She said they wanted to buy a new home and she wanted to be married before they made the purchase so her name would be on the title."

After exposing Rebecca's avarice, Hum aimed his questions at her sexual indiscretions. Bertha hid nothing about Rebecca's relationship with male stripper Dave Romero and details of the wild bachelorette party in which Rebecca ended up in bed with him.

"Did Rebecca Cleland ever express to you any concern about her reputation prior to moving into that house?"

"She did. She said that she had told Bruce she hadn't been intimate with anybody for a long time and she wanted to wait until after the church wedding for him to move in."

"And based on conversations you had with her, did you know that wasn't true?"

"Yes." Bertha gave the same answer to Hum's inquiries about Rebecca sleeping with other men after she met and married Bruce. She had abused his loving trust in her. "Rebecca would be nice to him a lot of times and then, depending on what she wanted, she would be mean. It all depended on what was going on that day and her mood."

"Did she tell you anything about what she made Bruce do before he could come to the house in Whittier?"

"He had to call her in advance and let her know he wanted to come."

Hum revisited the subject of gifts. "Did you see a ring the defendant got shortly after she started dating Bruce?"

"Yes. It had a lot of diamonds. Very beautiful ring." Bertha thought it had cost $7,000 or $8,000. Others mentioned a figure of $10,000.

Hum asked how many men Bertha had seen visiting Rebecca in the Whittier house. "Was it one, or two, or five, or six, or do you recall?"

Thinking it over for a moment, Bertha couldn't come up with a number. She said, "That's a hard question because she had a lot of male friends." She mentioned only one by name, Dave Romero.

"I want to ask you about a bachelorette party held in January, just before the church wedding. Did you attend?" Bertha said she had attended, but had left early.

"At that party, did defendant Cleland tell you anything about why she was marrying Bruce?"

Bertha again considered her answer before speaking. "Well, she said she didn't want to marry him, but she wasn't sure about it because she was really confused. But that everything had been planned, so she had to go through with it."

Cutting right to the bone, Hum asked, "Did she tell you whether or not she loved Bruce?"

Bertha didn't hesitate this time. "She said she did not love him."

"Did she tell you why she would marry him if she didn't love him?"

"Money, financial security. She was going to marry Bruce, eventually divorce him, and get spousal support."

Back to the bachelorette party, Hum asked if male strippers had been there. Bertha said that Dave Romero had danced and stripped. She told of walking in the bedroom where she saw them "hugging." To additional questions, Bertha also revealed that Rebecca had continued an affair with Romero after the church marriage to Bruce. She had admitted sleeping with him.

Bertha described the wedding as huge and beautiful with perhaps "a couple hundred" guests.

Stepping gently into a sensitive area, especially with Bruce's parents sitting in the gallery, Hum asked, "Immediately after they got back from the honeymoon, did defendant Cleland start complaining about Bruce?"

"Yes. She was upset with his sexual performance."

If the jurors hadn't fully perceived the picture of Rebecca's wicked ways, Craig Hum elicited information to brand it into their minds. Bertha testified to observing Rebecca purchase underwear for Romero, which she charged to Bruce's credit card. After kicking Bruce out of the house, said Bertha, Rebecca had arranged for her attorney to draw up a separation agreement. When Bruce balked at signing it, Rebecca had responded by accusing him of molesting her son, and threatening to inform his employer and the police.

Prior to the trial, Hum had interviewed several people to see if any credence should be put on Rebecca's allegations, and found no one who really believed that Bruce had engaged in any sexual contact, or molestation attempts, with the young boy. He asked Bertha, "Had you seen Bruce and the child together previously?" She had, perhaps ten times. "Did the youngster ever seem to be afraid of Bruce?"

"No."

"When she told you that, what did you tell her to do?"

"To call the police and take her son to the hospital."

Asked how the defendant responded, Bertha said that Rebecca ignored the advice. She never reported the alleged molestation to law enforcement and never sought medical or psychological treatment for the little boy. Jurors could be seen furiously writing in their notebooks.

Probing Rebecca's behavior even deeper, Hum questioned Bertha about subsequent events regarding the marriage. The witness told of Bruce leaving the home in April after an argument and moving in with his parents. A few spectators stole glances at Harold and Theda, who sat in stoic silence. "Later," Bertha said, "Rebecca was going to talk to an attorney, have separation documents drawn up so she could legally separate from Bruce—and asked him for financial support. She wanted him to continue paying the mortgage and to keep on giving her spending money."

"Did Bruce go along with it?"

"No. Bruce wouldn't sign the document. And he was very upset that she was requesting it. He told her that he had given her everything, and asked what more did she want."

"Do you know if she planned to divorce him?"

"She wasn't dumb. She was not going to divorce him. She was very angry."

"Did she tell you she was going to threaten Bruce in any way?"

"Yes. If he didn't sign, she was going to call his employer and tell them that he had molested her son, and ruin his reputation."

The second part of Bertha's testimony centered on events after Bruce's death. She recalled hearing about the murder the next day and rushing over to Rebecca's place to comfort her. But Rebecca didn't want to talk about it. Instead, she spoke only of herself, whining about being hit over the head. Paradoxically, she wouldn't allow Bertha to examine the alleged injury. It puzzled Bertha when Rebecca disappeared into another room with a man she identified as her attorney. Even more bizarre, Bertha told jurors, a couple of days later she had attended a viewing of Bruce's body on the evening before the funeral. There Bertha saw Rebecca holding hands with the attorney. Her old friend was devoid of any tears or grieving.

Bertha's testimony revealed yet another degree of Rebecca's self-serving behavior. The new widow asked Bertha for money to sustain her until she could collect on Bruce's accidental-death insurance policy and his 401(k) investments. It had embarrassed Bertha to be put in that position. Also, said the witness, in subsequent visits to the Whittier house, she saw that Alvaro had moved in, and Rebecca had given him Bruce's old Honda. They seemed quite affectionate with one another.

After Rebecca's arrest, said Bertha, she had agreed to help her by putting some personal things in storage. While collecting them, she had found Rebecca's checkbook and noticed that a check for $500 had been written to A. Quezada.

Hum concluded his questioning of Bertha by spotlighting a strange, disconnected comment made by Rebecca. Bertha had visited her old friend in jail. The prosecutor asked, "During either of those two or so visits, was there a discussion between you and defendant Cleland about a movie or book rights?"

A hint of mirth illuminated Bertha's face in her reply. "She joked about it. She joked about making a movie about her story, her life story."

"Did she say she had somebody in mind to play her part?"

"Yes."

"Who?"

"I think it was Carmen Electra."

The defense conducted their cross-examination of Bertha, but she didn't waiver in her testimony against Rebecca. Hum trumpeted, "Call Dolores Salcedo." Rebecca's sister made her way forward, took the oath, and replaced Bertha in the witness chair. Insiders had heard about the explosive relationship between Rebecca and Dolores. A question hung in the air. Could a woman denounce her own sister and testify truthfully if it meant her sibling might be found guilty of murder?

Chapter 23

A Heartless Conspirator

After she spelled her name and gave her age, Dolores identified her sister and her two cousins sitting at the defense counsel table. Following a few questions about the witness's knowledge of Bruce and how they met, Hum asked if Rebecca had told her of Bruce's financial situation.

"Yes," Dolores replied. "She said he was a good catch and that she checked his credit reports. . . . She wasn't in love with him, but he was just basically a good catch."

"Did she say anything about Bruce's intelligence?"

"She referred to him as a dumb American."

"If that was what she expressed, do you know why she was with him?"

"He bought her a lot of stuff. A Honda Accord. She thought she would be set for life with him." Rebecca, said Dolores, had acquired other things at Bruce's expense, some without his knowledge "She went for a nose job. She had her lips done. And she didn't tell him she was going to have her breasts done, but she did it, anyway, and he paid for it." The witness also described the diamond ring and trips to Hawaii and Mexico given to Rebecca by Bruce.

Dolores's answers corroborated for the jurors what they had heard from the previous witnesses. She went through the civil and church weddings and the home purchase. She said Rebecca moved in, but she wouldn't allow Bruce to live there. "He was supposed to call her before he came over. She wanted to make sure that if somebody was there, that he wasn't coming over when she had guests."

"What kind of guests?"

Vitriol dripped from Dolores's words as she virtually spit them out. "Her male friends."

"Did she tell you she was sleeping with these men?"

"Yes. One was a guy she had worked with. Another one was Dave the stripper."

"Did she tell you she was sleeping with any women, even after she met and married Bruce?"

"Yes, with Diana."

Craig Hum knew from the detectives' reports that Rebecca had met with her sister in a bar not long before the bachelorette party, and had said some harsh things. He asked the witness about it.

Dolores answered without hesitation. "She said that basically she was unhappy, that she wanted to get Bruce out of the way. And I asked her what was wrong. She told me that she wanted me to help her get rid of him. I asked her, 'What do you mean?' She goes, 'Well, you know a lot of people. You're in the bail bond business and you know a lot of people who can do things.' She went on to say, 'Well, it can be done like if he had an accident or cutting the brakes or just making it— having something happen to him, but that it would be like an accident'—that it wouldn't come back to her."

Craig Hum knew that his next question could be pivotal in the trial's outcome. He had pondered the exact way to ask it, and settled on the most direct, uncomplicated wording.

"Did your sister, defendant Rebecca Cleland, specifically say she wanted Bruce killed?"

The reply came equally unadorned. Dolores said, "Basically, yes."

"What did you say to her?"

"I couldn't believe what I was hearing. I told her that I didn't know anybody like that and said I didn't want her ever to talk about something like that or even think about it again. Then I asked her, 'How do you know I'm not going to call the police and tell them what you just told me?' She looked me straight in the eye and goes, 'I'll just tell them that it was all your planning, that you were having an affair with Bruce, and it was all your doing.'"

"Did you tell anybody about this?"

"Yes. I told my coworker Jovita Garay, and I told my cousin Robert Diaz."

Dolores said that the sibling relationship temporarily smoothed out afterward. Rebecca even invited her to the bachelorette party. Dolores attended and saw Dave Romero and two other strippers dance. Hum asked, "Did you see your sister interacting with Dave Romero?"

"Yes. She was being flirtatious and rubbing herself all over him."

Dolores acknowledged being a bridesmaid at the church wedding. Later, Rebecca had informed her, along with many others, about Bruce's dismal sexual performance during the honeymoon. By April, the witness said, Rebecca revealed her plans to kick her husband out of the house.

Regarding personal feelings about Bruce, Dolores said she really thought he was a nice guy and felt sorry for him. She also held his parents in high esteem.

Following up on that theme, Hum inquired, "After you heard that your sister wasn't in love with Bruce, planned to kick him out, and was sleeping with these other men and women, did you tell Bruce's parents?"

"Yes, I did. I told Mrs. Cleland she should hire a private

investigator, and that the PI could get proof, and that pictures wouldn't lie." But Rebecca apparently found out. She had called Dolores and left a threatening message on her phone recorder.

Dolores told the jury about hearing of Bruce's murder on her telephone answering machine after returning from a trip to Rosarito, a community south of Tijuana, with her friend Diana and her cousin Robert Diaz. A detective had left the message. The news had stunned and sickened her, Dolores said, and she had subsequently contacted the police and told Detective Herman about Rebecca's attempt, months earlier, to enlist Dolores's help in a plan to get rid of Bruce.

To end his direct examination, Hum asked, "Why are you coming to court and telling us this?"

Dolores snarled, "Because it's the truth, and it needs to be told."

To corroborate Dolores's testimony regarding Rebecca's sinister plan, Hum invited Jovita Garay to the stand.

The young woman, not quite twenty-three, had relocated to another state the previous year, making a long trip necessary to testify for the prosecution. Hum asked if she had worked with Dolores back in 1997, and he got an affirmative reply. She had also met Rebecca, and could identify her as the woman at the defense table, wearing a black suit.

"Did you attend a bachelorette party in Whittier given by this defendant?"

With a slight blush, the woman admitted that she did go. The embarrassment may have stemmed from knowledge that jurors had heard about male strippers entertaining in the Whittier house. Jovita had been only eighteen at the time.

To her relief, Hum didn't linger on the subject. He asked, "Sometime before that, did you have a conversation with Dolores regarding something her sister had said?"

The witness said she had: "Dolores was taking me home that day and she mentioned that she was very scared. She told me that Rebecca had asked her to help hire someone to kill Bruce. I was scared, too. At first, she had told her that she wanted to get rid of him, actually. But she didn't know exactly what she meant by that."

The garbled answer needed some clarification for the jury. "Who said they wanted to get rid of Bruce?"

"Rebecca. Becky told Dolores that she wanted to get rid of Bruce."

"Who didn't know what was meant?"

"Dolores." Jovita again tried to explain what had happened, but it took a series of questions from Hum to make it understandable. With patience, the prosecutor drew out the entire story of Rebecca's plan and her threat to pin it on Dolores.

None of the three defense attorneys wished to cross-examine the witness.

Continuing his exploration of Rebecca's reputation as a heartless conspirator to murder, Hum summoned Patricia Medina to the witness chair. Witness Medina had worked in a doctor's office alongside the defendant's mother. While still a child, Rebecca had sometimes accompanied Lucy to the workplace. The witness said, "When Becky got a little older, her mom was ill, and Becky would come to the office and actually take her place."

Years later, said Medina, she had heard about Bruce. And Rebecca had confided the reasons for her interest in him. "She said he was very well-off. He had parents that were elderly and had a lot of money. So, basically, when his parents were to pass away, he would inherit a fortune."

"Did Rebecca Cleland tell you anything with regard to her relationship with Bruce?"

"Well, Becky planned on getting married, having a child, possibly staying married for about a year, divorcing him, and collecting child support." Medina added, "She used to tell that to a lot of people."

Even the expensive ring Bruce bought for Rebecca had been leveraged by coercion. Bruce, the witness said, would have done anything to keep Rebecca in his life. "She [told Bruce] she could not introduce him to her family unless, you know, he at least bought her a diamond ring. That would be good faith. . . . She told him it was a custom in her culture to do that."

Raising the subject of insurance policies on Bruce, Hum's questions spurred Medina to recall a salient remark from Rebecca. She had said that Bruce's accidental death would pay off more than three times his annual salary.

So far, Hum's last four witnesses, all women, had created exactly the image he wanted to implant in jurors' minds. Now, just to keep things balanced, the prosecutor decided to offer corroboration from a male point of view. He called the cousin who had moved from Texas and then back again, Robert Diaz.

A stout man in his early thirties, with coal black unmanageable hair and darting brown eyes, Diaz walked forward as if it was his last mile. He obviously did not relish being a witness. And when Hum asked him if he knew the woman dressed in black at the counsel table, Diaz frowned while saying he did. Diaz told of being invited to the church wedding and flying all the way from Texas to attend, compelled by family loyalty.

He had met Bruce Cleland, Harold Cleland, and Ed Brown when they rented tuxedos together. Bruce, he said, had shown personal interest in him by accepting a work history from Diaz and agreed to see if he could help him get a job at TRW. But by the time Diaz relocated to California, in April 1997, Bruce had already moved out of the Whittier house.

"When you arrived at the Cleland home, who was there?"

"Rebecca, Dave Romero, the pool guy, and my cousin Ana. That's all I remember."

"Did she say anything regarding your job prospects?"

"Yeah. She basically said that I could kiss that job—the one Bruce might be able to help me get—kiss it good-bye. This was in front of the pool man and Dave, people I really didn't know. So I was a little embarrassed, you know."

Diaz had suddenly found himself with no job prospects and no home. Dolores had rescued him with an invitation to live with her for a while. Hum asked if Dolores had said anything to Diaz regarding a conversation she'd had with Rebecca. The witness replied, "Yeah. Dolores told me that Becky had asked if she knew anybody that could kill Bruce. I said, 'You are joking!'" Dolores had said it was serious, and mentioned Rebecca's threats to shift the blame.

"The weekend of the murder, where were you?"

"We were in Rosarito, down below Tijuana, Mexico. Me, Dolores, and Diana."

"When you came back, where did you stay?"

"I ended up staying with Dolores's friend Diana." Diaz told of answering Diana's phone while she showered, and how Rebecca had sounded abrupt and cold in saying, "Let me speak with Diana." It had bothered Diaz, especially when he learned the purpose of the call—to announce that Bruce had been killed.

Hum asked Diaz if he knew the man sitting at counsel table and wearing a white shirt. Diaz said, "It's Al. He has gained weight, but it's Al." He knew the other man, Jose, "only in passing." Diaz said he had once seen the brothers together at a family barbecue.

On cross-examination by Rebecca's attorney, Diaz thought he remembered hearing a "couple of people," maybe Dolores and Bruce's mother, say that Bruce had married the wrong sister.

Diaz appeared to breathe a sigh of relief when none of the other lawyers had any questions for him. Excused, he wasted no time getting out of the courtroom.

* * *

Jurors had heard testimony, all based on conversations, about Rebecca being unfaithful to Bruce after the marriage. Now Hum called someone who could speak from firsthand experience about it.

Dr. Randy Ellison took the stand. Hum established background facts about him, then asked, "In May 1997, did you take a vacation to Mexico?" Yes, said Ellison, he had gone alone to Cabo San Lucas. He explained about a breakup with his wife and deciding to follow through with prearranged plans, anyway, without her. Near the end of his trip, he had met Rebecca and her female companion in a bar. "I think I was watching a couple of girls dancing on a table and I noticed that Rebecca was kind of staring at me. So I went over and introduced myself." Observers wondered if she had given Bruce that same kind of stare she had use previously at a drive-in swap meet.

Ellison took jurors through the entire encounter and how it had lifted him out of depression. He had noticed a diamond ring on the third finger of her left hand, and heard Rebecca's explanation that she was going through a divorce.

Hum asked, "Did the defendant make reference to any particular part of her anatomy during the conversation?"

"Yes. I found that we shared the same sense of humor, and she referred to her—"

An objection from the defense tried to interrupt Ellison, but not before he said, "—breasts."

At a whispered sidebar conference with the judge, Hum explained, "She told him about her breasts and she called them 'the twins.' It goes to the relationship she's trying to strike up with this doctor." Hum wanted to contradict an opening statement by the defense portraying Rebecca's ongoing desire for reconciliation with Bruce. "Discussing her breasts with a man she has just met in a bar is certainly indicative of a different attitude than someone who's trying to reconcile with her husband." The judge ruled against allowing jurors to hear Rebecca's reference to her breasts as "the twins," and asked, "Is that the extent of this witness's testimony? Where is he going? Did they end up in bed?"

Trying to answer the multiple questions, Hum replied, "They exchange phone numbers. He goes home. She's constantly calling him. Our position is that he's basically her next victim. They make plans to see each other, and they do, one time. She tells him about this separation agreement she's trying to get Bruce to sign."

Rancorous tension seemed to radiate from the growling voices. Hum turned to one defender and demanded, "Don't shake your head." The attorney disagreed with Hum's narrative. Finally the judge managed to restore calm and allowed Dr. Ellison to continue, without reference to "the twins."

Resuming his direct examination, Hum asked Ellison if Rebecca had made any comments about her husband. He replied, "She told me of two major reasons for the planned divorce. Number one, she alleged that he had sexually abused her son, and number two, they didn't have a very good sex life."

"Please describe how she was behaving. Did she seem sad or happy?"

"I'd have to say she was the most fun person I have ever met. Very outgoing, center of attention." He saw nothing to indicate Rebecca felt morose or depressed.

Ellison's testimony took jurors through contacts with Rebecca after they both returned to their respective homes. They had spoken numerous times by telephone and discussed getting together. A parade of obstacles popped up, but they finally succeeded with a meeting in Las Vegas. He admitted they occupied the same room, but denied having sex.

At one point, Ellison said, Rebecca mentioned the possibility of moving to Arizona near him, and getting a job at "one of those exotic dance places."

He recalled Rebecca's subsequent invitation to join her in a July 4 outing at Lake Havasu, which he had to decline. In late July, she had called him with a stunning announcement of Bruce's violent death. A week later, in another call, she had spoken of the funeral and "how some people were starting to point the finger at her." Even more telephone conversations had taken place, said Ellison, in which Rebecca had spoken about insurance money she expected to collect, possibly in the hundreds of thousands of dollars.

Finally, in November of 1997, the witness recalled, she had invited him to visit her for the Thanksgiving holiday. "I purchased tickets, and then a friend of mine talked me out of it. So I didn't go."

On cross-examination by Mr. Orr, the defense attorney elicited testimony that Rebecca, despite talking about moving to Arizona, had never actually done it. He also wanted the jury to hear that Rebecca had not initiated all of the telephone calls, but many had been made by Ellison. The defender also inquired whether Rebecca, in talking about the alleged child molestation by Bruce, had specified the number of times it took place. Ellison couldn't recall, but he said he had advised her to contact a child protective services agency.

Following through on redirect, Hum asked, "Did she indicate whether she had reported the molestation charges to law enforcement?"

Ellison replied, "She had not reported it."

In a 2008 interview, Hum described Ellison as a cooperative and helpful witness. "He was very willing to testify. I think Rebecca had originally flattered his ego, but he became suspicious that something bad was going on, so he finally broke it off. He definitely was not naive or sheltered like Bruce, but had been going through some bad times. When an attractive woman showed interest in him at the Cabo San Lucas bar, it made him feel good. He was one of our best witnesses to show Rebecca's real side."

Chapter 24

The Voices of
Virtue and
a Villain

The next testimony came from a woman who had played two roles in the morbid saga. Elizabeth "Beth" Lamb had first been sought out by Rebecca as a wedding photographer, but she soon found herself being courted by the new client as a friend and confidante. Elizabeth, while amicable and gregarious, regarded it as nothing more than a business relationship. As a religious person, she had seen and heard much more than she had wanted or had ever bargained for.

From the witness chair, Elizabeth Lamb spoke of her eighteen-year background in photographing weddings, and of owning her own business for eleven of those years. Proud of her personal life, she told jurors of her own marriage and four children.

Initially, said Lamb, she had been delighted at the prospect of a lucrative deal. Rebecca wanted the most expensive package of wedding photos and candidly admitted she didn't care how much it cost, since Bruce was paying for it. Lamb's first visit to Rebecca in the Maywood house, she told jurors, had amazed her. The high-quality interior furnishings didn't match the modest exterior, and Rebecca commented the purchases had been Bruce's mistake for leaving his credit card with her during his absence on a business trip.

In scanning the expensive trappings, Lamb had noticed most of the photographs displayed were of Rebecca. "There were some of her and Bruce on a cruise. And a picture of Rebecca in a bathing suit. She told me it was in Hawaii."

Rebecca's expensive tastes didn't seem to jibe with her description of Bruce's spending patterns. "She said he drove an old car, was very tight with his money, and never spent a penny. But she was going to spend it for him." To prove it, Rebecca had regaled Lamb with accounts of Bruce's gifts: the furniture, a boat, and a "Jacuzzi to calm her Latin nerves because she had such a temper." The sparkling diamond ring caught Lamb's eye. Prosecutor Hum asked her about it, and Lamb said, "She told me the secret to getting a ring like that is you refuse to sleep with them until they marry you. 'Why buy the cow if you can get the milk for free?'" Jurors and observers could barely stifle their laughter. Lamb told the jury that first meetings with prospective clients usually take about an hour, but she spent a full three hours talking to Rebecca.

Spectators liked Lamb from the first moment she spoke, and jurors probably did too. Her demeanor and words rang with honesty and pure motives. It surprised no one to learn that she was a "Mormon mom."

In the weeks leading up to the wedding, and afterward, Rebecca continued to embarrass Lamb with intimate revelations. "She told me she had boob jobs done twice and Bruce paid for it all. She said he was stupid because he didn't know she was getting a boob job. She told him she was only getting her lips done and he believed her." Moreover, Rebecca bragged, Bruce didn't even know that his credit cards had paid for the surgery.

Years later, recalling her testimony, Lamb laughed with a slight blush, saying, "I can't believe I said the word 'boobs' in court."

Hum asked if Lamb had attended the bachelorette party. Rolling her eyes skyward, she snapped an unequivocal "no."

Lamb told of fulfilling her duties at the January wedding and reception. The photos she took included a close-up of Rebecca's and Bruce's hands, showing their rings. Hum introduced them into evidence.

Immediately after the honeymoon, according to Lamb, she had received a phone call from Rebecca. "She told me it was a nightmare. She found out that Bruce was a virgin. He didn't bother to tell her until the honeymoon was over. She said that answered a lot of questions, that he was very inexperienced and couldn't perform." The reddish flush of Lamb's face while delivering these words could be seen all the way to the gallery's back row.

On February 3, said the witness, she had driven to the Whittier home to show Rebecca proofs of the wedding photos, and take orders for prints. Rebecca, as usual, turned the conversation to matters much more personal than Beth Lamb wanted to hear. Rebecca piled on additional intimate dirt about Bruce's inept sexual performance. "She said she had brought all this trashy lingerie, and nothing worked. He couldn't perform. She gave me all those details."

In a March telephone conversation, Lamb divulged, Rebecca had criticized Bruce again. "She said the marriage was going bad, that he was driving her crazy. He had gone on a business trip and she was glad to see him go, because he was like a sick puppy following her around. He ended up coming home early and it upset her."

Hum asked, "Did defendant Rebecca Cleland tell you anything more with regard to her and Bruce's sex life?"

"Yes. She told me they didn't have a sex life, that they only

had sex once in their entire marriage, and it was on their honeymoon. She said he could never get an erection, but that he had
no problem masturbating in bed next to her. And she finally told
him—she would just pretend to be asleep—but finally told him
to just leave, you know, have the decency to go into the bathroom. She said at first it made her angry, but then she was glad
because she didn't want to sleep with him, anyway." Lamb's
face glowed even more crimson.

The most stunning disclosure came during a mid-July
meeting between the two women, said Lamb. Rebecca told
her that Bruce had made a pass at her uncle Arturo and had
molested her young son. Shocked and angry, Lamb had asked
Rebecca if she had notified the police. The witness quoted
Rebecca's reply: "'Why would I do that? . . . He would do me
no good in jail. I am going to get him where it hurts, in the
pocketbook. When I am through with him, he will not have
a penny left to his name.'"

"Did defendant Cleland say anything to you with regard to
the timing of what she was going to do?"

"She said that they were going through counseling and he
thought there was a chance they were still going to get back
together. But she was waiting for the right moment to drop
the bomb on him."

"Did Rebecca say whether or not there really was a chance
to salvage the marriage?"

"She said, 'No way in hell would we get back together.'"

Hum asked, "What did the defendant do about the wedding
photo order after talking about the molestation of her son?"
The prosecutor knew the answer would give jurors a glimpse
of this woman's devious nature.

Lamb's voice grew higher and indignant. "She proceeded
to place her order, including the five large wall portraits that
she had wanted." The largest portrait featured Bruce, Rebecca, and her son, with Bruce holding the little boy. "And at
that point, I asked her, 'What are you doing? You're going to
divorce him, and this is the man that has molested your child?

Why are you ordering this huge wall portrait? For your son alone, it would be a nightmare.' She kind of laughed and said, 'You don't understand. I have to play this facade that there's still a chance we're going to stay married. And my family is so angry at him for what he's done, and I wouldn't be surprised if somebody kills him, and I can't be a suspect.'" The conversation had taken place on July 17. In a little more than a week, Bruce would be dead.

The witness next told jurors of a bizarre telephone conversation in which Rebecca alternately sobbed about losing Bruce, then calmly ordered pictures for the funeral and asked if Lamb could recommend a videographer. Later, said Lamb, she had visited the Whittier house on the morning of the funeral. A few eyebrows arched when Lamb stated that she had noticed Rebecca wearing the "stolen" diamond ring and ostensibly crying, but shedding no tears.

A few days after the funeral, said Lamb, she had called a police officer friend to discuss her suspicions about Rebecca. At his advice, she contacted the LAPD.

On his cross-examination, Rebecca's defense attorney, Joseph Orr, asked, "All your [suspicions] at the time were just a hunch. Is that correct?"

Lamb replied, "Yes." He had no more questions.

Judge Connor thanked Lamb and said, "You are excused."

Rebecca's chances for nomination to sainthood had suffered a serious hit. If a scale existed to measure witness credibility, Beth Lamb would score at the very top. Her moral values and frank honesty rang with absolute veracity.

Hum later gave her superlative marks. "Elizabeth Lamb was one of the most significant players. It took courage for her to contact the police. Obviously, Rebecca's assertion that someone in her family might harm Bruce led to suspicion. And her comment about not wanting to be a suspect, after which Bruce ends up dead, made for compelling evidence. Beth was a good witness for the prosecution all the way through. She was obviously so honest, there was no way at all for the defense to attack her."

The next witness could be a little more problematical, and would be a sharp contrast to Beth Lamb. If the Mormon mom represented virtue, Pierre Lebec could play the perfect villain.

Muscular, early thirties, with his hair cut in a flattop, Pierre swaggered up to the witness chair. Dressed in jeans and a dark polo shirt, he obviously meant to impress no one with sartorial elegance.

Knowing full well that the defense would fill the courtroom with Lebec's misdeeds in an attempt to discredit anything he might say, Hum beat them to the punch by allowing jurors to hear Lebec's own admission of an iniquitous background, including running guns and selling drugs. The witness didn't bother to deny his dishonorable past, with one exception. He had once been arrested in a department store for alleged theft. He told Hum, "I didn't steal anything from that place."

Hum asked the witness if he knew Jose and Alvaro Quezada. Pierre stated that he had grown up with the brothers, but he hadn't seen them lately. He recalled that sometime in 1997 Jose had looked him up and asked about acquiring a gun and a driver for a job he planned. At a second meeting, Jose still needed the gun, but no longer a driver. Jose had said that he and his brother had a hit to do.

Lebec tried to recall exactly when the conversations had taken place, but could only guess. He said it was probably three or four months before Bruce was killed.

All three defense attorneys ripped into Lebec with a vengeance. They worked to discredit every aspect of his testimony, and him personally, making his criminal background comparable to a Mafia godfather. It surprised no one when Lebec sometimes let his temper flare. Richard Lasting produced arrest records from the department store incident, and

Lebec grudgingly rationalized that maybe his memory failed him. "I got charged with something, but I don't know exactly what it was. I guess I did it."

When Lebec stepped down, he exited with the same swagger.

Dr. Randy Ellison had allowed jurors to see Rebecca's unfaithful behavior, but only after she had kicked Bruce out of the Whittier house. Now Hum wanted to give them a view of her infidelity before and during the marriage. He called a witness who had close, personal knowledge.

Dave Romero glided up to be sworn in. After taking the oath, he acknowledged first meeting Rebecca in 1986, when she was about seventeen and he was a twenty-year-old stripper.

"About how long did you date her?"

"I don't know. Maybe five, six months." After that, they had gone their separate ways, until January 1997 when she called him with a request to supply entertainment for her bachelorette party. Romero said he agreed to dance, but he would arrive late, so he sent two other strippers to keep the women happy until he could show up.

"At that party, did you have any contact with Rebecca?" Hum's question brought an immediate objection from the defense and a sidebar conference. Rebecca's attorney said, "The offer here is about a sexual contact between the defendant and the witness. It's pretty bad. You know, he's a stripper and it's touchy-feely and things like that. It's to show that she didn't really love Bruce, but I think the court can limit that type of character assassination. The jury is not going to like the defendant when they hear how she behaved, and I'm just wondering if the court is going to exercise its discretion and limit this." The appeal went for naught, and Hum received permission to proceed.

With the question repeated, about having contact with Rebecca at the party, Romero grunted, "Yes, I did."

"Did she tell you she wanted to have sex with you?"

"She didn't tell me," he said, "but we did have sex."

"At some point, did you receive a phone call from the defendant while she was on her honeymoon?"

"I believe so, yes."

"What did she say?"

Romero mistakenly believed Rebecca had called from Mexico. "She said when she gets back, she wanted to see me. I thought it was gonna kinda be like friends, so I said sure." They had met one week after her return from Hawaii. According to Romero's recollection, they had done nothing more than get together for lunch at the club where he worked.

Unsatisfied with vague allusions by Romero, Hum came directly to the point. "Did the two of you ever have sex again?"

Twisting uncomfortably in the blue-padded chair, Romero muttered, "Yeah, we did." It took place at the Whittier house. He also admitted that she bought him many gifts. And after Bruce left in April, Rebecca invited Romero to move in with her, but he declined the offer. Still, he occasionally spent the night with her there. The final overnight stay took place after the small gathering of people to watch the televised Mike Tyson fight with Evander Holyfield and the famous ear-biting episode.

Romero also confirmed that he had brought Alvaro into his stable of dancer/strippers and taught him the business. Hum asked if Alvaro had worked on the Saturday night of Bruce's murder. Romero had previously checked, at Detective Tom Herman's request, and found that Alvaro had not worked that night.

"Did you ever—except for the night of the fight party— did you ever socialize with Alvaro?" No, said Romero. With the exception of carpooling a few times to dancing gigs, they did not socialize. "Other than the fight night, did you ever go out drinking with Alvaro?"

"No."

"How about your other employee Mark Garcia? Did you ever go out with him and Alvaro?"

"No." Romero stated that he had worked late at night at Pepper's club on July 25, and had not seen Alvaro.

Defense attorneys questioned Romero briefly before the judge allowed him to step down.

In Hum's opening statements, he had mentioned a couple of witnesses to the shooting, and beckoned the first one. The middle-aged teacher's aide, Virginia Selva, came forward and settled into the chair. Later speaking of her, Hum said, "She was a very nice lady who didn't want to be there, but knew it was the right thing."

Selva stated that she had been awakened by the sound of gunfire. Hum asked, "When you looked out the window, tell us what you saw."

She replied, "I saw the flash from a gun. The flashes were going so fast. There were four or five shots."

"Did you see a person holding the gun?"

"Yes. It was a man and he was wearing dark clothing, He had short hair, and he was, like, stocky. His black jacket was open to the waist." She added that the person ran toward Concord Street and disappeared around the corner.

Selva had also seen the 4Runner and a woman lying on the pavement behind it. "At first, I thought she was hiding so they wouldn't shoot her." After the police and fire department personnel arrived, the witness had also seen a body lying on the neighbor's driveway.

Judge Connor called for a short break. While bailiffs escorted Jose Quezada out through a side door, Virginia Selva caught sight of him. The image struck a chord in her memory. She later testified that it brought a flashback recollection of the night she saw the shooter run. To her, Jose's physique, size, and movements, from the rear view, looked exactly like the man she had seen running away.

On cross-examination, the defense tried to dislodge her serendipitous identification, but she stuck with it. They also established that she wore glasses and asked if she had them on when she was looking out her window at those events. Yes, said Selva. She had hurriedly picked up her glasses and put them on downstairs. Regarding her statement about hearing what sounded like people "arguing," Selva couldn't say with certainty if one of the voices had been a woman's.

Another challenge came about being able to see anything clearly that night in the darkness. Selva said, "Well, it was dark, but there are lights right down on the corner."

Selva's in-court identification of Jose's back had been an unexpected bonus for the prosecution, but Craig Hum had no way of measuring whether or not the jury would give it much weight.

Chapter 25

Eyewitnesses

Another crime scene witness replaced Selva. Roberto Suarez had rounded the corner of Concord and Beswick, then stopped his small truck when he saw the parked 4Runner with lights on and door open. He said, "I saw a woman lying on the ground behind the car with her feet out toward the street and her face toward the tire."

Hum asked, "How were her hands positioned?"

Suarcz tried to demonstrate it by cradling his head in his right hand, then told of talking to the driver of a taxi, which had also stopped. They had seen paramedics cutting away the shirt from a man lying on the nearby driveway.

To make certain the jury had a clear impression of Rebecca's posture and hand position, Hum asked Suarez to lie down on the carpeted floor and demonstrate. "Don't worry," Hum assured him, "they just vacuumed." Suarez complied, and jurors craned their necks for a good view.

After Suarez completed his turn on the stand, and stepped down, Hum called a procession of five fire department employees and LAPD officers who had worked the crime scene. They took jurors, step-by-step, through their experiences and observations that grim night. The jury learned of Rebecca's statements about being knocked unconscious, the absence of any corroborating injuries to her head or body, and her remarkably calm demeanor with no interest in the status of her husband lying dead across the street. They also heard about her high heels placed neatly side by side on the pavement, and her cell phone call to Arturo Quezada, father of Jose and Alvaro. One of the witnesses, EMT Carlos Gallegos, had overheard the conversation and recalled hearing her ask if *"Papi"* was there. She waited for a moment, and then said, "Something has happened. We're on Beswick. They killed him."

In addition, the jurors listened to gruesome descriptions of Bruce's condition as he lay in a pool of blood from multiple bullet wounds.

The first officer to interview Rebecca had talked to her at the crime scene while she sat in the backseat of his patrol car. In the witness chair, Sean Hoffman recalled the account she had given of the reconciliation dinner at a Mexican-food restaurant, the stopover at her uncle's home, and the subsequent attack after she got out of the 4Runner to check the back hatch door. The woman, he said, had claimed, upon regaining consciousness, that someone had stolen her diamond ring.

Rebecca, Hoffman recalled, had asked if Officer Robert Zavala was on duty, and she wanted to talk to him. Zavala didn't happen to be working that night.

Hum asked Hoffman, "Do you recall what she was wearing that night?"

"She had a black dress and nylons." No, the witness said, he could see no rips, tears, or runs in her clothing, nor any injuries to her.

"Did she say anything in regard to the route that she had taken that night?"

"Yes. She stated that it was not her normal route."

After talking with her, Hoffman said, he and his partner, Jerry Morales, had transported Rebecca to the Hollenbeck Police Station. Hum inquired, "Did she say anything to your partner regarding her personal appearance?"

"Yes, sir. There was a conversation brought up about the type of work she did. She stated she did not work because before their marriage, she had gotten cosmetic surgery for breast enlargement and was dieting to lose weight for the marriage." Observers wondered just what this woman was thinking. She had been through one of the most horrific experiences imaginable, costing the life of her husband, and she was casually chatting with police officers about her breasts? If Rebecca had, indeed, been in collusion with her cousins to kill Bruce, why in the world would she take this cavalier attitude? Wouldn't it have served her purposes better to put on a histrionic display of grief, or at least pretend to be under the effects of shock?

To amplify her strange behavior, Hum asked, "So your partner asked if she worked, and Rebecca volunteered this information about how she got breast implants and she was dieting?"

"Yes, sir. At the time, it seemed a little, in my opinion, flirtatious and friendly toward him."

If jurors wondered why Officer Morales had not been brought in to testify, Hum clarified it by asking, "Jerry Morales is now deceased. Is that correct?"

With a pained expression, Hoffman replied, "That is correct." He offered no details.

On cross-examination by a defense attorney, Hoffman asserted, "She was nonresponsive to questions my partner was asking."

"What do you mean by that?"

"Basically, in asking her questions about noticing anybody in the area following them, or any information regarding possible suspects. She didn't provide anything."

* * *

Detective Walter Angulo supplied the next testimony. He told jurors about visiting the crime scene, returning to Hollenbeck Station, and interviewing Rebecca. When he had entered the room where she waited, Angulo thought Rebecca seemed cold and obtained a jacket for her to wear.

After allowing Angulo to establish those facts, Craig Hum asked what Rebecca said about events leading up to the incident on Beswick Street. Angulo said, "She told me that she and her husband were having marital problems, and that they had gone to a restaurant on César Chávez Boulevard, where they ate and drank. They were celebrating getting back together. Afterward . . . she left with her husband to her father's house on Fresno Street, where they had some more drinks, then left to go home." The witness quoted Rebecca's story of stopping on Beswick, being knocked out, and then waking up. "She indicated to me that she was calling for her husband, then saw a taxi stop. She said she called for her husband, but he didn't come to her."

A few more questions from Hum allowed Angulo to say, "About her husband, she was asking me when they were going to let her talk to him. I asked if she was not aware of what had happened to her husband. She said no, no one had told her anything about that, so then I told her that her husband was dead."

In the gallery, some saw the amazing contrast. Rebecca had made a call to her uncle and said, "They killed him." But a short time later, she suddenly developed an interest in her husband's welfare and wanted to talk to him. Did this reveal her deceitfulness, or was she suffering from shock? Spectators wondered if jurors had noted the sharp turnabout.

"When you told her that her husband was dead, what reaction did she have?"

"She appeared to be hysterical, quite upset, crying, very emotional." But, said the detective, Rebecca calmed down enough to reiterate her complaint about the diamond ring being stolen.

At the interview's conclusion, Arturo Quezada came to the station; Rebecca left with him.

The detective assigned to investigate Bruce's murder, Tom Herman, replaced Angulo in the witness chair. His answers to Craig Hum's questions gave the jury details of the crime scene. The detective explained photographs introduced into evidence. "This is a close-up of the right front passenger seat in the SUV. Shows the blood on the center console and the passenger seat. This next one shows the running board with blood down here, where it dripped onto the ground." He described a ghastly trail of blood. "It led outside the passenger door, back toward the rear of the vehicle. And then southbound across Beswick to the driveway." That's where Bruce's body lay.

Herman gave the jury an explanation of bullet casings, slugs, and unexpended cartridges found.

Since the murder had taken place long before dawn, Hum wanted jurors to understand the lighting conditions at the scene. Defense attorneys had already made allusions to it. Could witnesses have seen the shooter clearly enough, with illumination from streetlamps, to later identify him? Introducing a diagram showing locations of overhead streetlights, Hum asked the detective if all of them were working on that night. Herman said they were, and the light from them provided more than adequate ability to see another person from a considerable distance.

Another looming matter might have been concerning jurors. Was the route Rebecca had chosen, which took her to Beswick Street, significantly out of the way if she planned on going to Whittier? Herman used maps to show that it would have been more direct and easier to take the I-60, which Rebecca had passed under. The I-5, which would be accessed via Beswick Street, was farther and notably inconvenient if she was really headed toward their home.

* * *

Herman's turn on the witness stand lasted only about an hour. He stepped down, giving the seat to Officer Robert Zavala.

Zavala's friendship with Rebecca had put him in an embarrassing position, but he handled it with professional dignity. He responded with articulate confidence to Hum's interrogation, taking jurors through every contact he had with Alvaro and Rebecca, including the trip to Lake Havasu and the Tyson-Holyfield fight party. Zavala made it clear that he had met Jose only once, for a very brief time, when he gave Alvaro a ride.

Hum focused on a few phone calls Zavala had received on the weekend of Bruce's death. At two-thirty on the morning of July 26, Alvaro had called to have Zavala commiserate with him about a breakup with his girlfriend. He claimed to be calling from near a taco stand in East Los Angeles, and said that Dave Romero and Mark Garcia, the fellow dancer/strippers, were with him. Romero had met both men at the party to watch a boxing match. At four-twenty, the same morning, Alvaro called again, this time to say, "They shot Bruce," news he had heard from Arturo, his father. Two hours later, Rebecca had called, and in a confused statement, she had also spoken of Bruce being murdered.

Hum asked, "Did you get another call from Rebecca about one-thirty the same afternoon?"

"I did. Basically, she was concerned that she didn't have her house or car keys. She was afraid that the suspect, or suspects, had taken them and she was in fear of her safety at home in case they got possession of her wallet and her identification, which would reveal where she lived."

"Did she say her purse and her keys had been stolen?"

"Yes, she did."

Muffled whispers rippled through the gallery. Full-color

photographs had been introduced to the jury showing the purse in plain view inside the 4Runner.

Zavala told the jury he had driven out to Whittier the evening of July 26 to visit Rebecca and check on her welfare. He had examined her head and found no sign of injury. Asked if she had said any more about the murder, Zavala replied, "She didn't elaborate other than they were drinking and somebody had attempted to carjack them and they knocked her out." Rebecca, he said, seemed more interested in other subjects, as shown by her asking how the investigation was going.

On cross-examination, a defense attorney asked, "Is it fair to say that you got to know Rebecca Cleland pretty well?"

Sparks shot from Zavala's eyes as he snapped, "No, that's not fair. No, I didn't get to know her that well." The defender did elicit a comment from Zavala that Rebecca had never mentioned Jose to him.

The jury had heard of Alvaro's early-morning call to Zavala in which the defendant had claimed two men were with him at the taco stand shortly after Bruce had been murdered. One of the men, Dave Romero, had already testified that he had not been with Alvaro during that time frame. Now Hum sought to erase the other half of Alvaro's apparent alibi by showing that he had not been accompanied by fellow dancer Mark Garcia on the crucial night.

Garcia took the oath and answered Hum's questions. "Back in July 1997, what was your profession?" The witness said he worked as a dancer/stripper for Dave Romero. Yes, he did know Alvaro Quezada. The three of them often worked together. Hum zeroed in. "Did you ever go out and socialize with your friend Dave Romero?"

"Occasionally."

"Did you ever go out drinking in the evening with Al Quezada?"

"No." Specifically, he had not been with Alvaro the night Bruce was murdered.

On a roll, Hum called the other key eyewitness who had identified Jose as the man running away from the crime scene, Lupe Hernandez. Her testimony closely followed the same information she had given to Detective Tom Herman during the extended investigation. Lupe said she had been in her backyard, went into her bedroom, and heard the noise of shouting plus gunfire. She also spotted an SUV parked at the intersection a block north of her house. A few moments later, she had seen a dark-clad man running downhill on the other side of Concord Street. Racing from her bedroom to her kitchen, Lupe had watched his progress until he disappeared. She had heard a car engine start up and accelerate into the night.

In 2008, Hum spoke of Lupe's testimony. "She was warned by her family not to do it, but refused to back off. She called the police because she thought someone needed help. We wanted to overcome obvious concern about her identification of Jose under those conditions. I went out there with the detectives, both in daylight hours and late at night. There actually is a significant amount of light right there. We went inside her house, window to window, and stood where she said she was. We crouched down, and you could see quite well where Jose ran. Plus, what are the chances she just happens to pick out the same guy whose cousin arranged the murder of her husband? A guy who had asked somebody to get a gun for a hit he wanted to do, whose brother has a cell phone pinpointed down there on the corner. All those things together fit perfectly. We went out there and looked the scene over for bushes, trees, poles, and obstructions to her view. And you could see everything she said she could see. Regarding the car, she said she couldn't see it. That fit, too, because by process of elimination, where she could see, it could only have been where we thought it was. There were four directions, and she could see in three of them. It had to be the fourth."

Continuing his direct examination, Hum asked, "Miss Hernandez, the man you saw running down that street, is he in the courtroom today?"

The witness raised her hand, pointed her finger like a pistol at Jose, and replied, "Yes, he is the man in blue."

A couple of loopholes in Lupe's call to 911 needed to be closed. She admitted saying at the time that she could not tell the runner's ethnic heritage. But to Hum's questions, she said, "He looked Hispanic."

"Why did you tell the 911 operator that you didn't know the race of the person?"

"Well, I wanted them to hurry up and get to the location because of this lady crying, the commotion at the top of the street."

"Do you recall about how much time it was that you watched the man running down the street?"

"Yes. It was about eight seconds." She acknowledged talking to Detective Herman the next Monday and giving a more detailed description of the runner, and repeated it for the jury. "A guy in his twenties, wearing black. Black everything. Black top. Black pants. Black shoes. Shaved head or very short hair." She thought he looked like a gang member. At the time, though, she didn't know if he was being shot at or was the shooter. "I just saw a man."

Lupe had later picked Jose's photo, number four out of a six-pack of pictures. On the reverse side of the layout, she had written, *Of the six photos, photo four is the closest to the person I saw running down Concord after the shooting.* Her slight equivocation had given defense attorneys a crack in the identification, and they had tried to pry it wide apart during opening statements.

"Why did you write that down?" Hum asked.

"Because I didn't want to be the only one accusing this man of the crime."

"When you looked at the photos, were you sure he was the

one?" She replied in the affirmative. "Was there anyone telling you not to get involved in this case?"

"Yes, my mother." That pressure had been part of the reason for her written comment. But none of the investigators or officials, Lupe declared, had exerted any influence on her selection. At a later live lineup, Lupe had also picked out Jose, number six this time. But she had again put a damaging chip in it by writing, *From the six men, I would say that number six looks most like the man I saw that night.* Lupe again rationalized that she did not want to be the only person responsible for accusing Jose. Even worse, when leaving the lineup auditorium, Lupe had said to Detective Peterson that she was "ninety-eight percent sure that was the guy."

Hum again asked another pointedly direct question to verify her selection, and Lupe said, "He is the man I saw running down the street that night."

To the onslaught of defense attorney cross-examination questions, Lupe stood her ground.

The prosecutor could only hope that the spackle he had applied to Lupe's cracked identifications would stick and hold.

For an additional reinforcement, Hum next summoned Detective Rick Peterson. The investigator went through a detailed description of how live lineups are conducted. He told the jury that after Lupe had selected number six, Jose, she left the building. Outside, said Peterson, Lupe had joined him and made the comment about being ninety-eight percent sure. However, she left the impression of having no doubts in her mind that the runner was Jose.

Peterson had also been part of another important discovery of evidence. He told the jury about serving a search warrant at the Whittier house, and finding Rebecca wearing the diamond ring she had reported as stolen. She had tried unsuccessfully to hide her hands. The incident proved her a liar.

Chapter 26

The Prosecution Rests

Nearly all murder trials feature gruesome testimony from pathologists who conduct autopsies of the victims. Family members often choose not to attend this painful segment.

Dr. Irwin Golden, deputy medical examiner (ME) for the Los Angeles County Coroner Office, began his turn in the witness chair by telling jurors of his expertise as a board-certified forensic pathologist. He had performed thousands of autopsies.

Before Craig Hum could ask anything about the case, the defense attorneys asked for a sidebar conference. In the usual whispers, they argued against showing jurors certain photos taken during the autopsy of Bruce Cleland. In one picture, a rod had been inserted into a bullet hole in the victim's head to demonstrate the bullet's path. Hum said, "I think it is significant in this case because it is our position it was an execution, not just a random shooting."

After examining each print, the judge ruled they could all be presented to the jury. With his questioning, Hum drew information from the witness to establish that Bruce had died by homicide from four gunshot wounds. Dr. Golden spelled out in stomach-wrenching detail the effects of each slug tearing through Bruce's flesh and bones. He also explained to jurors about stippling, which had been noted on Bruce's cheek, nose, and face. The "peppering marks," Golden said, are left on a victim's skin from a gun fired within close range. He defined "close" as "the gun's muzzle being between six inches and two feet from the skin." But, for a precise conclusion of the distance, tests would be required using the original weapon. And the murder weapon used on Bruce had never been found.

Handing Golden the primary photo that defenders had objected to, Hum asked, "Does this show the entrance and exit in the skull of a projectile, including the path of travel?"

"Yes. This is the front view. It shows the path of travel from the decedent's right temple to the left side of the scalp going across the skull and brain, from right to left and slightly upward." It had been the coup de grace shot delivered by a cold-blooded killer.

Additional stippling appeared on the backs of Bruce's hands. According to Golden, this would indicate that Bruce had raised his hands to his face just before being shot through his upper lip.

The pathologist next explained the term "fouling." He said it applied to pieces of metal or debris from the gun barrel, as opposed to gunpowder, that could leave marks on the skin. Because the material is heavier, it can travel farther, perhaps three to four feet.

"Do you see any evidence of fouling in any of Mr. Cleland's wounds?"

"Yes. On the back of the scalp, there were several marks." The projectile, he said, had traveled several feet. "There's no way of reading the exact distance, but it would be in terms of feet rather than a greater distance, like yards."

Another finding by Golden proved that Bruce had consumed a large amount of alcohol. His blood alcohol level was measured at .33 percent. In California, a person is legally intoxicated with a .08 reading. According to accepted medical charts, Bruce had consumed at least fifteen drinks within a two-hour period, each one equal to a twelve-ounce can of beer, four ounces of wine, or one and one-quarter ounces of eighty-proof liquor. If Rebecca had wanted him drunk, she got her wish.

Golden said that he had noted other wounds, abrasions, and scrapes consistent with falling onto the pavement.

After establishing a probable sequence for each of the four gunshot wounds, Hum announced he had no further questions. The defenders, perhaps wishing to quickly end Golden's testimony and get it out of the spotlight, declined cross-examination.

Three representatives of insurance companies occupied attention in the courtroom for the next hour, providing information about policies that would pay Rebecca handsomely as the beneficiary in case of Bruce's accidental death.

Carmelita Barron, the waitress who had served Rebecca and Bruce their last meal together, testified next. She told of seeing Rebecca use the pay phone in a corridor out of Bruce's sight, and then later standing in the hallway while using a cell phone.

The pay phone call had gone to a wrong number, answered by Ilma Lopes. She followed Carmelita as a witness, and told jurors that the caller had been a woman speaking in Spanish and asking for "Jose." As soon as Lopes told her that no one named Jose lived there, the phone went dead. Detectives, using telephone company records, had visited the witness several months later. She told them that she did remember receiving the call, plus the first name of the person asked for. It had lodged in her memory because she had a relative named Jose. But, Lopes admitted, she could not recall the last name.

"Did the detectives ask you if the last name was Quezada?"

"Yes."

"And did you tell them that it was?"

"Yes."

"Did you tell the detectives that was the last name of the person the lady asked for because that was the name they said, or because you recognized the name when you heard it?"

"Because I remembered." At Hum's inquiry, the witness said she had never seen defendant Rebecca Cleland or either of her cousins, nor did she know anyone by the name of Quezada or Cleland.

Questions from defense attorneys attempted to undermine Lopes's recollection of a wrong-number call from so long ago, and suggested her memory of the names had been prompted by the detectives. But Ilma Lopes stood by her testimony.

A man named Saiful Huq next stepped forward to provide an hour of complex, technical testimony about how cell phones work. In 1997, he had been the manager of network engineering for Pacific Bell Wireless company. Huq explained what happens when a user makes or receives a cell phone call, how it goes from the originator's phone to a tower, or cell site, and is relayed from there to one of many central switches and computers. The computer, in turn, sends the signal to a tower closest to the phone being called.

Craig Hum had prepared a chart to illustrate the process, and Huq confirmed its accuracy. The expert informed jurors that cell phones, while switched on, constantly scan the system for the nearest cell site. This enables the computer to easily find the phone being called. He also stated that records are kept of every call, and the cell sites through which the connections were made. A few observers thought they were hearing an example of George Orwell's book *1984,* and the incarnation of "Big Brother."

Witness Huq provided evidence that eleven calls had taken place between Rebecca and Alvaro's cell phones on the night of Bruce's death. The records also pinpointed Alvaro, putting him in close proximity to the crime scene.

Adding a new twist to testimony about cell phones, the prosecutor called another expert, Brad Hooper. He had been a police officer in 1997 specializing in cellular phone fraud, and later employed by L.A. Cellular as supervisor of fraud investigation. Hooper revealed that Rebecca had made two calls to the phone company on the afternoon and evening of July 26, just hours after her husband had been killed. The first call canceled Bruce's service, and the second suspended her own service. Two weeks later, she reported that her phone had been stolen.

During a fifteen-minute break, spectators buzzed about what Hooper had said. Had Rebecca foreseen how her calls could tie her to Alvaro and the murder? Did she plan to say the phone had been stolen before the killing? And had these same questions registered in jurors' minds?

After the court reconvened, a third expert, Phillip Brown, gave additional clarification to how cell towers functioned and bolstered earlier testimony linking Alvaro and Rebecca to the crime scene by their cell phone connections.

To end his parade of witnesses, Craig Hum re-called Detective Tom Herman just to clear up a few loose ends related to people he had interviewed during the investigation.

A few minutes later, he announced, "The prosecution rests."

Chapter 27

Alibi: The Back Side Is the Front Side?

The trio of defense attorneys opened their part of the trial by placing relatives of the defendants on the stand, pretty much as character witnesses. The first person to take the stand, Arturo Quezada, tried to show his sons in a positive light. One of his daughters, sister of the two defendants, followed Arturo with more laudatory comments about Alvaro and Jose. A doctor came next to tell jurors about Jose's injured arm, which might have limited his ability to hold and fire a gun.

Alvaro needed a strong alibi, and his attorney, Richard Lasting, questioned a young woman who identified herself as Eneida Moreno, the mother of Alvaro's young son. Lasting directed her to events of 1997, specifically July 26. Eneida said that Alvaro had shown up at an East Los Angeles restaurant where she worked as a bartender. He had arrived before closing time, between 1:00 and 2:00 A.M.

"Was he alone or in the company of someone else?"

"He was walking ahead of—he was with somebody else, but he was walking ahead of the individual—his friend." After some hesitation, Eneida came up with a name. "It was his friend Jerry."

"Did he say where he was going when he left the bar?"

"Yes. He was going to a taco place."

"Do you remember anything particular about his clothing that night?"

"He was wearing a really bright red shirt. It's like a satin shirt."

"Did you comment to him about it?"

"I told him it was very tacky."

Lasting wanted to know about their relationship after she and Alvaro had split up in July 1995. Eneida answered, "He said that we weren't going to be typical parents who separated and would hold grudges with each other. So we did everything possible to maintain a good relationship, you know." She added that it was for her son's sake.

Guided by Lasting's queries, Eneida described Alvaro's compassion in helping others at the YMCA. "He assisted handicapped people, fat people, thin people, anybody that needed help at the gym. And if somebody needed help elsewhere, he would go." She asserted that he was a "peaceful person."

The defender also inquired about Alvaro's job as a dancer/stripper at bachelorette parties. Eneida said she knew about it and that it did not make her jealous.

Craig Hum, on cross-examination, established that Alvaro had used his cell phone to call Eneida's number at 1:37 A.M. on July 26, and had left a voice mail message. The witness said she had no memory of retrieving the message. She began sobbing and dabbing at her eyes with a tissue.

Hum asked, "Do you need some time to compose yourself?" Eneida said she would be okay. The prosecutor next probed Alvaro's financial status, and elicited from her that he earned limited income and usually needed money.

Regarding Alvaro's friend Jerry Morales, Eneida stated that she had met him before that night. But when reminded by Hum of previously telling an investigator that she didn't know Morales, Eneida's memory went blank.

Hum needed to deal with the witness's direct testimony about Alvaro's alleged visit to her workplace, near the time Bruce had been killed. He asked about the bar's floor plan.

Years later, in a 2008 interview, Hum explained the reason for his interest in the site's configuration. "The mother of Al's child said they came to the bar to see her. I went there with the detectives and looked the place over very carefully. We found a serious flaw in what she had said to investigators. It would have been impossible for her to see Jerry from where she stood, according to her own words, and where Alvaro and Jerry were supposed to be. A wall between her and the bathroom area would have prevented her from seeing what she claimed to see."

A series of replies from Eneida gave jurors a mental picture of the bar's layout. Hum asked, "If someone comes in the back entrance, that is where the bathrooms are?" Yes. "And you can't see the bathrooms from the bar?" No. "And you worked in the bar?" Yes.

After a few more exchanges, Hum asked, "Ms. Moreno, when was the first time you went to the police and told them, 'You have got the wrong guy. He couldn't have done it?'"

"I didn't go to the police."

For Hum, jurors should see the implicit message in her answer. Wouldn't a caring person rush immediately to the police if they had information that might save someone they loved from a wrongful arrest for murder?

* * *

Defense attorney Richard Lasting worked to restore the witness's credibility. "Do you remember telling an investigator that when you saw Jerry, you were cleaning the tables?"

"Yes, I was cleaning. I wanted to get out of there."

"Does that require you to walk around from place to place inside the bar, where you might see the restrooms?"

Eneida answered in the affirmative, but left the impression that she could see only the women's restroom. Jurors made entries in their notebooks.

To complete his redirect, Lasting drew more character witness testimony from Eneida. She told jurors the story of an incident in which she and Alvaro had witnessed a child buying ice cream from a mobile ice-cream vendor. A passing van had struck the little boy, after which Alvaro chased and subdued the hit-and-run driver.

The prosecutor, meanwhile, had been studying his records. On recross he asked, "Ma'am, you said if you were at the back tables of the bar, you could see the restroom?"

"I could see one restroom."

"Is that where you saw Jerry?"

"He was in the back, where I was cleaning tables."

"Didn't you tell police officers that he was in the front, looking at girls?"

The witness mumbled something about "the back side."

Hum produced a short transcript and read aloud from it, quoting her words to an investigator: *"This is like the bar and so Al's here . . . and Jerry is like at the front, looking at the girls, you know."* Eneida said she could not remember the conversation.

The defender leaped to his feet again. During that interview, he asked, hadn't the police brought up Jerry being in the front area? Eneida snapped a quick "yes."

Hum's turn came again. "Ma'am, when I just read that

portion, and asked you if you remembered that, you said you didn't remember. Correct?"

"Yes."

With a puzzled expression, Hum asked, "When Alvaro's lawyer asked you about it, you testified that you remembered. Is that correct?"

The witness answered in a whisper, "Yes." She gave a one-word explanation. "Parts."

"So you remember parts of those ten lines?"

"It's been so long, I'm sorry. It's been a long time. I remember parts, yes."

"And do you remember the parts only when the defendant's lawyer questions you?"

"He is asking me because people can see the back side in the front side, and the front side in the back side."

In a calm voice, Hum asked, "The back side is the front side of the restaurant?"

After a few more attempts to clear up the bar-restaurant's layout, Hum let it hang in an amorphous cloud. The jury had seen and heard all they needed to help them decide if this witness had provided Alvaro with a credible alibi.

The other ostensible alibi witness, Jerry Morales, testified that he knew Alvaro and often went out with him. But he could not remember exact dates or times. Regarding Eneida Moreno, Morales said he had never met her, nor had he ever seen her in the bar where she worked. If he had gone there with Alvaro, at any time, he might have gone inside, but only to use the bathroom. He had never even been in the bar area.

A physical-education director at the YMCA in East Los Angeles testified about Alvaro's good work with teenagers at the establishment. She acknowledged helping him develop choreography when he became a stripper. The woman concluded by expressing her shock upon learning of his arrest, and saying that Alvaro was not the type of person who could be involved in a murder conspiracy.

Observers had been eagerly waiting for the next development, and were not disappointed.

Chapter 28

Alvaro's Version

Court watchers love it when defendants testify. Even though it's not likely a person standing trial for murder is going to dramatically confess—as often portrayed in old black-and-white television dramas—the potential for surprises still rivets spectators. Maybe it's the same reason fans attend car races or watch high-speed police pursuits on television, to experience delicious tension while waiting for the possibility of a spectacular crash.

Neither Rebecca nor Jose chose to speak in their own defense, but Alvaro sprang to his feet when given the opportunity and marched athletically from the counsel table. He raised his hand and swore to tell the truth. Would he really keep his oath?

His defense attorney, Richard Lasting, took direct aim at the case's heart with his first question.

"Mr. Quezada, did you conspire to murder Bruce Cleland?"

In an unwavering voice, Alvaro's answer came loud and clear. "No, sir."

"Did you in any way help plan the murder of Bruce Cleland?"

"No, sir."

"Did you drive your brother to the area of Beswick and the I-5 freeway on the night of July 25, 1997?"

"No, sir."

Alvaro gave the same short, crisp answers to the next few inquiries, emphatically denying that he had taken anyone to that area, acted as a getaway driver, or was even remotely linked to the killing. Lasting next established that Alvaro had moved out of a residence shared with his girlfriend in early 1997 and lived for a while in a camper near his sister's residence. The defendant couldn't recall exactly how long he had occupied the dilapidated shell, but he estimated it to be two or three months. In May 1997, he had accepted Rebecca's invitation to move in with her at the Whittier home.

"During this period of time did you see your brother Jose on a frequent basis?"

"No, not really." But he had seen him "from time to time."

"After you moved into the house, did you occasionally do favors for Rebecca?"

"Yes, I did." He had sometimes given her son a ride from school, and helped around the house. "You know, just the normal things anybody would do to help out. Pick up around the place, do chores and stuff."

"Were you employed during this period?"

"Man, it's been such a long time. I don't know if I was going to school at that time. I was probably going to school, I think. To my best recollection, I was in school through unemployment. I think they were sending me to school."

In the gallery, a few coughs and grunts sounded more like skeptical responses rather than colds or viruses. Alvaro's rambling answer sounded too vague. Surely, a person accused of murder would have sharper recall of whether or not they were going to school in that crucial time period. But perhaps the trauma of jail had blurred his memory.

"After you moved into Rebecca's house, at some point, were you offered the opportunity to do some nightclub dancing?"

"That's correct. . . . I danced at a place called Pepper's. And a lot of other places." He named several communities in the region where he had stripped at clubs or private parties. "I danced all over the place. They would send me to different parts of the city and I would go there to perform."

"Did you have a car at the time?"

"No, I didn't. I had a motorcycle." But he admitted sometimes borrowing a car from Rebecca, including the 4Runner.

"Did Bruce Cleland ever live at the house at the same time you did?"

"No, sir." However, said Alvaro, he did see Bruce now and then.

Lasting asked Alvaro if had ever told anyone about his perception of the relationship between Rebecca and Bruce, but Rebecca's attorney, Joseph Orr, objected and the judge sustained it.

Unperturbed, Lasting moved on. "At some point in 1997, did you have a temporary job in Las Vegas?"

"Yes, I did, sir." Alvaro explained his work as a limousine driver in the service of champion boxer Oscar De La Hoya. He acknowledged meeting Robert Zavala, an officer with LAPD at that time. They had developed what Alvaro regarded as a friendship and agreed to socialize in the future.

"Did you later spend a lot of the time at the YMCA in East Los Angeles?"

"Yeah. That was one of the problems with my girlfriend. She had a hard time dealing with that. I would do a lot of free work for them, and she couldn't understand that."

"Did Officer Zavala come to the YMCA to pick you up?"

"Yes, he did. He asked me if I wanted to go on a ride-along with him to see how the job was, and I told him that I wanted to be a police officer."

If that ambition had little to do with Alvaro's guilt or innocence, it might still be useful to the defense in showing his character. Would someone with ambitions to be a cop willingly become an accomplice in murder?

Alvaro commented, "So, you know, he just basically says, 'Come with me and I'll show you what it's like.'" He described in detail the day he had been in a patrol car with Zavala, spotted Jose on the sidewalk, and stopped to talk with him. He had hugged his brother and had given him some money. Alvaro couldn't recall the amount, but said, "It wasn't much. I know that. Maybe five or ten dollars."

Zavala, said Alvaro, had revealed something very personal to him. "The day of the ride-along, we had lunch at Denny's. He began to—he looked hurt, you know, like something was bothering him. He started talking to me about the fact that this younger officer was dating his wife."

In the gallery, the grunts and sniffles ceased, and several people appeared to lean forward, wanting to catch every drop of this juicy revelation.

Lasting asked, "Your recollection is that he discussed a younger officer that was with his wife?"

"That's right. His wife was a police officer, and one of the—his own people that he worked with was dating his wife. And they were fooling around."

A few observers wondered just how this could remotely bear any importance to the case.

"Did Officer Zavala—without going into all of the details about his personal life, did he tell you whether or not his wife had left him?"

"Yeah. Yes, he did. They got separated, but she was trying to come back into the relationship. And he didn't want to see her anymore."

Probing Alvaro's own broken relationship, Lasting asked if, after moving out of the residence shared with his girlfriend, the couple had continued to see one another and date. "Yes, sir," Alvaro answered. "We were still together." But eventually she had ended it. "She said she didn't want to see me no more."

"Do you recall the specific date she told you that?"

"Yeah. It was the night that Bruce got killed. Actually, the morning. The twenty-fifth or twenty-sixth of July, I think."

Lasting inquired what Alvaro had done when she had informed him of the decision. Alvaro said he had called a couple of friends, named Jerry and George. They came over and picked him up at the Whittier house. "It was about nine or ten o'clock that night. We went to Club Pepper's in Industry."

"Did you have a cell phone with you at the time, on the morning of July twenty-sixth?"

"Yes, I did."

"Did you make and receive calls on your cell phone during that time period?"

"Yeah. I used it a lot." Alvaro agreed that numerous calls shown on a prosecution exhibit had been either placed or received by him, and that no one else had used his cell phone.

Lasting approached a key issue: "Do you have a specific recollection of any particular conversation among the various calls back and forth that night?"

"No, sir," Al answered. "It's been three years."

"In any of those calls, did you discuss arrangements to meet Rebecca Cleland in the vicinity of Beswick and the I-5 Freeway?"

"No, sir."

Alvaro's memory appeared sharper with that answer, considering that he had just denied recalling the subject matter of any telephone conversations that night. It remained lucid with his next response, too.

"Do you remember what time you left Pepper's on the morning of July twenty-sixth?"

"A little bit after one-thirty or so." He related it to the club's closing time.

With another flash of recollection, he spoke of calling his son's mother. "I tried to get hold of her because I wanted to make arrangements with her based on the schedule with my boy, and I might have called her at home."

Seizing on the "might have" comment, Lasting popped a question that sent Alvaro's memory plunging into blurry depths again. "Do you have a specific recollection of making that call or not making the call?"

Perhaps realizing that his defense relied heavily on poor retention of past events, Alvaro gasped, "No, no. I mean, it's been so long, but it—"

The attorney cut Alvaro off by inquiring if he had left Pepper's and gone elsewhere at any time before exiting at one-thirty. The defendant stated a firm no. He had trudged around inside or sometimes sat in a front patio area. "I really didn't want to, you know, be around—how can I say? It kind of sounds funny. I didn't want to be around people, but at the same time, I didn't want to be by myself. So I just hung out in the patio and drank by myself." He had made several phone calls, but couldn't recall to whom.

When Alvaro and his two companions finally walked out, he explained, he and Jerry had stopped by a bar where his baby son's mother worked. Lasting asked if he remembered what he wore.

Spectators, who silently asked themselves what they had worn three years ago, expected Alvaro to say he had no idea. But he answered, "I don't recall exactly what I was wearing, but I remember she said something about my shirt. She made fun of it and said I looked like a clown or something like that."

After leaving the bar, the trio had driven to a taco stand in East Los Angeles, said Alvaro, and arrived at approximately two or two-thirty that morning. "We wanted to get something to eat, because it's a hangout where everybody goes, and, you know, kind of—it's like an after-hours place. They cruise and, you know, just party-scene type of thing." The comments struck some as gratuitous.

"Had you been drinking?"

"Yes, sir."

"Did you make a telephone call while you were at the taco place?"

"I called Mr. Zavala." With another flash of clarity, he added, "I remember talking about the breakup between me and my girlfriend. I mentioned to him that I was at the taco stand."

"Did you tell Officer Zavala that you were with Dave Romero and Mark Garcia?"

"No, sir. No."

Alvaro's answer directly contradicted Robert Zavala's testimony, in which he recalled Alvaro telling him that Romero and Garcia stood nearby. Would jurors believe an accused killer who needed an alibi, had admitted drinking on the morning of the murder, and professed to have a hazy memory? Or would they accept the word of a police officer who had no reason to lie?

Lasting asked if Alvaro knew Dave Romero and Mark Garcia. Yes, he did, but they had not been with him. He had left the taco eatery with "Jerry and George," who "took me back home to the Cleland residence."

"Do you know what time you got home?"

"It would be sometime between three and three-twenty or so. I'm guessing. Around there."

"At some point that morning, did you learn of anything that had happened with regard to Bruce Cleland or Rebecca Cleland?"

"Yes. I will never forget it. My dad called me, and he sounded troubled, you know. I could tell something was wrong with my dad. And I said, 'What's wrong, Dad?' And he kind of wanted to cry, and I knew something had happened because my dad doesn't normally cry. And he said he wanted to say something, and he just says, 'Here,' and he told his girlfriend to get on the phone. And she said something had happened, something terrible had happened. I'm like, 'What? What are you talking about?' And I said, 'What happened to Becky?' And she's like, 'she's okay, but they killed Bruce.' And I remember I was in shock. I cried. I· remember crying, and I was—I wanted to get over there. I wanted to know what happened. I—I was just in shock."

Speaking softly as if in sympathy, Lasting asked, "At some point after that telephone call, did you re-call Officer Zavala?"

"Yeah. Yes, I did."

"Did you have any way to leave the Whittier house?"

"No, I didn't have a car. I sold my motorcycle and didn't have anything to get around with." Alvaro said he called one of his sisters, who gave him a ride to his father's house.

Moving on in time, Lasting established that Alvaro had continued living with Rebecca for several months. The defendant admitted that Rebecca gave him money. "She would buy me stuff, yeah, and she would help me out."

"Did Rebecca , on one occasion, write you a check for some sum of money that you recall?"

Observers familiar with the case realized Lasting probably wanted to deal with Bertha Awana's testimony about discovering records in Rebecca's checkbook indicating she had written a check to A. Quezada for $500.

Alvaro answered with a shrugging motion, as if to make the matter unimportant. "Umm, I recall her helping me with my car, you know. I was trying to fix it so I could get my transportation going. And she did, she helped me out. She wrote a check for me."

A few in the gallery wondered where that car came from. He had admitted using Rebecca's vehicles. And without any money, how had he suddenly acquired a car? Maybe the funds came from the sale of his motorcycle.

Lasting asked, "Do you know how much that check was for?"

"About five hundred dollars, I think. It could be more. I'm not sure."

"Do you remember when you got arrested?"

"It was sometime in April, I think. Something like that." Alvaro's memory bank seemed to delete important matters and retain inconsequential subjects. He could recall gibes at his shirt, but not when he was first arrested on suspicion of murder.

The attorney inquired if Alvaro had ever tried to influence any of the people he claimed to be with at the time of the killing, and tell them how to answer questions from investigators.

"No, sir. No. No," Alvaro replied.

"I have no further questions," the defense lawyer announced.

But Craig Hum had plenty to ask.

Chapter 29

I Don't Remember

After a ten-minute break, Craig Hum began his cross-examination of Alvaro Quezada.

The first few answers established that Alvaro knew the man sitting at counsel table, wearing a blue shirt. "Yes, sir, that's my older brother, Jose Quezada."

"Do you love him?"

"Yeah."

"Are you close to him?"

Sounding combative, Alvaro shot back, "What do you mean by 'close'?"

Hum repeated the question. Alvaro asked, "Like how? Buddy-buddy? Hang out every day? What do you mean, 'close'?"

Calm and collected, Hum said, "Well, let's not talk about whether you hang out every day, but back in 1997, would you see your brother?"

"Not all the time," said Alvaro.

"Would you say you were really close to him?"

"Not really." The defendant affirmed that Jose hadn't been

working then, needed money, and had accepted a small amount from him.

Taking the same line of questioning in regard to Rebecca, Hum elicited from Alvaro admissions of being close to her and loving her.

"Back in July 1997, would you say you behaved affectionately toward her?"

"Yes, I do."

"Hug her a lot?"

"Yes."

"Kiss her a lot?"

"Yes."

"Touch each other a lot?"

The personal probe had apparently crossed a line to Alvaro. He barked, "No."

"Did you ever take off your clothes in front of each other?"

Sounding petulant, Alvaro replied, "We grew up together as kids. Used to change in front of each other. That is how we grew up. That was normal."

Hum kept it up. "I am not talking about when you were six years old. I am talking about when you were an adult. You would take your clothes off in front of your cousin when you were an adult?" The prosecutor didn't specify whether or not his inquiry included Alvaro's professional stripping.

Nor did the defendant mention it. He answered simply, "That's correct."

"She would take her clothes off in front of you?"

"That's correct."

"Did you ever sleep in the same bed?"

"Yeah. We did." A little more defiant, Alvaro repeated, "Yes, we did."

"Would that be at the Whittier house?"

"That's correct."

"Did you also sleep in the same bed with her at Lake Havasu?"

"No."

"Did you ever have any pictures taken of you with your cousin topless?"

"No, not that I recall, sir." A few of the jurors scribbled quick notes. Wouldn't most men clearly remember if they had been photographed with a topless, attractive female cousin?

Hum repeated the question, but he placed the inquiry in Lake Havasu. His emphasis on the topic created an impression with spectators that he must have seen such photographs. Alvaro again couldn't recall such pictures being taken, but he did remember Rebecca being with him when they had their tongues pierced.

Rebecca had been arrested before Alvaro. Hum asked if he had ever visited her in jail. Yes, he said, once with his father.

"Now," said Hum, "I want to ask you some questions about these calls from your cell phone the night of July 25, 1997, to the morning of July 26, [1997]. You said you made and received a number of calls, correct?"

"Yes, sir." One of them, he admitted, had gone to Officer Zavala, at about two-thirty in the morning. And another to the mother of his son.

"What other calls do you remember?"

"I think I remember calling Rebecca." But he couldn't say how many times.

"Well, let me ask you this. Before that evening, had you ever used your cell phone to call your cousin Rebecca Cleland on her cell phone?"

"Not that I recall. I don't know, sir."

"So, to the best of your recollection, the night or evening of July 25, 1997, would have been the first time you ever called [her] using your cell phone to call her cell phone?"

"Yeah, that sounds right."

"How many times did you call her that night?"

"I don't recall, sir."

"Was it more than once?"

"Several."

In consecutive questions, Hum asked if it had been more

than one, two, three, four, or five times. To each, Alvaro replied, "Might have."

"When you called her the first time, at about nine-eighteen that evening, did you call to talk to her?"

"Yeah. Why would someone use the phone—?"

Hum wouldn't allow him to finish the retort. "Did you call to talk to her? Yes or no?"

"Yeah."

"Did you talk to her?"

"I don't recall if I did. Might have. I don't know. I don't recall."

Once more, Hum asked in rapid succession if Alvaro had talked to Rebecca on the second, third, or fourth calls—the last one being at 11:56 P.M. To each one, the defendant said he couldn't recall.

"Do you remember if you talked to her on any of the calls?"

Alvaro's voice rose a couple of notches, betraying his escalating tension. "I never denied that I talked to her. I don't remember speaking to her. [That's] my best recollection."

"Do you remember speaking to Officer Zavala?"

Hedging his answer, Alvaro said, "Not everything. But, yeah, to the best I can recollect, I can say that I spoke to him."

"How many times do you remember speaking to your cousin Rebecca on the night of July twenty-fifth?"

"I couldn't tell you. I don't know." Finally retreating a half step, Alvaro said, "Several times, probably. To my best recollection, several times."

Thrusting to seize the minuscule advantage, Hum inquired, "In addition to calling your cousin—defendant Rebecca Cleland—she called you, using her cell phone to yours?"

Unwilling to give another inch, Alvaro replied, "I don't know what she did, sir."

"Do you remember receiving calls from Rebecca Cleland that night?"

"Might have. Don't recall. Maybe."

"Let's talk about a call at nine-thirty in the evening. Do

you remember receiving a call from your cousin on that Friday night?"

"I don't recall. It's been so long."

Hum's strategy couldn't be missed by anyone in the courtroom. Cell phone records introduced into evidence had shown numerous calls, back and forth, between Alvaro and Rebecca. His continued pummeling of Alvaro with repetitious questions steadily built a huge signboard that said: "He's lying!" Alvaro had never called her cell phone before, but he couldn't remember even one, after repeatedly doing it on the fatal night.

Hum kept chipping away. Enumerating several calls by Rebecca, he asked if Alvaro remembered receiving them. The defendant would say no more than "She might have called me" or "Not to the best of my recollection." He did acknowledge one call. "I remember receiving one from my father at the house. That is probably the best one I can remember. I don't know what time that took place."

"Did you call your father's house in the early-morning hours of Saturday, July 26, 1997?"

"Umm, somewhat. Not everything. I don't remember vividly. I remember I spoke to them, yeah."

Hum fired back. "I'm not asking if you somewhat recalled. I am asking, did you call your father's house in the early-morning hours of Saturday, July twenty-sixth?"

Now peevish, Alvaro grunted, "I don't remember." He recited the same words to Hum's next four questions, and similar words to the next dozen.

Just before putting the matter to rest, Hum asked where Alvaro had been while making cell phone calls that night. He claimed he had been at Pepper's club in the city of Industry for all of them.

For the next few minutes, the prosecutor concentrated on Alvaro's living with Rebecca at the Whittier house, and all of the advantages it offered him. "Living in that house was a lot better than living in a camper, wasn't it?"

"Yeah, sure." He had even changed his driver's license to that address.

Up to this point, Alvaro had said he had used a motorcycle and the 4Runner for transportation, but he had never mentioned the Honda. Hum asked, "After Bruce's murder, did you start driving a particular car?"

"Umm, I would borrow it sometimes."

"Which car?"

"The green Honda." He denied using it on a regular basis, but he conceded that he often drove it to distant dancing gigs.

Hum wanted to know about Alvaro's relationship with Rebecca in 1996. The defendant claimed he hadn't even spoken to her that entire year. Moreover, he estimated that in the first few months of 1997, he and Rebecca had spoken to each other no more than two or three times. In late May, she had asked him to move in with her.

Inquiries about all the presents Bruce had bought for Rebecca brought only a claim of ignorance from Alvaro. "What about the plastic surgery? Did she tell you that Bruce bought that for her?"

"Not that I recall, sir."

"After you moved into the house, you saw each other naked?"

"Yes."

"She never mentioned the plastic surgery?"

Alvaro's answer brought stifled laughter in the gallery. She had never talked about her enlarged breasts with him. He said, "People grow. You know, people grow and they are adult."

"Did your cousin Rebecca talk to you about her sex life with Bruce?"

"Not that I recall, sir."

If spectators had allowed themselves muffled laughter at the "people grow" comment, they tried to suppress groans at this latest answer. Rebecca had told everyone she knew about

Bruce's poor sexual skills. She might as well have rented an aerial banner. It certainly didn't ring true that she wouldn't mention it to her macho cousin while they shared a bed.

Before turning Alvaro over to cross-examination by Rebecca's attorney, Joseph "Joe" Orr, Craig Hum asked once more if, before the night of the murder, Alvaro had ever used his cell phone to call Rebecca's cell phone. The defendant replied, "I don't know. I might have, might not have. I don't recall."

Hum announced, "I have no more questions."

The towering Joe Orr started his extremely brief cross-examination with basics. He asked Alvaro the same question in four different configurations, if he had ever "inspired" a plan with Jose and Rebecca, or discussed it, or entered into a conspiracy with them, to kill Bruce Cleland. Mentioning no memory problems, Alvaro answered Orr with a resounding "no" to each one. After eliciting a few comments about Rebecca's generosity, Orr sat down.

While sitting at the prosecution table during those few minutes, Craig Hum came up with only one more question. On recross he asked Alvaro if he and Rebecca spoke Spanish. The defendant said they did.

At long last, the defense rested. Now jurors and observers would be able to hear the four lawyers spell out their versions of what all the evidence had meant.

Chapter 30

Closing
Arguments

In the courthouse cafeteria, officers, witnesses, jurors, and others ate lunch on Tuesday, June 27, and read newspapers purchased in a row of vending machines out on the sidewalk.

Front-page articles covered campaigning by George W. Bush and Al Gore for the presidential election coming in November 2000.

Some readers worried about more prosaic announcements. The average price of gasoline had leaped up to $1.64 per gallon. In other financial news, President Clinton announced that the government's anticipated budget surplus would exceed projections by almost $2 trillion over the next decade—a cornucopia of cash that would make social programs achievable. GOP presidential nominee George W. Bush said the estimates validated his claim that there would be plenty of room in the federal budget for his ambitious plan to cut taxes and still have money for other priorities.

Lawyers and legal buffs devoured news about a U.S.

Supreme Court decision affirming the 1966 Miranda ruling requiring law enforcement agencies to advise arrested suspects of their right to a lawyer and the right to remain silent. No one in the building could guess how that subject would eventually impact a trial scheduled for closing arguments up on the ninth floor.

At ten minutes after one o'clock, Judge Jacqueline Connor advised the jury that each side would now proceed with their arguments. Even though she, and all other judges, always warn jurors that statements from lawyers are not evidence and must not be considered in deliberations, many attorneys feel that summations from both the prosecutor and the defenders are exceptionally important elements of a murder trial. The process of formulating and delivering these presentations may be compared to a movie editor splicing together miles of film in order to tell a cohesive, understandable story.

This stage allows each attorney to highlight important elements of evidence supporting his or her case. It gives jurors the opportunity to rearrange facts in their own minds, since confusing fragments of evidence are often presented out of logical order. Some see the process as similar to assembling a giant jigsaw puzzle.

In Judge Connor's courtroom, four men were scheduled to speak. Jurors and spectators would see a quartet of remarkably different personalities, styles, vocabularies, and techniques used in attempting to convince a dozen triers of fact to see their points of view and to agree with them.

Craig Hum took a deep breath, stood erect at the lectern to study his notes for a final moment, then made friendly eye contact with the jurors. In his relaxed, youthful voice, he said, "Good afternoon, ladies and gentlemen." With his hallmark sincerity, he thanked the twelve weary people for their attention, time, and effort. "I know that sometimes jury service can be a bit of an inconvenience. I know that people have jobs and some of you have private businesses of your own that you would like to get back to. And I certainly appreciate your continued attention to this matter." He reminded the men and women of their duty to determine exactly what happened in the early-morning hours of July 26, 1997. "And you decide whether or not each ·one of these three defendants is guilty of murder and conspiracy to commit murder."

After explaining how the law specifically applied to the charges against Rebecca Cleland, Jose Quezada, and Alvaro Quezada—and the jury's responsibility to reach separate verdicts for all three defendants—Hum illustrated it in the case against Jose. "Let's talk about express malice and intent to kill. Did defendant Jose Quezada intend to kill Bruce Cleland when he shot him? Clearly, he did. . . . We have his actions at the murder scene. I mean, he shoots Bruce in the face, and then when Bruce gets out and runs, Jose Quezada chases him down, shoots him in the back, and then executes him with two shots to the head. That clearly shows the intent to kill."

Without a doubt, jurors understood that would be the intent of any killer who pulls a trigger. But what about the other two defendants? How did the intent to kill apply to Rebecca and Alvaro?

Hum tackled the problem head-on. "They certainly didn't actually kill Bruce. They didn't shoot him in the head. But they are guilty because they are aiders and abettors." He cited the legal example of a getaway driver in a bank robbery being as culpable as the accomplice who enters a bank, points the gun at the teller, and runs out with a bag of money. "In fact," said Hum, "that's what defendant Alvaro was, the getaway driver."

Most people have heard the term "abettor" many times, but never bothered to look up the definition. Abet means simply to encourage, support, or countenance by aid or approval, usually in wrongdoing.

Hum scanned jurors' faces to see if anyone looked quizzical about his explanation. Satisfied, he said that Rebecca and Alvaro were guilty of exactly the same crime as defendant Jose Quezada. "They stepped into the shoes of the actual killer, and they are responsible for his actions. They assume the same mental state, the same intent as he had." In legal terms, the two codefendants "had knowledge of the unlawful purpose of the perpetrator, the intent of committing or encouraging or facilitating the commission of the crime by act or advice, aids, promote, encourages, or instigates the commission of the crime."

Pausing to let the legalese sink in, Hum pointed an accusing finger at Rebecca, saying, "Stop for a minute and apply the facts to this defendant. Does she know what Jose Quezada is going to do? Of course, she does. I mean, she planned it. She instigated it. It was her idea."

Relying on the long-proven speech technique of repetition to drive home a point, Hum asked, "Does she intend to encourage or facilitate the murder? Of course, she does. That's why she set the whole thing up. Does she do anything to aid, promote, encourage, or instigate the commission of the crime? Again, of course, she does. She's the one who gets it started. She planned the whole thing. She made the phone calls. She stopped the car. That makes her guilty as an aider and abettor—just as guilty of the murder as if she pulled the trigger herself."

Hum next aimed his accusing forefinger at Alvaro Quezada. "Let's talk a little bit about this defendant. He is the classic example of an aider and abettor—the getaway driver. Does he know what his brother is going to do? Of course. Clearly. All three of them had planned this out. Does he have the intent to commit, encourage, or facilitate the crime? Absolutely." Hum articulated each word in saying that Alvaro had made a series of cell phone calls to Rebecca within a short time frame prior to the shooting, and that he drove the car for his brother.

The jurors needed to understand certain requirements

stated in the law for finding these defendants guilty of first-degree murder. The crime must have been willful, deliberate, and premeditated, and evidence must show they were lying in wait for the victim. Hum explained and defined each term, with emphasis on Jose's acquisition of a weapon and going to the crime scene before Rebecca and Bruce arrived. He said that Rebecca and Alvaro "stepped into the shoes of Jose Quezada, making them equally guilty of first-degree, willful, deliberate, premeditated murder."

Lying in wait, said Hum, would be simple to decide. "Jose and Alvaro Quezada are waiting near the I-5 Freeway on-ramp about a block away. They're waiting for Rebecca to drive up with Bruce and stop the car. They're waiting and watching for a chance to take Bruce by surprise. Defendant Rebecca Cleland calls defendant Alvaro Quezada, says she's on the way, and they're lying in wait for her to stop. That makes this first-degree murder." Hum repeated that Rebecca's role made her equally guilty of lying in wait.

In California, if prosecutors seek a sentence of death or life in prison without the possibility of parole, they must prove to the jury that certain "special circumstances" apply to the murder. This includes intentional murder carried out for financial gain, multiple killings, slaying someone to prevent them from testifying in a trial, intentionally killing a victim by lying in wait, and a victim being intentionally killed because of his or her race, color, religion, nationality, or country of origin. "Every person, not the actual killer, who, with the intent to kill, aids, abets, counsels, commands, induces, solicits, requests, or assists any actor in the commission of murder in the first degree" may be eligible for maximum punishment as well.

Craig Hum had already discussed the allegation of lying in wait as a required element to convict defendants of first-degree murder. He explained that it also applied as a special circumstance, and asserted that the special circumstance of murder for financial gain would apply in this case. "It really is as simple as it sounds. They killed Bruce for money. That is crystal clear. The only thing Rebecca Cleland wanted from Bruce was his money, and that was clear to everyone—except Bruce. Her plan from the very beginning was to marry him, get a divorce, and take his money. But she found out that if she got a divorce, it wouldn't happen. So she tried blackmail, to force him into signing an agreement to give her money. She threatened to accuse him of molesting her child if he didn't pay her off. That didn't work. So, in order to get his money, Rebecca Cleland decided to have Bruce killed. That's murder for financial gain, and it really is that simple."

Just to make certain jurors wouldn't underestimate the greed, Hum enumerated the specific monetary value of Bruce's life. "Rebecca Cleland wasn't even satisfied with the car, the boat, the furniture, the jewelry, the TRW benefits. That's not enough for her. So she forges his name on a mortgage insurance policy on Bruce's life, and she takes out another policy." (A TRW accidental-death policy for $517,000. A Minnesota Mutual mortgage insurance, accidental death, $200,000. Bruce's TRW employee stock savings plan, $196,829. TRW basic life insurance policy, $44,000. JCPenney accidental-death policy, $25,000. His final paycheck, $3,858.) "Ladies and gentlemen, Bruce Cleland was murdered for $986, 687. That's the motive for this murder, and that's murder for financial gain."

Anticipating the possible questions jurors would have about the payoff for Jose and Alvaro, Hum made it clear they expected to be rewarded for their parts in the murder. "They did not do it for free. They both needed the money, but it does not matter whether they were actually paid or not. Even if they didn't get a dime, the special circumstance for financial gain is still true." He didn't mention the check Rebecca had made out to Alvaro for $500, found in her records by Bertha Awana. No proof existed to show unequivocally the reason for that payment. The prosecutor put his trust in the jury to reach a logical conclusion that both men had anticipated collecting cash for killing Bruce.

Hum next addressed the conspiracy to commit murder charge in regard to the evidence involving the conspiracy among them. "What does that mean in real life? It means that all three defendants agreed to kill Bruce, they intended for him to die, and at least one of them committed the overt act." Letting that comment sink in, Hum added, "It wasn't just some big coincidence that they all showed up in the same spot at the same time."

Hum knew he had to deal with one of the biggest problems—that much of the evidence was entirely circumstantial. He realized that jurors, trained by television crime stories to look for DNA, fingerprints, weapons used, and other direct forensics physically tying a defendant to murder, sometimes fail to understand the importance of circumstantial evidence. Hum acknowledged the issue, and used an analogy to educate the jury. "Most of us know that the Los Angeles Lakers basketball team recently won a championship. Right? Let's say that three coworkers all show up at the game in the same car. They get out, all dressed in purple and gold, raise their fingers to indicate 'Lakers number one.' They all have tickets, they all walk in and watch the game.

"Okay. Can't we tell from those facts that they all have agreed to get together and go to this basketball game? Of course, they did. Now, there's no direct evidence that they met in advance to plan this, but we know they did. It's the same thing that happened here. You can infer from what happened that the three defendants agreed beforehand to do this killing."

Hum planned to highlight testimony from several prosecution witnesses, one by one, to assemble a full picture of what happened, and show how all of the testimony pointed to guilty verdicts. Eventually he would have to mention the important puzzle piece supplied by Pierre Lebec. In Hum's experience, he knew jurors had probably been skeptical of Lebec's veracity, and wondered if the ex-con's testimony had been influenced by police threats or other self-serving purposes.

To lay a foundation, Hum said, "One of your responsibilities is deciding whether or not a witness is telling the truth. You must use your common sense to determine if there is any bias or other motive for them to lie." He reminded the panel of a packet that had been provided to each one of them. It contained instructions related to measuring witness credibility by applying a list of numerous factors to consider. This included any obvious bias, special interests, or other motives to shade the truth. Hum hoped the jurors would take his advice and apply the sensible measures when they came to Lebec's testimony. He would have more to say about Lebec a little later.

With that, the prosecutor said, "Now let's talk a little bit about some of the witnesses and what they said on the stand. We heard from Mr. Cleland, Bruce's father and best friend, about what they did together, including going to ball games and the swap meet. That's where Bruce met defendant Rebecca Cleland. Mr. Cleland told us he and his wife had been encouraging Bruce to meet somebody, because his sister had just died, and they weren't as young as they used to be. They didn't want Bruce to wind up alone."

The mention of Bruce's father brought back a touching moment in the prosecutor's mind, something he really couldn't share with the jury. The elderly man had impressed Hum as a kind, gentle soul—soft-spoken, courteous, and dignified. During the final month of 1999 while preparing for the trial, Hum and Detective Tom Herman had visited the Clelands at their house in South Pasadena. "We were just chatting, touching bases and letting them know what was going on. And I wished them both a good holiday, under the circumstances. In his frail voice, Harold said, 'Mr. Hum, do you have any children?' I said, 'No, Mr. Cleland, I don't.' He said, 'Neither do we.' It was so sad. You've lived your life right, you have two great kids, you think you can retire and live out your days in peace, and then it all falls apart."

After allowing himself a brief, private, sentimental moment, Hum reminded jurors of testimony from Ed Brown, Bruce's brother-in-law. He had testified about Rebecca throwing Bruce out of the Whittier house and trying to get him to sign a separation agreement that would enrich her. Brown had also revealed the defendant's threats to accuse Bruce of child molestation in an effort to extort money from him.

Hum next cited testimony from Bruce's divorce attorney, who said the community property value would equal less than $10,000. "Well, that's obviously not what Rebecca Cleland had in mind. And Mr. Ziff corroborated defendant Rebecca Cleland's threat to accuse Bruce of child molestation if he refused to sign an agreement to give her money."

Subsequent witnesses, said Hum, had filled in other blanks. "When you put it all together, the picture it paints is absolutely devastating."

During the next twenty minutes, Hum used crucial pieces of witness testimony to re-create a chronological vision. Observers in the gallery could easily picture events beginning at the swap meet encounter and culminating in murder.

Listing all the gifts Bruce purchased for Rebecca, including cosmetic surgery, the prosecutor made her greed obvious. The secret civil marriage, Hum said, took place so Rebecca could have her name on the Whittier home deed. He stated that she never intended to cohabit the house with Bruce, just to profit from it.

Some of the most damning testimony had been given by Rebecca's own sister Dolores. Hum spotlighted it. "She said that Rebecca didn't love Bruce, that he was just a stupid American." Dolores had asserted that Rebecca was using Bruce for his money while sleeping with other men and other women. Hum said, "And then, in late December 1996, defendant Rebecca Cleland solicits her sister Dolores to help find someone to kill Bruce."

After allowing a long moment of silence to serve as a huge punctuation mark, Hum added that Dolores had made these same statements to mutual friend Jovita Garay and cousin Robert Diaz. Both Diaz and Garay had confirmed it from the witness stand.

Even though information about Rebecca's antics with other men couldn't link her to the murder, testimony about her infidelity had demonstrated abject disloyalty to Bruce. Hum said, "She had an affair with Dave Romero, only one of a number of people that she is having sexual relationships with while she is supposedly with Bruce." Hum named her lovers—two men and one woman.

Each of the twelve people on the jury appeared to be riveted by Hum's presentation. It played like a dramatic daytime television soap opera. He moved on to Rebecca evicting Bruce from the Whittier home, her trip to Cabo San Lucas, and her attempted seduction of Dr. Randy Ellison. The doctor had testified and given jurors all the details.

The underlying motive for killing Bruce, Hum asserted, was money. He reminded jurors of the insurance policies Rebecca had purchased by forging Bruce's signature. "They don't pay off if he has a heart attack. They do pay off if he is murdered."

Originally, said the prosecutor, Rebecca had intended to divorce Bruce and take half of his wealth. But that all changed when she found out she would gain little from ending the marriage. "We know that in July of 1997, defendant Rebecca Cleland tells Bruce that she will never agree to a divorce. Dancer/stripper Dave Romero heard it. 'I'll never give you a divorce, no matter what you say.' Why? Because she knows she won't get anything.

"Then comes the meeting with Beth Lamb where Rebecca says that she would not be surprised if someone in her family killed Bruce, and she can't be a suspect. Nine days before the murder, Dr. Ellison tells us that Rebecca Cleland was trying to get Bruce to sign an agreement to pay her thirty-five hundred a month forever. And we know Bruce wouldn't agree to that.

Bertha Awana, the defendant's best friend, tells us how Rebecca Cleland became upset when Bruce wouldn't sign the separation agreement and how she threatened to claim he had molested her child."

Hum had observed jurors' reactions to Elizabeth Lamb while she occupied the witness chair. They loved her honesty and unimpeachable dignity. About her testimony, Hum said, "She contacts the police on her own after she finds out that Bruce is dead, because she knows what's going on here." He recounted the disgusting, intimate things Rebecca had told Lamb, and then said, "On July 17, 1997, only eight days before this alleged reconciliation dinner, defendant Cleland said to Ms. Lamb, 'Well, Bruce thinks there might be a possibility for us to get back together, but there is no way in hell we're going to get back together.'"

Deepening his voice to an indignant growl, Hum said, "Ladies and gentlemen, from this evidence alone, we know who had Bruce Cleland murdered, and we know why. The person who cared only about Bruce's money. The person who thought she was set for life when she married Bruce and found out differently. The person who used men for what she wanted, and the only person who would profit directly from Bruce's murder. Almost a million dollars' worth. Defendant Rebecca Cleland.

"We all know it. But we also know that Rebecca Cleland didn't do it alone. She needed help. Who is she going to turn to, to help her murder her husband? Sister Dolores already turned her down. Do you think she is going to go out on the street and solicit a complete stranger? I don't think so. Who is she going to turn to? Who can she trust? Who is she closest to? Who is she living with?" The evidence pointed to only one person.

"Defendant Alvaro Quezada. That is who she is going to get to do the murder. And he knows just the person to help him, his brother, Jose, who needs the money and who knows where to get a gun. It all makes sense. It all fits together."

Witnesses Virginia Selva and Guadalupe Hernandez, Hum

reminded jurors, had heard gunshots, seen the shooter running away, and had later identified Jose Quezada as that man.

Keeping the jury's attention on the crime scene, Hum talked about Rebecca's behavior there, as described by police officers and firefighter personnel. "They see defendant Rebecca Cleland lying on the ground, on her side, facing the rear tire of the 4Runner, with the side of her face cupped in her palm. Remember, I even had one of the witnesses demonstrate it here and show us. Why is that important? Rebecca Cleland claims she was hit on the head and knocked unconscious and fell to the ground. Do you really believe that she fell and just happened to land with her face in her hand? Of course not. She wasn't knocked unconscious."

In addition, said Hum, Rebecca had shown no interest in Bruce, whose body was stretched out on a driveway across the street. No questions about him, no effort to go over there and check on him. That was not the action of a wife who cared whether he was dead or not.

Also, the emergency medical personnel had checked her head and limbs for any sign of injury. They found none. "She claimed she was knocked unconscious and fell to the pavement, but she didn't have a scratch. Not even a run in her nylons. Nothing. Ladies and gentlemen, we have all smacked our heads on something, and we know what happens." She had no lump, bleeding, or any type of injury. "They also noticed her shoes sitting at the back of the 4Runner, like she had just stepped out of them to lie down on the ground."

The defendant's actions, said Hum, pointed directly to her guilt. "What does she do? She immediately goes to her vehicle and calls her uncle, whom she refers to as her father. She says, 'They killed him. They killed him.'"

Hum rubbed his chin, as if in deep thought, then spoke. "Number one, nobody told her Bruce is dead. Number two, if she was knocked unconscious, how does she know that *they* did anything? She knows, because she set it up. And she knows who *they* are. Her own cousins. Don't forget, Bruce

Cleland is shot several times, and defendant Rebecca Cleland doesn't have a scratch."

Officer Edson, said Hum, had arrived within a minute or two after the killing. "He sees her purse and cell phone in the car. Why is that important?" Answering his own question, Hum said it provided unequivocal evidence that the crime was not a robbery or carjacking.

Another police officer, Sean Hoffman, had asked Rebecca why she took that particular route if she was going to Whittier. She answered, "I don't know. I never go that way."

In a skeptical voice, Hum said, "Gee, what a coincidence. The one time you decide to take this quiet, secluded route home, you just stop your car and your husband gets murdered." And, the prosecutor stated, her conversation with the officers certainly did not reflect the trauma of the situation. "She was talking about her diet and her breast implants while her husband is lying dead on the street."

The story Rebecca had given about a warning light on the instrument panel also raised Hum's hackles. "Why does it take so long to notice this light? Why does she first notice it right here at this nice, secluded on-ramp? She claims she got out and went to the tailgate, and the next thing she remembers is being on the ground with her head hurting. . . . What a coincidence that she just happens to notice this warning light and stopped the 4Runner right where this so-called robber/carjacker is hanging out with a gun. What a coincidence."

Hum's face looked as if a bad odor hung in the courtroom air. "And after this robber decides to knock her out, he says, 'I'm going to go around to the passenger side and kill the man in the passenger seat.' Why? He puts his gun inside the open window and shoots Bruce in the face. We know that because one of the bullet casings is in there."

None of this made any logical sense, said Hum. "First of all, if you are going to steal the car, why would you shoot the passenger? Now you have a dead body inside the vehicle. You have blood all over the place. What kind of a carjacker is that? It's not a carjacking.

"But Bruce is only wounded, so he tries to run. And what does our robber/carjacker do then? Does he take the purse, which is sitting right there? No. Does he take the cell phone in plain sight? No. Does he take the car, which is sitting there with the engine running, lights on, within a few feet of a free-way on-ramp? No. He chases Bruce and shoots him in the back, then executes him with two shots to the head. And then he runs down Concord to the intersection with Garnet, where a getaway car just happens to be waiting to take him away. What a coincidence."

One other anomaly to this scenario stood out, and Hum wanted the jury to grasp it fully. "The killer doesn't take any property except for—defendant Rebecca Cleland says—he took her diamond ring. The purse, cell phone, car, and Bruce's wallet are all still there, and we are supposed to believe this is a robbery or carjacking? Absolute nonsense. And something else to think about—when exactly was it that this robber took the diamond ring? I guess it would have to be *after* he knocked her senseless, but *before* he decided to go around and shoot Bruce. And you might ask yourself, 'How did he do that if she is lying with her face on her left hand?'"

To hammer home the lie about the ring theft, Hum held up the photographs taken by detectives of Rebecca at the Whittier house, in which she wore the diamond. "Ladies and gentlemen, common sense tells us there was no robbery, no carjacking—and we all know it."

Judge Connor, always considerate about jurors' comfort and personal needs, suggested a five-minute break. Each person in the courtroom allowed himself a short respite from the palpable tension.

With everyone reseated and quiet, Craig Hum resumed his arguments. He had concentrated heavily on Rebecca, and now shifted gears. "Let's talk for a few minutes about defendants Jose and Alvaro Quezada. We know that two people helped Rebecca Cleland. There was a shooter and a getaway driver." To the prosecutor, no doubt existed about who those two helpers were.

Two eyewitnesses had identified Jose as the man fleeing from the crime scene, and Hum took the jury through their testimony once more. Lupe Hernandez said she had watched him run for about eight seconds. To give the jury a feeling of how long that is, Hum asked for everyone to sit still in total silence for that length of time. It amazed observers how eight seconds seemed interminable, and would be plenty of time to brand an image of someone in the mind.

To further tie it down, Hum reiterated, "Lupe Hernandez gets six pictures she has never seen before, and she identifies Jose Quezada as the person she saw running down Concord. And what a coincidence, the person she picks just happens to be defendant Rebecca Cleland's cousin."

After the live lineup, Lupe had again selected Jose Quezada, but she had written the comment *This is the person who looks most like the guy.* That seemed to leave a little room for equivocation, and Hum wanted to erase that thought. He explained: "We know why she wrote that. Lupe felt bad. She didn't want to be the only person who put defendant Jose Quezada away. She also got pressure from her mother not to get involved. But, ladies and gentlemen, Lupe Hernandez tells us this was the man she saw running down the street. She knows this is the man, and she told us that here in court under oath, from the witness stand."

The identification, Hum noted, had been corroborated by the other witness, Virginia Selva. And the fact that Rebecca tried to call someone named Jose on that night, from the restaurant, could also be considered as corroboration.

Regarding that attempt, and additional cell phone calls, Hum pointed out that Rebecca had made them all behind Bruce's back. He added, "Is this just a big coincidence? She just happens to call her cousin three hours before her husband is murdered, and one of her cousins is the man identified as running away from the crime scene?"

Moving on to the day detectives arrested Rebecca and Jose, Hum said, "He is put in the backseat of a police car with his cousin defendant Rebecca Cleland. And what do we have? Absolute silence. We have 'How are you doing?' And then that's it. For fifteen minutes, not another word is spoken. No small talk. Nothing. Why not? Defendant Jose Quezada tries to claim, 'Gosh, I didn't know it was my cousin. I had never seen her before.' Nonsense. Of course, he knows it's his cousin. And even if he didn't, you are sitting in the back of a police car with somebody, you are not going to say a word to them? And defendant Rebecca Cleland admits that she knows this is her cousin sitting in the car with her. She doesn't say a word, either. Nothing. Fifteen minutes of silence. Why? Because they are afraid the police might be listening in and they don't want to say anything. Think about it. You have been arrested for something. You don't have any idea what you are doing there. You are in the backseat of a police car with your cousin, and you just kind of sit there for fifteen minutes. Nonsense.

"Ladies and gentlemen, that silence speaks volumes. What really happened? These three defendants had set up the murder of Bruce. They thought they had gotten away with it. All of a sudden, Jose Quezada and Rebecca Cleland are in the back of a police car, looking at each other, but they are not saying a word."

Satisfied that his verbal cannon had blasted another hole into the sinking ship of the accused killers, Hum paused a moment before moving on. He had no way of knowing the explosion would backfire on him.

One of the most powerful statements in the trial had come from the shady witness named Pierre Lebec, who had revealed Jose's attempt to obtain a gun. Most prosecutors eventually must come to grips with testimony from witnesses who have a criminal background, knowing that jurors tend to put little weight on their testimony, suspicious that they could say anything in trade for favors. One of the major building blocks to arresting Jose Quezada had been Detective Tom Herman's serendipitous discovery of Pierre Lebec. This witness had testified about Jose trying to obtain a gun and telling him that he and his brother had a hit to do. The defense, trying to discredit Lebec, had made his rap sheet a major issue.

The prosecutor wanted jurors to understand that such a witness does not necessarily lie. "You saw Pierre Lebec. You heard him. You saw him exactly as he is. Nobody tried to dress him up or pretend he was somebody he wasn't, because you are entitled to see him and hear him exactly as he is." Observers understood the oblique slap at defense attorneys who had gone to great lengths to change the appearance of Jose and Alvaro.

Hum continued: "He was a drug dealer. He was a gunrunner. But, ladies and gentlemen, Pierre Lebec has no reason to lie to us. He is friends with Jose and Alvaro Quezada. He grew up with them. He has known them for twenty years. He likes them. He has no reason to lie to us, or to say what he said, unless it's true. And he admits to us that in 1997, Jose Quezada approaches him and says he needs a handgun and a driver. And then a short time later, says he still needs the gun, but not a driver anymore. And Jose Quezada tells Pierre Lebec, 'Me and my brother are going to do a hit.'"

Once more turning to his "coincidence" theme, Hum said, "Defendant Jose Quezada needs a gun. He is going to do a hit with his brother, Al. What hit do we think they are talking about? Three hours before the murder, Rebecca Cleland tries to call Jose. He is identified by eyewitnesses and his photo is picked out of six pictures. And he is picked out at a live lineup. And when arrested and left alone in a police car with his cousin, the person who set up the murder, he says absolutely nothing. Again, it all fits together. Do we think this is all some huge coincidence? Of course not. Ladies and gentlemen, the testimony from Pierre Lebec is absolutely devastating to the defendants, and he has no reason to lie to us."

Two down, and one to go. Hum turned his attention to Alvaro Quezada, the only defendant who chose to testify. "He is a person Rebecca is very close to. A person she sleeps in the same bed with. The person who is living with her at Bruce's house in Whittier at the time of the murder. The person who would be back living in a trailer if Bruce and Rebecca got a divorce." Hum added that Alvaro regularly received money or gifts from Rebecca, that he had free use of Bruce's Honda, and he was the person Jose had named in saying they were going to do a hit.

Furthermore, said Hum, this is the man who had never before used his cell phone to call Rebecca, but used it five times to contact her on the night of the murder. "He calls her at his father's house two more times that night, less than a half hour before Bruce is murdered. And he received five calls on his cell phone from her in the three and a half hours before Bruce's murder—the last one less than ten minutes before the shooting."

Like Evander Holyfield or Oscar De La Hoya landing punches, Hum kept pounding away. "Alvaro Quezada is the person who gives a false alibi for the night of the murder to his police officer friend, then has to change it when he finds out his coworkers aren't going to back him up. Let's talk about Alvaro Quezada, the person who clearly remembers several calls he made that night to other people, but can't remember any of the ten calls he makes or receives from his cousin Rebecca Cleland on the night of the murder.

"We heard from Bertha Awana about defendant Alvaro Quezada's relationship with his cousin, and from Quezada himself. Hugging, kissing, naked together, sleeping in the same bed. They even got their tongues pierced together."

Hum named several witnesses who refused to back up Alvaro's alibis, including Dave Romero. This witness testified that Alvaro had not worked that night as a stripper. "We had Jerry Morales, who doesn't remember what night he was out with Alvaro. He had no idea." Hum reminded jurors that Morales had said he didn't know the mother of Alvaro's son, had never met her, and didn't see her in the bar on the night of Bruce's murder. "If he did go in there, it was only to use the bathroom. He never went into the bar." And he certainly wasn't in there during the early morning of July 26.

"And then we have Eneida Moreno, the mother of Alvaro's little boy. She claims that Alvaro came by her work between one-twenty and one-thirty that morning." She lied, said Hum. She wanted Alvaro out of jail, and lied to keep him free for her own motives. She said, "I saw Jerry there." But Jerry had denied it. According to Eneida's own testimony, Hum asserted, she could not have seen him if he had gone in only to use the bathroom. It would have been physically impossible, since a wall completely blocked the view. And Jerry wasn't even certain what night that had happened.

"Here's another interesting point," Hum offered. "If Alvaro was at the bar where she worked that night, why did he call her home on his cell phone? It's on the record. It's a lie."

Next, tackling the cell phone evidence placing Alvaro at the crime scene, Hum summarized the technical aspects, trying to keep it simple yet vibrant. None of the jurors appeared to lose interest. The prosecutor followed up with a vitriolic debunking of defense witnesses, one by one.

Winding down, Hum attacked the remaining testimony from Alvaro Quezada. "You saw him on the witness stand and the way he acted. Do you really believe what he said was the truth? Because if you do, let him go. If you believe him, turn him loose. Ladies and gentlemen, we all know he was lying. He has only one reason to do that, because he was involved in this murder."

If observers in the gallery had been looking for titillation during the trial, they had been treated amply with testimony about the relationship of Rebecca and Alvaro. Hum touched on it briefly. "We know Alvaro and his cousin Rebecca were extremely close. It was interesting that, although he claims they took off their clothes in front of each other all the time, they never discussed her plastic surgery. All I asked about was cosmetic surgery. He said, 'You know, people grow.' She didn't discuss it with him? She is talking about it with the police when her husband is lying on the street, dead, but doesn't talk about it with her cousin? That is nonsense."

To Hum, the phone call evidence on the night of the murder was an eighteen-wheeler smashing into a MINI Cooper. No contest. Any reasonable person, he concluded, would be able to see the crushing impact of those cell phone connections. Hum said, "I asked him about all those phone calls, back and forth, between him and his cousin on the night of the murder, and all of a sudden, he can't remember anything. He had never before called Rebecca Cleland on his cell phone. But he can't remember calling her that night. They are absolutely devastating to his case, yet he can't remember them."

After taking one more opportunity to demonstrate how cell towers linked Alvaro to the crime scene, Hum exhaled deeply, then launched his final volley.

"Ladies and gentlemen, the evidence in this case is overwhelming, as to all three defendants. We all know what happened that morning. And we all know why. Defendant Rebecca Cleland set this murder up, and her cousins carried it out. It was all about money and all about greed. In the early-morning hours of July 26, 1997, Alvaro Quezada called Rebecca Cleland at Arturo Quezada's house. This took place at twelve forty-nine in the morning. Thirteen minutes later, Rebecca calls him back. She leaves her uncle's house, and her two cousins are waiting. She drove to the intersection of Beswick and Concord, then stopped the car and got out. Defendant Jose Quezada walked up to Bruce, sitting in that passenger seat, stuck the gun in his face, and pulled the trigger.

And when Bruce tried to run, Jose Quezada chased him down, shot him in the back, and then executed him. He then ran to the getaway car, which was right where the cell phone records show it was. The car driven by defendant Alvaro Quezada, where Lupe Hernandez said it was. And they sped away.

"Ladies and gentlemen, that makes each one of these defendants—Jose Quezada, Alvaro Quezada, and Rebecca Cleland—guilty of first-degree, special-circumstances murder.

"Thank you."

Craig Hum would have one more chance to address the jury following the presentations by lawyers for the three defendants.

Judge Connor called for another five-minute break after which defense attorney Jeff Kelley would offer his final arguments to show the innocence of his client, Jose Quezada.

Chapter 31

The Defense
Attack

One of the better orators among defense attorneys, Jeff Kelley stood to his full height, considerably below six feet, wiped his spectacles, replaced them on his nose, and spoke in a deep, sonorous voice. "Your Honor, counsel, ladies and gentlemen of the jury—good afternoon."

He voiced the usual gratitude for jurors' attention and devotion to their work, then opened fire with his defense of Jose Quezada, taking aim at the prosecution's case. "Now, I don't know what you think of Rebecca Cleland, and, quite frankly, I don't really care. The evidence in this case has not shown that Jose Quezada had any involvement with her in the planning and execution of Bruce Cleland. . . . Whatever she did, if anything, whatever you find her activities to be, she did them without the aid of Jose Quezada." Kelley repeated assertions from his opening statement that no matter how tragic the event, Jose had no part in Bruce's murder.

Defenders must walk a fine line to avoid offending jurors'

sensibilities by disrespecting a victim's family. Kelley tagged that base early and sounded absolutely sincere. "Bruce Cleland seemed like a very nice man from all accounts. I have been seeing his family in court since this case has been in the justice system, and they are very nice people, too. We have always exchanged greetings, and I would give my heartfelt condolences to them. They have been through a lot in the past few years."

Despite recognition of this pain, said Kelley, the jurors must face their responsibility to avoid any emotion or sentiment in reaching a verdict. "Mr. Hum will have one last opportunity to address you, because he has the burden of proof in this case. And I submit to you that he has not proven his case against Jose Quezada."

In recent years, the public has been made acutely aware of failures and inaccuracies related to eyewitness testimony. Scores of criminal convictions based on eyewitnesses have been overturned through the use of DNA evidence. Defense attorneys recognize this vulnerability, and routinely use it to their advantage.

Pointing out that the prosecutor had "spoken at length" about testimony from witness Lupe Hernandez, Kelley said, "Now, I'm not here to tell you she is a bad lady. I don't know her. I'm not even saying she was lying. I am, however, saying she is wrong. History is replete with circumstances in which people have made mistaken identifications. It's nothing new. It's nothing earth-shattering. That is what we have in this case.

"This is not me spin-doctoring what she said. The things I'm going to talk about are the words that came out of her mouth or the words she wrote in her own hand on paper." Kelley understood the need to put a dynamite charge under Lupe Hernandez's identification of Jose as the man running away from the crime scene, then light the fuse.

Hernandez had called 911 immediately after the shooting, and a recording of it had been made. Kelley advised jurors they would have the tape, plus a transcript, to use during deliberations, but he wanted to play it for them now. After experiencing an embarrassing technical problem that delayed the audio for a few minutes, Kelley succeeded.

As soon as he finished playing it, Kelley commented that the prosecution had tried to suggest Hernandez had been nervous when she made the call. He said, "You heard it. Did she sound nervous?" To some people seated in the gallery, Lupe spoke in a coherent, perhaps urgent tone, but had remained calm.

In interviews with detectives, and in her trial testimony, Hernandez had said the runner looked Hispanic, and that she had moved out of her bedroom to another window from which she got a second look at him. Referring to the 911 call, Kelley noted, "She was asked if she could tell what race the person was. She said. 'No, I couldn't see. I'm from my bedroom window.' That's what she said after making the observations. Again, these are words out of her own mouth." If she really couldn't see Jose for some of the time, could her identification of him be trusted?

Turning to the telephone interview with Detective Herman on July 28, Kelley stated, "That was the first contact any detectives had with her . . . and she said the person was one hundred fifty to one hundred sixty pounds, had a shaved head, and was definitely a gang member. Now, when Detective Herman testified, he tried to infer that she said he resembled a gang member. But when I referred him to his own records, he had to admit that she indicated the person was definitely a gang member."

If Kelley meant to suggest that Lupe's brief description did not fit Jose, he needed to dig a little deeper, and proceeded to do so.

Even more important, the defender declared, was another statement by Hernandez during the telephone conversation. "She said that she did not see the man's face, which is consistent with what she told the 911 operator. But, over four months later, not a couple of days later, the detectives have their first in-person interview with Lupe Hernandez. She gives a description similar to the one she gave earlier by telephone. In addition, she says that she lost sight of the person as he ran past bushes in the front of her house. She didn't say she lost sight of him as he entered the shadows of the trees across the street. Those are two completely different things."

Craig Hum had drummed repeatedly on the theme of specious "coincidence." Kelley said, "The prosecution made reference to the big coincidence that Lupe Hernandez selected a cousin of Rebecca Cleland." Bristling with righteous indignation, Kelley growled, "Who put the photographic six-pack together? It was the detectives. Do you think Jose Quezada just dropped out of the sky by magic and happened to appear in that six-pack? No. They put him there because he is the cousin of Rebecca Cleland, and that is the only reason they put his picture in that six-pack."

Pushing harder on that issue, Kelley pointed out that Lupe had described the suspect as eighteen to twenty years old. His client was thirty at the time. The defender also complained that the six-pack photo apparently had been taken years earlier, when Jose was younger. Exploring another chink in Lupe's identification, Kelley read aloud what she had written on the reverse side of the photo six-pack. *"Of the six photos, photo number four is the closest to the person I saw running down Concord after the shooting."*

In an accusatory tone, Kelley said the prosecution had just glossed over the equivocal statement. And Lupe had been equally vague in what she wrote after the live lineup: *From the six men, I would say number six looks most like the man I saw running that night.* And later, in the parking lot, she had said to the detectives she was "ninety-eight percent" sure of her selection.

Defense attorneys want identifications to be unqualified, and to Kelley, Lupe's selection of Jose Quezada fell considerably below that standard. He made his opinion clear to the jury. He also let them know that Lupe had refused his interview request. .

"I believe that person she saw running down the street that night shot Bruce Cleland, but that man is not Jose Quezada," he declared.

Observers wondered if Kelley's argument had undermined Lupe's eyewitness identification of Jose enough to create reasonable doubt in jurors' minds. The defense needed only one of the twelve to hold out, which would cause a mistrial.

The next witness to fall under Kelley's scythe was Ilma Lopes, who had received a call on the night of July 26, but couldn't remember the full name of the person a female voice had asked for. Kelley suggested she had received hints from the detectives. "Think about it," he said. Could any of the jurors think back seven months and remember receiving a wrong-number phone call on a certain date and time? And on top of that, could they remember the name of the person asked for? Kelley painted the entire incident with doubt, suggesting that detectives had influenced Lopes's recollection and that Rebecca hadn't even used the restaurant's pay phone.

Moreover, he said, telephone records showed that no calls had been made that night to either residence where Jose was living at the time. Observers didn't buy into that one. If Rebecca had been trying to reach Jose, and if a conspiracy had been planned, she probably would have assumed he was with Alvaro.

With renewed contempt, Kelley took aim at one more prosecution witness. "They trot out Pierre Lebec. You have got to be kidding me with this guy. He is an admitted liar and criminal, every which way you want to cut it. . . . He is a snitch, who is involved in criminal activity." Kelley didn't dispute Lebec's long-term acquaintance with his client, but denied that the conversation about guns and doing a hit ever took place. And, he asserted, the alleged timing of Lebec's meeting with Jose was too vague for reliability.

Kelley finally attacked the conspiracy theory. "People who saw Rebecca the most never saw her with Jose. If they are alleging a conspiracy, when did it take place?"

The incident of placing Jose and Rebecca in the backseat of a police car also bothered the defender. "They are trying to infer something sinister because nothing was said."

Kelley wound down his presentation by focusing on Jose's broken wrist. Spectators gave it little weight, since cross-examination of the doctor revealed that Jose could probably still have held and fired a gun, albeit with some pain.

"This is not a case of guilt by association," Kelley stated. "I submit to you that the burden has not been met by the government in this case. The Clelands deserve to have justice, but that cannot come at the expense of convicting an innocent man. Jose Quezada did not shoot Bruce Cleland, didn't have anything to do with it. He is here because he is the cousin of Rebecca Cleland, which put him in a lineup and a photographic six-pack prepared by the detectives. Also some tentative identifications made by witnesses who said they could not see the man's face on that night. That is the essence of this case.

"The only verdict in this case for Jose Quezada is not guilty."

Kelley sank into his chair. Observers speculated that he may very well have hit the most vulnerable parts of the people's case.

Judge Connor thanked him, and announced that closing statements from Mr. Orr and Mr. Lasting, plus Mr. Hum's final argument, would take place the following morning at nine-thirty.

On that Wednesday morning, Joseph Orr would be up first to argue on behalf of Rebecca Cleland. Ron Bowers had known Orr for some time. Describing in retrospect the time they worked together, Bowers said, "[When I was] a new deputy, Joe took a liking to me and would pull me aside and give me a whispered account of ways he had discovered for getting around the burdensome office policies. I appreciated his suggestions, but Joe's whispers were so loud that people at the end of the hallway could overhear every word he said. Eventually he retired from the regimented hours of the DA's office and sought out private practice, where the work schedules were more flexible and to his liking. Over the years, I often ran into old Joe in the courthouse elevators. When he entered one of the crowded cubicles, his shoulders were at the same level as the top of most people's heads. He would be able to turn around and survey the group to see if he recognized anyone. Occasionally he would see me on the other side of the elevator and immediately start talking to me. [Because of] his loud, booming voice, everyone in the elevator could hear him complain that he should never have left the DA's office, because he'd had it made there. He would grumble about how much harder he had to work in private practice. Joe was totally oblivious to the other twenty-five or so people sardined into the tiny space, all of whom were dead silent as though mesmerized by his lamentation. Joe would put me in an edgy spot by asking, 'Isn't it true? Isn't the DA's office easier?'" I would remain mute as long as possible, trying to find the appropriate thing to say, but most of the time would avoid the embarrassment by getting off as soon as the elevator doors opened, no matter what floor I was on."

Shortly after the appointed hour on Wednesday morning, Judge Connor briefly attended to a couple of housekeeping matters, then said, "Okay, Mr. Orr, it's all yours."

The tall defender approached the lectern, placed his notes on the slanted surface, greeted the jury, and began speaking in a conversational tone. He reminded jurors that they had heard a lot of evidence, very little of which he had refuted. "For example, you heard stipulations about insurance companies, policies on accidental death. You've heard about the acquisition of materialistic things, about greed, and about someone being selfish.

"No one is arguing with that part of the evidence. In other words, I'm conceding what you know is the obvious." But, he said, he would deal with more important matters. Orr noted that detectives had arrived at the crime scene and observed the 4Runner stalled at the intersection limit line. Deciding to use that as a metaphor, he said, "I'm contending to you that the limit line is where I break off from the district attorney. The DA says there was a conspiracy—that three people entered into an agreement to kill Bruce Cleland. . . . I do not agree, and I take issue with the [accusation] that Rebecca Cleland entered into an agreement to kill Bruce Cleland."

The DA, Orr proclaimed, did not prove the case. Detectives had looked around for someone to fit the picture, he suggested, and began trying to fit people into a theory of conspiracy. "They say an opening statement is just like a puzzle, and they're going to give you the overall picture so that when each part fits in, you'll understand where it goes and it won't be confusing to you. The point I'm making with you [is] that when they took Jose Quezada, and they took Alvaro Quezada, they tried to put them into the puzzle, just like they took Texas and tried to jam it into Rhode Island."

A few faces in the gallery registered confusion, but they remained attentive to the defender's booming voice and style.

"So what I'm telling you is there are people out there who killed Bruce Cleland. The bullet was popped by some gunman into his body, but they haven't proved who did it." Orr had no problem with labeling his client, Rebecca, as materialistic, but he disagreed that proof had surfaced of her involvement in first-degree murder. "They stopped at the limit line, and it never went any further than that because they have got the wrong people."

Citing an example of weak evidence, Orr put it in the form of a question. "Because someone lives with Rebecca Cleland, and because someone gets their lips pierced with her, that means they conspired to commit murder?" Observers recalled Elizabeth Lamb mentioning that Rebecca and Alvaro had matching tongue piercings, not lips, but they allowed the defense attorney a margin of slight error.

Orr introduced a new slant with his next comment. "The investigators and the DA don't understand the Latin culture, and they don't understand how those folks related to each other. So they take that kissing and hugging and try to make that into a murder case."

Echoing Jeff Kelley's condemnation of testimony from a street criminal, Orr said, "And they take Pierre Lebec, who is hanging around East L.A., where a lot of people know him, and try to run him into this case."

Orr expressed agreement with other points Jeff Kelley had made, and concurred with his compassion for Harold and Theda Cleland. But he cautioned the jury not to make a decision based on sympathy, and he suggested that Bruce's family would also wish for a fair trial.

Returning to the crime scene, Orr noted that an empty beer bottle had been found along with bullet casings. Neither the shells nor the bottle bore any fingerprints. Using Lupe Hernandez's comment that the man running away had looked like a gang member, Orr advanced a theory. "There's a very good chance that whoever was lying in wait was drinking a beer, sitting around the area, and the 4Runner came up randomly, or not randomly. If someone was lying in wait, that doesn't mean it was Jose Quezada. Anyone could have been there. . . . See, if you want to take the district attorney's argument, where he tried to push Texas into Rhode Island, he's got it all figured out that Al was the driver." Orr paused a moment to peek at his notes, then said that no real evidence had ever surfaced to prove that Alvaro had driven the getaway car. Lupe Hernandez had spoken of hearing a car, but what did that prove?

"A car could have driven off in one direction, and whoever shot the victim could have run off in another direction. He could have got on a bike. He could have hid in the bushes nine blocks away in some ravine, and when it was all safe, he took off."

Orr accused the police of failing to search the area and "standing around" with the 911 responder personnel. No evidence surfaced, he asserted, to show that the killer or killers ever used a car. And according to the defender Orr, Lupe Hernandez had gradually changed her identification of Jose from 0 percent to 98 percent by being programmed, pushed, and lied to by investigators.

He rhetorically asked, did the people prove their case? Did the people get the right ones in front of the jury? Did the people prove that Rebecca Cleland hired two killers to murder Bruce Cleland? Where was the gun? Without overtly answering his own queries, Orr challenged the idea that any conspiracy, or even an agreement, ever took place among the defendants. "That is so far out there, you need a moon shot to find it."

Circling back around to the gunrunner, Orr asked, "How about that worthless street criminal Pierre Lebec coming up here?" The defender answered himself this time with an impassioned rant. "He was an informant for the FBI, the CIA, and the police department. I never found out how he ever contacted LAPD or how they contacted him. He goes around and he sells information. He has other people selling drugs for him. He sells—according to him—weed, heroin, and crack. If he sold one of each, every day, that would be three felonies a day. That would be about a thousand felonies a year. And do you know what street dealers are? Not only do they poison the public, but they're the biggest cheats, thieves, and dishonest people out there. They'll do anything to get what they want."

Cranking it up one more notch, Orr suggested that maybe Lebec had shot Bruce Cleland.

Observers wondered if Orr was not only defending Rebecca, but was a de facto attorney for Jose and Alvaro as well. Orr asked, "Where does Al Quezada fit into this picture? They infer that since Al lived with Rebecca, they must have conspired. How do they know that? Al didn't have any place to go. . . . He's on the fringe of being broke. What have we got to show that he had anything to do with this? These phone calls? What does that show?" Orr reminded jurors that Alvaro had been drinking that night, which might account for his hazy recollections.

The scientific cell site information from telephone company experts failed to impress Joe Orr. He dismissed it as inconsistent. And in his view, those ten or eleven telephone calls between Alvaro and Rebecca proved nothing. "That has about the same value of telling you because he hugs and kisses her that he is involved in a conspiracy with her."

With a glance toward Jose Quezada, Orr stated, "Oh, and by the way, no one ever found any phone for Joe. How were they supposed to be contacting Joe all this time he was supposedly entering into this agreement, which was not proved. How are they going to dream that up?" Maybe through that Lebec guy, Orr said. He expressed contempt for the prosecution's use of Ilma Lopes, the woman who had received a wrong-number call asking for Jose. "That was a joke. That's police corruption. When you force people to say things that aren't true, that's not right."

With a final blast at the absence of conspiracy evidence, while still acknowledging Rebecca's greed, Orr said to jurors, "I'm asking you to make a judgment. . . . Again, there's no evidence of that agreement, and that takes away the heart of the district attorney's argument, as I see it.

"I ask you to acquit Rebecca Cleland."

* * *

Following another short break, Judge Connor gave Richard Lasting the nod to go ahead with his argument for Alvaro Quezada. Spectators wondered what he could say to make his client's testimony appear to be trustworthy.

After offering the customary greeting and gratitude, Lasting told jurors their role. "You are the judges. Judge Connor has repeatedly told you, members of the jury, that you are the judges of the facts and she is the judge of the law. You decide the facts."

His role, he stated, was to talk to them about the evidence they would use to reach this goal. "You twelve citizens . . . are going to be asked to make . . . the most far-reaching, important decision you will ever be asked in your entire life to make that affects someone else. You are asked to decide about Al Quezada's life . . . based upon what's been presented to you here in this courtroom."

He put one key word in a bright spotlight. *Truth.* "You are here to find the truth. And sometimes the truth is easy to find. It might not take much analysis or much looking, but it's right there in front of you. But sometimes it's a little harder. And what I ask you to do is to carefully evaluate the testimony, look at the evidence, and find the truth."

An additional duty rested on their shoulders, Lasting said. They needed to separate the evidence, as it applied to each defendant, and make a separate, independent decision for each one.

The first piece of evidence Lasting wanted jurors to examine came from testimony of Pierre Lebec. This witness had emerged into a far more important status as a villain than anyone could have expected. In a short prologue, Lasting said, "It's not a hard thing to do to walk in here, stand in front of the jury, raise your right hand, and swear to tell the truth, and then to sit up there in the witness chair and lie. People do that.

"Pierre Lebec is in here to tell you that Jose Quezada came to him and wanted a gun to do a hit, and later said Al was going to do it with him.

"So what do we know about Pierre Lebec? Is he a liar? Is he the type of person who will swear to God that he's going to tell the truth, and then lie? And you know the answer to that question. You know he is willing to lie." A prime example, said Lasting, related to Lebec's arrest for theft at a department store. In his testimony, Lebec had denied stealing anything. "I gave him a chance," Lasting declared. "And what did he do with it? He told you he did not steal anything. And then I showed him the charge sheet. And he said, 'I got charged with something, but I don't recall exactly what it was, but I did it.' He came into court and he lied."

Gaining speed, Lasting snorted, "Let me ask you, would any one of you ever make an important decision that affected your life and future on the say-so of Pierre Lebec? Talk about proof beyond a reasonable doubt, are you going to rely on Lebec for the truth?" Lasting spent several more minutes roasting the witness's credibility and chipping away at the time frames in which the alleged meeting between Jose and Lebec took place. He then asked the jurors to base their decision on real evidence, not on the lies of a snitch.

Leaving the subject of Pierre Lebec, Lasting challenged testimony from Officer Robert Zavala, suggesting that he had possibly made some mistakes in his recollection of the two calls from Alvaro in the early-morning hours of July 26. The prosecution, he said, had smeared Alvaro with the allegation, using the call in an attempt to fabricate an alibi. Lasting sought to erase that idea.

Regarding Zavala, Lasting turned apologetic. During his client's testimony, the attorney had asked questions about Zavala's wife leaving him. "He seemed like a nice guy, and at one point, I may have embarrassed him. It was not my intention. But Officer Zavala was asked on direct examination if Alvaro's call was unusual, given the nature of his relationship with Al. And he said it was. . . . I felt it was appropriate to show the nature of their relationship and whether or not the officer had a similar conversation with Al in which he told him about problems in his own personal life. You may have thought I was being a jerk at the time, but I asked him that because I would suggest to you that it's not unusual—if you've talked to someone about a breakup with your wife, and your wife left you—is it really so unusual, on the very day that Al had broken up with his girlfriend . . . that Al calls Robert Zavala so he can confide in him?"

Spectators and reporters had wondered why Lasting had asked those personal questions during Alvaro's testimony, and the lawyer had provided reasonable justification. Jurors might discount the idea that Alvaro had made that odd call to establish an alibi.

The cell phone records had been especially damaging to Alvaro. His attorney implored jurors to examine all the documents carefully. For one thing, he said, they would find the prosecution's statement inaccurate about Alvaro never calling Rebecca before the murder night. "That is not true. He never called Rebecca on her cell phone before, but he had previously used his cell phone to call her home." He explained that Alvaro had completed calls to Rebecca's landline on several occasions in the middle of July.

While arguing for Rebecca, Joe Orr had tackled the reliability of cell tower technology, and Lasting picked up the cudgel. He pointed out that Alvaro and Rebecca's service provider had activated their system only three weeks before Bruce was killed, suggesting that all the bugs hadn't yet been ironed out. Lasting quoted testimony from a company representative that the cell sites required maintenance and fine-tuning, and no records could be found to determine if any of them had been malfunctioning on that weekend. The witness had also used words such as "less than scientific" and "many variables" that affected Alvaro's cellular calls.

Remarkably, during Lasting's speech, a cell phone belonging to someone in the gallery buzzed loud enough for everyone to hear. Looking less than happy, Judge Connor said, "Can everyone who has a cell phone turn it off, please?"

A weak voice came from among the spectators: "I'm sorry."

Lasting didn't allow the interruption to distract him. "The evidence does not prove that Al Quezada was at the crime scene. It only proves that he was somewhere within sixteen miles of the cell site at that particular time."

A couple of defense witnesses, including Alvaro's mother and his former girlfriend, had both testified regarding Alvaro's qualities, and Lasting spent a few moments summarizing them. "He is a compassionate person always ready to help others—a stranger broken down on the freeway, a kid trying to buy an ice cream, a victim of [a] hit and run. Al is the guy who stops to help an old lady cross the street. He is not a murderer. And he is not somebody that conspired with his cousin to commit murder."

Alvaro had been the only defendant to testify in his own behalf, and had professed memory failure to numerous questions, particularly about telephone calls on the night of the murder. Lasting rationalized the memory loss by challenging jurors to recollect every call they had made or received eight months ago. "Do you remember every dropped call? Do you remember if you actually talked on a particular call, or what you talked about? I couldn't tell you what I talked about at lunch yesterday. Wait, yes, I can. I talked about this case." His abrupt insertion of a little humor brought a chortle from jurors and the gallery.

Nearing conclusion, Lasting said, "Al didn't try to hide

from the stuff that actually makes him look bad. With Rebecca. He did favors for her. Got his tongue pierced at the same time she did. Took his clothes off in the house. But Al Quezada did not conspire to murder Bruce Cleland. He did not participate in the murder. He didn't drive anybody over there on Beswick to kill Bruce. And the evidence doesn't prove that he did.

"You are going to make the most important decision ever about someone you don't know. You have two choices, guilty or not guilty. . . . I would suggest to you that Al Quezada is innocent. He didn't do it. For the sake of us all and for the sake of justice, I pray you make the right decision. Thank you, Your Honor."

Everyone in the courtroom welcomed a two-hour recess for lunch.

At one-thirty in the afternoon, Craig Hum addressed the jury one last time to rebut statements from the three defense attorneys. Because prosecutors bear the burden of proof, California law allows them the final word.

Wishing the jurors a good afternoon, Craig Hum promised that he didn't plan to spend a lot of time standing in front of them repeating everything he had covered the previous day. Instead, he wanted to comment on a few things said by defense attorneys. The important thing, he explained, would be to avoid letting the attorneys' statements distract everyone from the essential truth "that these three defendants murdered Bruce Cleland."

Attacks by the defenders, said Hum, included criticism of the investigators, denigration of witness Pierre Lebec, and negative comments about the prosecution.

One of the elements of the defense strategy needed clarification, Hum stated. It centered on the lawyers' allegations that Jose and Alvaro had been singled out as suspects simply because of their familial relationship with Rebecca. The defenders had charged the prosecution with seeking guilt by association.

Basically, said Hum, at least two of the defense attorneys wanted to distance themselves from Rebecca Cleland and her relationship with Alvaro. But plenty of evidence, Hum asserted, had been presented to show the guilt of both male defendants, as well as Rebecca's.

Joe Kelley, Jose's attorney, said Hum, had tried to show that portions of testimony from witnesses Lupc Hernandez, Ilma Lopes, and Pierre Lebec were false. "But one thing he never did is tell us why they would lie." None of them had anything to gain by coming to court and giving the jury untrue information.

Kelley had also suggested weaknesses in the identification of Jose by Lupe Hernandez. Hum vehemently disagreed. "Ladies and gentlemen . . . Lupe Hernandez said, 'That's the guy. That's the guy I saw running down Concord.' She took the oath to tell the truth and kept her word. She told us why she made the prior statement about looking 'most' like the runner." Hernandez hadn't wanted to be the only one sending Jose to prison, even though "when she saw the picture, she knew it was the person."

Another statement from the defense rankled Hum. The lawyer had intimated that Hernandez had picked out Jose because he was Rebecca's cousin. The prosecutor protested: "She did not have to pick any one of those six people. She was shown two other six-packs and did not pick any of those men out. Included in one of those groupings was a picture of Alvaro Quezada, another cousin of Rebecca. She didn't pick him out. She picked the person she saw, and she didn't even know of the relationship."

Charging to the rescue of Ilma Lopes, the woman who had received a wrong-number call for Jose, Hum said no reason existed to accuse her of lying. Corroborating facts proved her truthfulness, Hum asserted. Only one call had been made from the restaurant's pay phone, and the waitress observed

Rebecca doing it. Ilma Lopes had heard the caller ask for Jose Quezada. "Yes, she tells us that she did not recall the name until she heard it again. Do you remember that she sat up there and said it was like if her phone number had been changed, and she wouldn't necessarily remember the old one, unless somebody said it? The very next witness was Mark Garcia, and I asked him what his cell phone number was back in 1997. He didn't remember. I asked if I mentioned it, would he recognize it? He said yes. And he did. It's a perfect example of what Ilma Lopes was talking about." Rebecca, Hum reminded jurors, had made that attempt to reach Jose only three hours before the murder.

It might have bothered jurors that no evidence had been introduced to show previous association between Rebecca and Jose. Defenders had pounced on the issue. Hum explained, "I'm not saying those two cousins were close. That's where Alvaro comes in. In fact, their lack of closeness shows why she called the wrong number when she was trying to get hold of Jose that night."

Hum once again needed to rehabilitate the ragged image of Pierre Lebec. "Everybody attacks him. Why? Because it's easy to attack Pierre Lebec. Alvaro's defense attorney spent about twenty minutes doing it. How tough is that? Jose's attorney said Lebec is a criminal every way you want to cut it. Of course, it's easy to attack him. He's a gun dealer and a drug dealer. Who do you go to when you want to get a gun? You don't go to your church and ask your pastor or priest to sell you a gun to do a murder with. So Lebec is a gun dealer, and he's the person Jose Quezada would go to. They were friends."

Taking a unique slant on charges that Lebec had lied, Hum remarked, "A liar? They all said he was a drug dealer. How do we know that? Because Lebec tells us he's a drug dealer. They obviously believe him. He admits he's a gun dealer.

How do we know he's a gun dealer? Because he says he is."
Hum's logic made sense. If Lebec wanted to lie while testifying, he probably would have shaded the truth about his own
criminal activity. He had no motivation to lie about Jose. The
defense lawyers couldn't have it both ways. If they believed
his self-incriminating statements, it would be logical to
believe his other testimony.

The second problem in Lebec's testimony may have been
stickier. In his cross-examination answers, he hadn't been
able to pinpoint the time frame in which contacts with Jose
had taken place. Hum scoffed at it. "What does that prove?
He simply doesn't remember exactly when it happened."
Street thugs don't keep planning calendars. Lebec had undoubtedly transacted hundreds of crooked deals, and he
couldn't remember the dates.

To make certain jurors hadn't forgotten his earlier comments about the silence of Jose and Rebecca in the police
vehicle, Hum brought it up again. "Jose Quezada's lawyer
can't explain it, so he just tries to brush it off. That's because
there is no innocent explanation. Of course, they know each
other, and Rebecca even admitted it. Why didn't she ask him,
'What are you doing here?' Why? Because they both knew
what they were doing there. That's why there was no conversation.

"It all fits together."

Rebecca's lawyer, said Hum, had argued that no proof of
a conspiracy had been offered by the prosecution. "Well,
ladies and gentlemen, it's clear they agreed on the plan, and
the evidence shows it." Hum spent several minutes reiterat-
ing supporting points from his previous summation.

With reference to attorney Joe Orr's comment that Rebecca is materialistic, greedy, and not a nice person, Hum
heated up the characterization. "It's a little bit more than that.

Somebody who kicks their dog is not a nice person. This woman is evil."

Turning to arguments from Alvaro's attorney, Hum said, "You notice that in the amount of time he took, he really didn't talk much about his client's testimony. Why? Because his client is a liar. You could tell that by how evasive he was. And by the fact that he kept saying, he didn't remember those phone calls." His lawyer had attributed the memory failure to the passage of time. Hum disagreed. "That's not really true, is it? He remembers conversations with his buddy about going out that night, and he remembers his conversation with Officer Zavala, and with his little son's mother. Interestingly, those are the only contacts his lawyer asked him about. But what about those eleven calls between him and his cousin the night of Bruce's murder, the ones I asked him about? Oh, he can't remember those.

"Of course, he remembers those, and he knows what they talked about. He can't tell us because they were talking about committing the murder. The only thing he can say is 'I don't remember.' How convenient."

Letting the image marinate in jurors' minds for a moment, Hum said, "You have to look at it all, and there is no reasonable interpretation that points to innocence. None."

Alvaro had changed the story he gave Officer Zavala that night on the phone, about being with Dave Romero and fellow stripper Mark Garcia at a taco stand. In Alvaro's testimony, the companions became "Jerry and George." He had also spoken of visiting a bar where the mother of his child worked. The young mom had also testified, placing Alvaro in the bar near the same hour Bruce was shot.

In Hum's view, the name of his companions had been substituted for a reason. "The defendant had figured that Dave Romero and Mark Garcia would back him. They are friends, and Dave is sleeping with his cousin Rebecca. But neither man would lie for him. And even the substituted person, Jerry Morales, said he didn't know where Alvaro was in the early morning of July twenty-sixth. And his girlfriend couldn't say where Alvaro was that morning. He has to get another alibi, and that is from his baby's mother. That is his only alibi. And we all know where her loyalties lie.

"Character witnesses came in and said he is a nice guy and helps old ladies across the street. Great. And that means what? Nothing. It's smoke. It's an attempt to distract us."

Once again, Hum brought up the unexplained telephone calls between Alvaro and Rebecca, dealing them out one at a time, like solitaire cards on a tabletop. He explained the timing, the originator, and the recipient of each call, ending by saying, "At one minute after one in the morning, ten minutes before Bruce is murdered, she calls him. Explain that to us. He can't. And his lawyer can't. Eleven calls in the three and a half hours leading up to the murder. This is a huge coincidence?"

Evidence about cell towers, or cell sites, had been technical, and juries sometimes have difficulty comprehending testimony about electronics and computers. Hum went through it again, emphasizing the bottom line, that telephone company records placed Alvaro's cell phone within close proximity to the murder scene during the calls and when the killing took place. The prosecutor rejected defense efforts to cast doubt when they suggested possible malfunctioning of the cell sites, that these might have been down for maintenance, or the existence of other mechanical problems. "There is absolutely no evidence of that at all."

Reaching his final moments of opportunity to erase reasonable doubts in jurors' minds, Hum said, "Ladies and gentlemen, in just a short time, you are going to go back into the jury room. All I'm asking is for justice. Simple justice. For

Bruce, for his mother, for his father, and justice for all of us. Your duty is to provide that, and to provide the truth."

Hum encapsulated his version of what that would be, according to the evidence.

"And we all know the truth is that defendant Rebecca Cleland married Bruce for his money, and when she found out she couldn't get it through divorce, and she couldn't get it through blackmail, she decided to have him killed. The truth is, she enlisted the help of the person she is closest to, her cousin defendant Alvaro Quezada and his brother. On the night of July 25, 1997, Rebecca Cleland took Bruce out, got him drunk at the restaurant and at her uncle's house.

"And the truth is that throughout the night, Rebecca Cleland and Alvaro Quezada exchanged phone calls to plan this murder. The truth is that at twelve forty-eight in the morning, on July twenty-sixth, Alvaro Quezada called his cousin Rebecca at Arturo's house and said, 'We're here.'

"And the truth is [that] at one-ten in the morning on July twenty-sixth, Rebecca Cleland called Al Quezada, and said, 'We're on the way.' A few minutes later, Rebecca Cleland pulled up at the intersection of Beswick and Concord, stopped the 4Runner, and got out of the car.

"And the truth is that defendant Jose Quezada walked up to the passenger side, stuck a gun in Bruce's face, and pulled the trigger. Bruce got out of the car, tried to run, and Jose Quezada chased him down, shot him in the back, and executed him.

"And the truth is that Jose Quezada then ran down Concord and got in the getaway car driven by his brother, Al Quezada, and they drove off.

"And that's the truth about what happened that night. Ladies and gentlemen, we all know what happened that night. All I ask of you is to tell them you know that's what the truth is, and find them guilty."

Hum nodded his appreciation to the attentive jury, walked back to his chair, and sank into it.

* * *

The last act in the drama of a murder trial belongs to the jury. After being sworn to do their duty, the twelve triers of fact would begin their deliberations on Thursday morning to decide the fates of Rebecca Cleland, Jose Quezada, and Alvaro Quezada.

Chapter 32

Verdicts and Upheaval

Harold and Theda Cleland showed up at the Los Angeles Criminal Courts Building on Thursday morning, even though they had been advised that the jury would probably deliberate at least a few days. After all, a dozen people had to unequivocally agree, and it's difficult for that to happen in far less stressful situations. This jury faced the arduous task of weighing evidence and delivering verdicts against three people. It sometimes takes a week or more to convict or exonerate a single defendant.

Unwilling to take a chance on missing the jury's findings, Bruce's parents sat patiently on hard benches in the ninth-floor hallway.

Craig Hum waited in his office up on the seventeenth floor, looking at his next possible case and fully expecting the Cleland-Quezada jury to extend their discussions well into the following week.

It stunned him, the defense attorneys, court officers, and reporters when word came that the jury had reached a decision before noon on that same Thursday. They had deliberated only three hours. By early afternoon, the courtroom and gallery filled with expectant, nervous, and amazed people.

Ron Bowers had been through the experience many times. "I know as a prosecutor when I heard that one of my juries had a verdict, I had mixed emotions. The first thing you do is look at the jurors as they walk into the courtroom to see if they are willing to make eye contact with you, or if they are looking more at the defendant or his family. But most times, jurors avoid eye contact with anyone, except perhaps among themselves. I can remember those agonizing moments, knowing that the defendant's and public's future was at stake. If the jury delivered a not guilty verdict, the defendant could be back on the streets that night. Conversely, if they found the person guilty, a celebration often took place in the hallways, and the public felt safe in the knowledge that justice had been done."

Judge Connor broke the silence by asking her bailiff to bring in the jurors. Twelve people filed through the door from their deliberations room and took their seats, avoiding any eye contact, just as Ron Bowers had predicted.

Asked by the judge if they had reached verdicts for all three defendants, the foreman rose and said they had. He handed the signed forms to the bailiff, who delivered the sheaf of papers to Connor. After a silent examination, she handed them over to her clerk, who read the verdicts aloud.

Rebecca Cleland: guilty of murder in the first degree with special circumstances.

Jose Quezada: guilty of murder in the first degree with special circumstances.

Alvaro Quezada: guilty of murder in the first degree with special circumstances.

All three defendants were also guilty of conspiracy to commit murder.

* * *

After Judge Connor announced a date for handing down mandatory life sentences, and the convicted trio were led from the courtroom, she thanked and excused the jurors.

Out in the hallway, Harold and Theda Cleland shook hands and hugged several of the jury members who lingered. Harold spoke to reporters and said about Rebecca, "She planned it from the beginning."

All three defense attorneys told reporters they planned to appeal. Craig Hum caught an elevator back up to the seventeenth floor to take a short break before opening files for his next case. Victory in a complex case such as the one he had just completed can't be celebrated very long in view of the ongoing workload.

In late July, Judge Jacqueline Connor assembled the three prisoners, the defense lawyers, and the prosecution to hand down formal sentences. Rebecca, Jose, and Alvaro listened with impassive expressions as she condemned them to serve the rest of their lives in prison without the possibility of parole. By all appearances, the book slammed closed on the Quezada-Cleland novel. Credits scrolled on the movie's screen. Newspapers and TV anchors delivered their denouement stories. Witnesses, attorneys, and other interested people resumed their daily lives.

But if Hum thought he was finished with Rebecca Cleland and her cousins, he was in for a rude shock.

Appeals can drag on for years. No exception, the Cleland-Quezada case wound its way through the next level for thirty-five months.

The process begins within weeks after the trial court settles the record and a new defense appellate attorney is appointed. In the case of death sentences, the case is automatically appealed to the California Supreme Court. Since the DA had not sought capital punishment against Rebecca, Jose, and

Alvaro, their initial requests for relief would be funneled to the California Court of Appeal.

The detectives and the prosecutor had worked long and hard to build a solid case against all three defendants. The evidence, even though circumstantial, had seemed overwhelming against Rebecca. The testimony from her sister Dolores and her friend Bertha glaringly proved that Rebecca had premeditated and deliberated the killing of Bruce months before the shooting. Wedding photographer Elizabeth Lamb's contribution—revealing Rebecca's statement that she wouldn't be surprised if someone from her family wanted to kill Bruce, and that she needed to deflect suspicion from herself—had been exceptionally powerful.

Jose's conviction had depended on eyewitness identification, plus testimony from an underground gunrunner. Jurors had apparently believed them.

In some opinions, Alvaro's conviction remained the most questionable. It had been built on a foundation of cell phone records, without any witnesses or forensics. The prosecution had suggested that process of elimination showed his culpability, based on Guadalupe Hernandez's report of hearing a car start up and accelerate that night.

The cell tower technology was in its infancy, and this was one of the first, if not *the* first, case in which pinpointing of a user's location found its way into court. Legal speculators guessed that Alvaro's conviction might be the most vulnerable on appeal. If he had received any financial benefits, they certainly appeared insignificant.

Most experts regarded the appeals for all three to be a mere formality with a slight possibility that the appellate court might establish some new rules as to the use of cell tower evidence in the courtroom. The California Attorney General's (AG's) Office handles all state felony conviction appeals. In other words, the process is no longer a concern of the local district attorney's office.

The procedure consists of the defense attorney submitting a brief of the legal issues, which is filed with the appellate court and a copy is served on the AG's office. The deputy attorney general reviews the copy and starts looking over the court transcripts to find answers, then files a response. At this level, no witnesses are called and no new evidence is introduced. The case is decided entirely on transcripts and records. Occasionally the trial prosecutor may be contacted to explain some detail, but his or her input is minimal.

Since most defendants are considered indigent, they are routinely eligible for free attorney representation at trial. If they are convicted, a new attorney is appointed to represent them, at taxpayers' expense. One of the most common tactics by the appellate lawyer is to suggest ineffectiveness of trial counsel. Rebecca, Jose, and Alvaro followed this process.

What happened next during the appellate process stunned the legal community.

Judge Jacqueline Connor, as one of the most experienced trial judges in the state, often advised others on procedural matters. Seldom had any of her well-reasoned rulings been challenged or overturned.

Craig Hum's reputation for faultless ethics and knowledge of the law made him one of the most reliable deputies in the office. He had taught many of the new prosecutors in the state. With Connor and Hum on the bridge, it seemed that no appeals court could sink their ship. Experts figured it would be impossible to dredge up any legal error caused by such knowledgeable professionals.

The defendants' appellate attorneys scoured the transcripts for the usual suspects, such as an incorrect jury instruction. Nothing notable could be found, but one little bulkhead crack caught their attention.

When the detectives had placed Jose and Rebecca together in the backseat of a police car, nothing had happened. And just maybe, something could be made of that nothing. During the trial, the defense attorney had asked Detective Peterson to explain why he did this, and Peterson had responded, "We did it to see what the topic of discussion would be if we put them together in the police vehicle."

The defense zeroed in on the notorious and oft-used Miranda ruling, in which suspects must be advised of their right to silence and legal representation. Neither Detective Peterson nor Herman had given the well-known admonition to Rebecca or Jose. They hadn't needed to, since no interrogation had yet taken place. The officers certainly would have read Miranda to them at the station, before asking any questions.

Although this concept of eavesdropping on a person in custody may seem unfair to some, the U.S. Supreme Court has upheld such tactics, ruling they do not violate a suspect's rights. How can there be a violation, since the investigators had not asked a single question? Merely listening to the suspects talking to each other is not illegal.

As a matter of fact, if Rebecca or Jose had said anything incriminating, those words would have been *admissible* in trial. The appellate court in this case ruled, *Police officers may monitor conversations in a police car between suspects in an effort to obtain incriminating statements, as Detectives Peterson and Herman attempted to do in this case. . . . Thus, it could have been constitutionally permissible for the People to introduce evidence of any post arrest statements made by Cleland or Jose Quezada when they were together in Peterson's police car, whether or not they had been advised of their Miranda rights.*

However, Rebecca and Jose hadn't just fallen off a turnip truck. When they found themselves in the backseat of the police car after their arrest, being fairly streetwise, they figured that the police car most likely was bugged. They cleverly outsmarted the cops by remaining silent.

Ironically, it was that very silence the appellate attorneys for Rebecca and Jose seized upon. They raised the issue that the trial court and the prosecutor had violated Rebecca's and Jose's constitutional rights to remain silent. This seemed remarkable, since the police and prosecution weren't trying to force the defendants to give up their rights to remain silent. As a matter of fact, Rebecca and Jose exercised their Fifth Amendment right to remain silent, since they didn't talk to the police or testify at trial.

Appellate defense attorneys for Rebecca and Jose, though, put the issue under a microscope and found a legal virus. They saw that courts had favored the defense with rulings to prevent the prosecution from commenting, directly or indirectly, on a person's right not to speak. Jurists had held it improper for a prosecutor to even remotely direct a jury's attention to a defendant's invocation of the right to silence during police interrogation. Such references by the prosecution might cause a jury to draw unfair inferences.

Sifting through every word uttered by Hum during his summary arguments, the defense lawyers hoped to find a nugget on which to base an appeal. Had he said anything to infringe on the right to silence protecting Rebecca and Jose while they sat mute in the rear of a police car? Transcripts revealed a potential problem. Hum had said:

> *Now, we also have defendant Jose Quezada's behavior when he was arrested on February 17, 1998. Remember the testimony? He is put in the back seat of a police car with his cousin, Defendant Rebecca Cleland. And what do we have? Absolute silence. We have, "How are you doing?" And then that's it. For fifteen minutes, not another word is spoken. No small talk. Nothing. Why not?*
>
> *Defendant Jose Quezada tries to claim, "Gosh, I didn't know it was my cousin, I had never seen her before." Of course he knows it's his cousin. And even if he didn't, you are sitting in the back of a police car with somebody, you are not going to say a word to them? And defendant Rebecca Cleland admits she knows this is her*

cousin sitting in the car with her. She doesn't say a word either. Nothing. Fifteen minutes of silence. Why? Because they are afraid the police might be listening in and they don't want to say anything.

Think about it. You have been arrested for something. You don't have any idea what you are doing there. You are in the back seat of a police car with your cousin and you just kind of sit there for fifteen minutes? Nonsense.

Ladies and gentlemen, that silence speaks volumes. What really happened? These three defendants had set up the murder of Bruce. They thought they had gotten away with it. All of a sudden, defendant Jose Quezada and defendant Rebecca Cleland are sitting in the back of a police car with each other and they are looking at each other but they are not saying a word.

The defense attorneys now hoped they could convince an appellate court to rule the prosecutor's wording to be improper comment, which reflected on Rebecca and Jose failing to take the witness stand and explain why they remained silent in the back of the police car.

Craig Hum had added more during his final rebuttal argument:

> *If they hadn't done anything and they are both sitting in the back of a police car, why didn't defendant Rebecca Cleland turn to her cousin and say, "What are you doing here?" And why didn't he say, "What are you doing here?" Why? Because they both knew what they were doing there. That's why there was no conversation. It all fits.*

Hoping they had found an Achilles' heel, appellate attorney Peter Gold, for Rebecca, and attorney Colleen M. Rohan, for Jose, filed their legal challenges. Peter Leeming, representing Alvaro, joined them, hoping to ride their coattails in case of reversal.

The California Court of Appeal, Second District, Division 7, held a hearing and heard presentations from the appellate team, along with counterarguments from a battery of lawyers for the California Attorney General's Office.

On May 7, 2003, the court issued a ruling: *Because Cleland and J. Quezada were the only people who could have answered the [prosecutor's] question "why" and provide an innocent explanation for their silence in the police car, this argument and the evidence upon which it was based constituted Griffin error.*

"Griffin error," the ruling explained, occurs if the prosecutor argues to the jury that certain testimony or evidence is uncontradicted, if such contradiction or denial could be provided only by the defendant, who, therefore, would be required to take the witness stand:

> *In the present case there can be no doubt the prosecutor's emphasis on Cleland's and J. Quezada's fifteen minutes of silence, during closing argument, impermissibly drew attention to their decision not to testify at trial to explain their conduct in the police car or otherwise to establish their innocence.*

This seemed to indicate the appellate court had agreed with the defense, and the case could be reversed. Still, the attorney general team had reason to hope. Usually, when an appellate court hears a minor legal infraction, they rule it "harmless error." Appeal judges generally try to protect the taxpaying public by upholding convictions when the error appears to be "harmless," and prevent unnecessary use of resources in the preparation and retrial of a case. It would cost taxpayers over $100,000 to hold another trial for Cleland and Quezada. So the odds were stacked against a reversal. Maybe the court would compromise by issuing a written opinion to simply clarify this new obscure interpretation of law.

A clear definition of "harmless error" appeared in the

ruling: *When federal constitutional error has been established, we must reverse the conviction unless the People have established, beyond a reasonable doubt, that the error did not contribute to the verdict. Under this test, the appropriate inquiry is not whether, in a trial that occurred without the error, a guilty verdict would surely have been rendered, but whether the guilty verdict actually rendered in this trial was surely unattributable to the error.*

In the prosecution of Rebecca, it appeared that evidence against her had been reasonably compelling and certainly adequate for conviction. So a "harmless error" ruling at the appellate level should have settled the matter. Most analysts would see the prosecutor's comments about silence in the backseat as insignificant, and believe the jury gave it little weight.

In the court of appeal, the chief judge saw it differently, and explained his reasoning:

The case against Cleland was entirely circumstantial. The prosecutor presented considerable evidence she was a person of bad character who apparently married Bruce Cleland for his money; she had affairs with other people during the time she was involved with Bruce Cleland; she took out insurance policies on his life and forged his signature on at least one policy application; and she attempted to obtain a favorable divorce settlement by threatening to accuse Bruce Cleland of sexually molesting her son.

With respect to events on the night of the murder, Cleland arranged a meeting with Bruce Cleland; she had multiple cell phone conversations with A. Quezada, who was apparently near the murder scene, that night; she suffered no discernable physical injuries as a result of the supposed attempt carjacking that led to Bruce Cleland's murder; she was wearing a wedding ring during *a postmurder search of her home, even though she claimed her diamond ring had been take by the carjackers; and she paid $500 to A. Quezada after the murder.*

At that point in the opinion, the prosecution felt relief. The panel of judges had apparently seen the light, and would concede that an abundance of evidence existed to uphold the conviction of Rebecca. Then, like a bolt of lightning out of the murky sky, the people in black robes struck at the heart of the prosecution:

> *Although this evidence surely established Cleland's greed and her poor treatment of Bruce Cleland, none of it tied her directly to the murder. Moreover, Cleland presented evidence to blunt some of the more damaging evidence. For example, she established the life insurance policies were purchased in response to solicitation by the insurance companies rather than as a result of her own initiative. She also presented testimony that A. Quezada was upset on the night of the murder and wanted to talk to her because he had just broken up with his girlfriend. On this record it is not possible to conclude that the finding of guilt as to Cleland was surely unattributable to the [prosecutor's] error in repeatedly commenting on her post arrest silence.*

What were the appellate justices thinking? What difference did it make who solicited the selling of the life insurance policy? The point was obvious—Rebecca would gain nearly a million dollars if her husband died by violence. The court apparently decided that phone calls between Alvaro and Rebecca were to talk about the breakup with his girlfriend. Yet, no testimony had been heard to support such a conclusion. That appeared to be mere speculation on the part of the court.

If any chance of reversal existed, the prosecution thought, it would be in Jose's case. At least part of the identification evidence against him might have been vulnerable. So it came as a surprise when the court wrote, *The evidence against Jose Quezada was somewhat stronger. . . .* Had someone mixed up the transcripts that were sent to the appellate court? How could they think that the evidence against Jose was stronger than that against Rebecca? It looked like they were going to overturn her conviction, but a glimmer of hope remained that they would uphold Jose's verdict.

That hope crashed and burned. The appellate justices reversed both convictions.

More than one person thought that evidence against Alvaro Quezada had been the weakest of all three. He appeared to be the least culpable, since the prosecution could prove only that his cell phone was used somewhere in the general area of the crime scene. His trial attorney put on a vigorous defense. Alibi witnesses had placed him fifteen miles from the crime scene, even though Hum had done a good job of discrediting them.

With so little evidence against Alvaro, the prosecution expected that if Rebecca and Jose were going to get off, so would Alvaro. However, the judges, in their mysterious ways, overruled every legal issue raised by his attorney.

In their findings, the judges wrote: *The convictions of Rebecca Cleland and Jose Quezada are reversed, and the matter is remanded for retrial. The conviction of Alvaro Quezada is affirmed.*

The decision escalated to the California Supreme Court. On August 27, 2003, they upheld the appellate court's decision.

Rebecca and Jose had anxiously waited in their state prison cells. They rejoiced when the news came. For the first time in five years, they had strong reasons to hope for exoneration and freedom. Officials prepared to transfer both of them back to Los Angeles County Jail to await a decision by the DA. Two choices faced officials: drop all charges or go through the entire trial process again.

Meanwhile, Alvaro Quezada had the appellate door slammed shut on him for the rest of his life.

Chapter 33

Rebecca's
New Strategy

Trial number two commenced in November 2006, some nine years after Bruce's murder. His parents, Harold and Theda, would not be there to endure the torture and suspense of going through it all again. Theda "Teddy" Cleland had died on September 27, 2003, just a few days after her eighty-fourth birthday, and exactly one month after the California Supreme Court affirmed the appellate court's ruling. Harold passed away on November 10, the same year. They left together, as they had arrived together. Incredibly, the remarkable couple had both been born in September 1919, only thirteen days apart, and died a little more than six weeks apart.

Another key player in the Cleland-Quezada story had also passed away. Arturo, the father of Jose and Alvaro, succumbed to illness in August 2004.

Other changes had transpired as well. County officials had given the downtown L.A. Criminal Courts Building a different identity. In 2002, it became the Clara Shortridge Foltz Criminal

Justice Center (but continued to be called the Criminal Courts Building by most people). The structure had been renamed to honor California's first female lawyer. When she passed the state bar examination in 1878, contemporary law allowed only white males to practice. But Clara bucked the "good old boys" network by having the law reworded from "white male" to "white person." More than another half century would pass before the "white" designation faded into shameful history.

Judge Jacqueline Connor no longer presided over criminal trials on the ninth floor. She had moved on to handle civil cases in the old Santa Monica Courthouse, not far from the historic pier that once marked old Route 66's western terminal. Connor had been admired for handling more major murder cases each year than anyone else in the Criminal Courts Building, and for being an efficient, no-nonsense judge. She ran her case calendar like a train engineer determined to guarantee on-time performance.

The judge who took Connor's place, Robert A. Perry, soon exceeded her prolific record. That November, he had recently completed a complex trial of a killer named Victor Paleologus (*Meet Me for Murder,* by Don Lasseter and Ronald Bowers, 2008, Pinnacle Books).

Perry had been appointed to the bench in 1992. Now, at age sixty-three, with a healthy thatch of nearly white hair and a trim build, his movements and articulate speech radiated the energy of someone twenty years younger. Well-known for keeping things moving at a brisk pace in his courtroom, Perry refused to allow unnecessary delays. He understood the law and allowed no shenanigans.

A few months earlier, when Perry had inherited the Cleland-Quezada retrial, he began to push for a calender date, ready to get it under way. He soon realized, though, that he wasn't going to be able to pressure the case to an early date in his courtroom. First he had to appoint a new lawyer to defend Rebecca. For Jose, his family somehow had found the resources to hire an attorney. These new defenders would need considerable time to prepare their cases.

Craig Hum had been transferred to the Torrance DA's branch, but would still handle the second prosecution. It would require considerable rearrangement of his busy trial calendar.

As a rule, retrials are quick and formulaic. Judge Perry didn't mind taking them on, for several reasons. Most of the issues have been previously litigated and orders from the appellate courts make it easy to rule on evidence. In this particular case, the court's decision had virtually eliminated everything related to Rebecca and Jose remaining silent in the back of the police car. Perry would allow no mention of Jose's utterance to Rebecca, nor of his denial to detectives that he even knew her. In pretrial hearings, Hum agreed.

To defense attorneys and their clients, retrials are beneficial for understanding what didn't work the first time, enabling them to revise their strategy.

Rebecca's new appointed lawyer, Edward "Ed" Murphy, had heard the wisecracks about his name, kidding him about being on *Saturday Night Live* and in numerous movies. Of Irish descent, lawyer Murphy, about six feet tall, slim, with white hair and glasses, looked to be in his midforties. He spoke in a clear, if somewhat nasal, voice. Highly respected by his peers, Murphy also had earned admiration from Craig Hum as not only a fine litigator, but a "nice guy."

Gary Meastas, of Hispanic heritage, would defend Jose. A little shorter than his colleagues, and heavier, with salt-and-pepper black hair, Meastas still spoke with a noticeable Spanish accent. Also well-respected in the profession, he had usually worked in counties east of Los Angeles.

Insiders speculated about what strategies the new defenders might employ. With Alvaro absent from the new proceedings, would they try to make him the bad guy? Would Rebecca and Jose work together on the most common defense, know in the inner circle as "SODDI"? Experienced attorneys know that the odd acronym stands for "Some Other Dude Did It."

The reversal gave Murphy and Measias wide-open opportunity to craft a new defense and weave new threads through the previous tapestry.

At last, on a cool November day, with a new jury listening, Judge Perry invited Craig Hum to begin his opening statements. It had a distinct feeling of déjà vu for him. Hum's delivery gave the appearance of gliding along on autopilot, but it resonated with power. He didn't need to look at his notes, since every fact had been branded into his brain. The whole scenario he described resembled the one he had used six years earlier, with a few exceptions.

He could see the opportunity to insert some special strategies himself, once he realized that the defendants would probably try to point fingers at each other. Hum didn't know any details of tactics they might use, but if the two defendants chose to testify, Hum knew he could slash them to bits in cross-examination.

When Ed Murphy stood to deliver his opening remarks, the two other lawyers paid close attention. Would he proclaim Rebecca's innocence and accuse her cousins Jose and Alvaro of doing the shooting of her husband on their own?

Following the standard greetings, Murphy said, "When Mrs. Cleland saw Mr. Quezada execute her husband on that street, she was thinking, 'I'm going to be implicated because I have brought my husband here, because I was asked to by Mr. Quezada and Alvaro so they could have a confrontation with my husband over homosexual advances that he made toward their father.' That's what was on her mind. And when she was waiting for the police, because she realized that she would be implicated, because she was the one that brought her husband, Bruce, to that location, she decided not to tell the police the truth."

The remarkable statement hit like a pinball bouncing from post to post and ringing bells. Murphy admitted that Rebecca saw her husband being executed, which refuted her original claim of being knocked unconscious by the attacker. And he acknowledged her deliberate lies to the police. To Hum and Meastas, it revealed Rebecca's intention to play the poor innocent girl who had been duped by her wicked cousins. But what type of tale could she create to cover all of her activities? The appellate court may have unwittingly suggested this idea to Rebecca with one single sentence: *Although this evidence surely established Cleland's greed and her poor treatment of Bruce Cleland, none of it tied her directly to the murder.*

Murphy boldly guaranteed, "You're not going to hear any evidence in this case . . . that she ever plotted his murder that was perpetrated by her cousins . . . because it never happened." On the contrary, Murphy presented a script in which Rebecca had been asked by her cousins to bring Bruce there so the two men could confront him about "various claims, true or untrue, regarding him and their father."

Even more amazing, Murphy said he would support it with testimony from wedding photographer Elizabeth Lamb. He cited Rebecca's conversation with Lamb on July 17, 1997, in which Rebecca had expressed fear that someone in her family would kill Bruce.

Commenting on the strategy, Ron Bowers said, "This was brilliant on the part of Rebecca's defense to rest its case on the foundation of the prosecution's case. Craig Hum and the investigators were entirely relying on Elizabeth Lamb's credibility. She was an unimpeachable witness. The prosecution's case centered on her testimony. Lamb's testimony that Rebecca had mentioned [that] her family was so mad at Bruce that one of them might kill him seemed to support the prosecution theory that it was a conspiracy by various Quezada family members.

But I started to wonder about the ingenuity of it. If she thought members of her family were angry enough to kill Bruce, why would she go along with this charade of taking him to an isolated area late at night so her cousins could confront him?"

Having given Hum and Meastas something to chew on, Murphy proceeded to paint a softer and gentler picture of Rebecca. He apparently wanted to show her as a victim to whom things happened that weren't her fault. Murphy took jurors through the entire history of Rebecca and Bruce, beginning with their initial encounter at the swap meet, through the lavish gifts, civil and church marriages, purchase of the home, the sexual "disaster," and a "big argument" that resulted in Bruce leaving her in April 1997. Shortly after that, Alvaro had moved in, Murphy said.

Observers who knew the story thought the attorney presented a dazzling spin on Rebecca's image, converting her from a master manipulator into the guiltless recipient of gifts from an adamant admirer. Murphy finally did acknowledge that Bruce's wealth had made him more attractive to Rebecca. He also threw in comments about Bruce's drinking problem.

Murphy said, "At this time, still concerned about everything falling apart, particularly the marriage not working out as she hoped it would, and concerned about her son and his financial security, she—after getting Mr. Cleland's permission—signed his name to the Minnesota Mutual mortgage insurance. There was no attempt to forge his name. She did it with his permission."

Spectators wondered how he planned to prove that. Other insurance policies followed, Murphy remarked almost incidentally. He also emphasized how frequently Rebecca and Bruce spoke by phone, even though they weren't living together.

Near the end of June, said Murphy, "Jose Quezada, the gentleman sitting at the end of the table," entered the scene.

In the presence of Officer Robert Zavala, "Alvaro Quezada and Mr. Jose Quezada were hugging each other that day."

Amazing, thought an observer, how the same story can sound so different depending on who is telling it.

"During all this time," Murphy said, "her cousin Alvaro, brother of Jose Quezada, was there living with Mrs. Cleland, sleeping with her and living the life of Riley. He didn't really have a place to stay until now. So he's really, you know, implanting himself in that house. And when it became obvious to Alvaro that a divorce wasn't going to keep his cousin-girlfriend living high on the hog, he hatched the plan, unbeknownst to Mrs. Cleland, to murder her husband. The plan was that Jose Quezada would go out on the streets and get a gun. And that Mrs. Cleland would not be told that they were going to kill Mr. Cleland. They would tell her to stop the car someplace to have a face-to-face with him over the claimed homosexual advances that her husband was making to their father."

Murphy tackled other thornier issues, one by one. He suggested that Rebecca's sister Dolores had testified against her in retribution for a falling-out over a mutual girlfriend they both loved. He portrayed Alvaro as the mastermind behind the whole evil murder scheme. It remained to be seen exactly how Murphy would go about proving this.

Turning to Alvaro's brother, Murphy leveled scathing charges. He said Jose had obtained a gun from Pierre Lebec, after which he and Alvaro told Rebecca they wanted a face-to-face with Bruce in a private, dark place. "No, they didn't want to intercept him on his way coming out of TRW, where he worked, or going to work in the morning. No, they didn't want to wait around his parents' house, where he was living in [South] Pasadena. They wanted it in East Los Angeles, in this dark entrance to the I-5 Freeway."

Rebecca, said Murphy, started to worry. She even told

wedding photographer Elizabeth Lamb of her concerns about her angry family possibly wishing to hurt or kill Bruce.

Murphy insisted that his client had not been involved in any planning or plotting to do away with her husband. He led jurors through events of July 25. "They are going out to dinner to discuss a hundred details about the marriage, the house, and many different things. After dinner they're going to stop at Mr. Quezada's father's house, and then from there, as agreed, pretend that something is wrong with the car at the place they told her, and they are going to confront Mr. Cleland.

"During the night, she is so concerned that she tries to call Jose, but gets a wrong number." Murphy explained that Rebecca's fears led to several calls to and from Alvaro. "She goes. She stops. And out of the bushes with a gun comes Jose Quezada and starts shooting her husband. She screams. The neighbors hear this. . . . She's in total shock. Her husband is dead."

Rebecca couldn't tell the truth, Murphy stated, because she thought it would implicate her in the killing. So she lied and said someone had knocked her unconscious. "She wasn't hit on the head. Her ring wasn't stolen. And that's what happened."

Murphy confirmed that Jose had been there, and that's why witnesses identified him. And Alvaro had been the getaway driver. "We know it was Alvaro, because it was he who masterminded the whole thing."

Ron Bowers understood the defense strategy. "Rebecca knew from the first trial that no one was buying into her story about an attempted carjacking. So she changed it to absolve herself, while implicating her cousins. She seized upon testimony by the responding police officer who overheard Rebecca's cell phone call to her 'father,' in which she said, 'They killed him.' The prosecution had used this to prove she knew Bruce was dead at the crime scene."

* * *

Ed Murphy tagged that base, too. "You'll find out about that telephone call she made right after this happened, to the father. What she was really saying was 'Your sons killed him.'"

The defender's words convinced everyone that Rebecca planned to testify and follow the road map laid out by Murphy. Perhaps she had been rehearsing it while locked up during the last five years. Few people who knew Rebecca doubted her dramatic skills to convincingly spin her tale.

If Murphy hadn't yet earned the jury's sympathy for Rebecca, he took one more shot at it. "Finally, when she received the first insurance payment, in November 1997, it was a little less than two hundred thousand dollars. Within a week of that, she executes her last will and testament, and attempted suicide. You'll find out about that.

"In conclusion, let me say this. Yes, you are going to hear that Mrs. Cleland had relations with other men, maybe even other women. Yes, you are going to hear the marriage was a total disaster. But as I said before . . . you're not going to hear during the course of this trial any testimony that Mrs. Cleland entered into some kind of an agreement with Mr. Quezada to kill her husband, Bruce Cleland. That wasn't part of the plan at all. And it was a total shock to Mrs. Cleland. And she's not guilty. Thank you."

Chapter 34

Protecting Jose

With jurors taking a break outside the courtroom on Tuesday, November 28, 2006, Judge Perry glared down from his elevated perch like an angry eagle. He had not given permission for any of the attorneys to leave. The look on his face reflected deep concern about something. He had obviously been surprised by statements from Rebecca's attorney, Ed Murphy. The new strategy had potentially raised a legal issue known as "antagonistic defense," which could force a severance, meaning separate trials for each defendant.

To clarify his misgivings, Perry read aloud from case law: *"No California case has discussed at length what constitutes an antagonistic defense. . . . Antagonistic defenses do not per se require severance even if the defendants are hostile or attempt to cast the blame on each other. . . . It must be demonstrated that the conflict is so prejudicial that the defenses are irreconcilable and the jury will unjustifiably infer that this conflict alone demonstrates that both are guilty [or that] the acceptance of one party's defense will preclude acquittal of the other."*

Noting that he hadn't yet heard a motion for severance, Perry stated, "I don't want to make a decision unless I fully research this." He asked Jose's attorney, Gary Meastas, if he planned to make opening statements at this time or reserve them for later.

Meastas replied, "Well, Your Honor, I think I feel compelled at this time to have the court hear a severance motion."

Perry replied immediately, "I'm not ready to grant this. I would prefer to just go ahead and get a couple days of trial in to see where we are. . . . I think no one, speaking for all attorneys, wants to see this case tried and then have Mr. Quezada's case be reversed on appeal. And I suppose if both defendants start shooting at each other, we could have a reversal, if there is a conviction. We may have to do it all again separately. . . . But I am of the belief that Mr. Quezada's defense has been surprised by Ms. Cleland's offense, and I wonder if I should sever Mr. Quezada and give him his own trial."

Turning to Craig Hum, Perry asked his opinion. Hum said, "Obviously, we're adamantly opposed to any severance," then explained why. Part of his logic came from long experience in gang prosecutions in which defendants often blame each other in order to save themselves. He reminded the judge that despite appearing to be antagonistic defenses, the courts try these cases together all the time, and appeal judges usually affirm them.

Perry said he didn't necessarily agree, but he would consider the matter. After a long recess, and still out of the jury's presence, Perry said, "Perhaps Mr. Hum is correct, that there's not much to this. But I want to really think it through. I stand by my decision to go forward with the case at this time."

Meastas announced he would reserve his opening statement for the time being.

Perry replied, "That's certainly your choice. And I'm still thinking about the issue. I have not made a final decision on it. I did deny your motion for severance at this time, though."

* * *

The choice by Meastas to defer his opening gave Perry the green light for the trial to proceed. He told Craig to call his first witness. Without any hesitation, Ed Brown, Bruce's brother-in-law, strode to the witness stand, where he raised his right hand and swore to tell the truth, just as he had at the first trial over six years earlier.

The prosecution witnesses came streaming in, one after the other, to testify in a virtual duplication of the evidence presented in June 2000. Only one noticeable difference could be seen. Previous testimony from a few witnesses who had passed away, including the late Harold Cleland, or found it impossible to travel, would be read to the jury.

Ten days later, Craig Hum rested his case. Judge Perry formally ruled against the motion for severance, reasoning that Jose's attorney would have the opportunity to cross-examine Rebecca when she took the witness stand. Thus, Jose's right of confrontation and cross-examination would be preserved.

Ed Murphy, though, had a surprise in store. Over the next couple of days, he presented witnesses to attack the prosecution, with limited success. Everyone in the courtroom expected Rebecca to take the stand and tell her side of the story. But Murphy's thunderclap announcement of "the defense rests" created a cloud that rained disappointment and washed away stories reporters had hoped to file.

Veins bulged in the forehead of Jose's attorney, Gary Meastas. In his opening statement, Ed Murphy had pointed the finger of blame at Jose. Now the opportunity for Meastas to cross-examine her, and shift the culpability, had been blown away in the storm. He still faced the challenge of presenting a defense case for Jose, but he believed it had been prejudiced beyond repair.

The issue of "antagonistic defense" had grown to gigantic proportions for Meastas. He stood and demanded a mistrial.

Judge Perry immediately recognized he had a tiger by the

tail. Had the opening statement by Rebecca's attorney poisoned the well for Jose? Could he still receive a fair trial after the jurors had heard such detailed accusations of his involvement? Gary Meas+tas voiced his reasons for requesting the mistrial for his client. "The opening statement basically polluted [the jury] against any defense that Mr. Quezada would present. . . . It was just inflammatory for them to hear that this individual executed the victim. . . . He was executed."

The defender's voice quaked with indignation. "So, basically, what we have is counsel for [Rebecca] Cleland testifying. I think it's almost impossible for these jurors to disregard that. It's just impossible. I can't cross-examine counsel, obviously. I can't cross-examine Ms. Cleland to find out why she said this." Extending professional courtesy to his colleague Ed Murphy, Measaas said, "I think Mr. Murphy had good faith when he got up there and presented his case. I'm not questioning that at all." However, Measaas said, "the only effective remedy is . . . to declare a mistrial in this case."

Judge Perry faced a profound predicament. He asked Craig Hum for the people's position. Hum tried to put things into perspective by saying that mistakes and legal errors are made during a trial. The proper remedy, he suggested, would be for the judge to give the jury an admonition instruction that anything stated by the attorneys was not evidence and should not be considered during deliberations.

A great deal of time and expense had already been invested in two trials, but Perry knew that he couldn't use that as justification for denying the mistrial motion. He asked Measaas his opinion of a jury admonition. Of course, as Jose's defense attorney, Measaas protested that it was too much to believe a mere admonition could make the jurors forget what Murphy had said about Jose's involvement. He ended his argument for a mistrial by stating, "It's not going to leave those jurors' minds. Listening to it myself, [I feel] it left an impact with me. And I have been doing this for twenty-seven years. I do know that Mr. Quezada is not going to get a fair trial. There's just no way we can overcome that opening statement. It's impossible."

Still optimistic about the ability of jurors to follow instructions, Perry denied the defense motion for a mistrial. He stated, "I am going to strongly admonish the jury regarding opening statements not being evidence. I presume they will follow the court's instructions."

With the severance issue out of the way, Gary Meastas stepped up to the plate to present Jose's defense. He decided not to make an opening statement, but to proceed with his witnesses.

First the defender called an experimental psychologist, Dr. Kathy Pezdek, who spent nearly two hours on the subject of eyewitness identifications. It appeared to be aimed at undermining statements from Lupe Hernandez and Virginia Selva. Pezdek delivered her opinions professionally, with crystal clarity. Craig Hum conducted a vigorous cross-examination, resulting in an admission from the doctor that she was not saying the eyewitnesses were always mistaken in their identification.

Meastas next brought Jose's mother into court. Rosario Quezada, age seventy, told the jury that Jose and his girlfriend stayed many weekends at her home in Riverside County, over sixty miles from the murder scene in Boyle Heights. She testified to remembering that she, along with her son and his lady, had stayed up and talked until one-fifteen on the morning of July 26, 1997. She also recalled receiving a phone call around three-thirty in the morning from her estranged husband, Arturo. He told her that Bruce had been killed. About four hours later, she told Jose and his girlfriend of Bruce's death.

This seemed to be the perfect alibi. It placed Jose miles

away at the time of the shooting. And it came from a mother, with whom jurors might easily sympathize.

Meastas asked why the phone call from Arturo stood out so clearly in her mind.

The mother replied, "Because I know that my son Jose was not the one who committed that crime. He was in my house. And I have been thinking and it's been going through my mind every single day that he has been incarcerated, day and night, knowing that he was not the one."

Hum objected to her answer as not responsive to the question. Judge Perry sustained it, but jurors had heard the plaintive words and the bell could not be unrung.

The defense attorney inquired about Jose's physical condition, and Rosario described her son's "red swollen arm" from having the cast removed. "He had a lot of pain and he couldn't even write."

Craig Hum faced a sensitive, difficult task in cross-examining an innocent, elderly woman. He started with the obvious, establishing that she loved her son and would do anything to help him.

Step-by-step, with obvious compassion, Hum allowed her to reiterate all of her previous answers. His questioning culminated with the query "And you know he couldn't have done it because he was with you, correct?"

She nodded, voicing her unqualified agreement.

In the same sympathetic tone, Hum asked, "So when was the first time that you went to the police and said, 'My son couldn't have done this, he was with me'?"

The woman's voice hardened defensively. "I never went to the police, and they never wanted my testimony in court."

The prosecutor had rung a different bell, and it resounded among spectators with new doubt about the mother's veracity. Anyone would respect a poor mother's pain in those conditions, but jurors might also understand a willingness to fudge the truth if it would keep her son out of prison. Yet, if her claims of Jose being with her were true, wouldn't she have clamored unceasingly to the police or anyone else who would listen to declare his innocence? People in the gallery also found it interesting that she never mentioned her younger son, Alvaro.

Hum thanked Rosario Quezada, and Judge Perry excused her.

The defense rested, and Perry informed jurors that all three attorneys would present their closing arguments after lunch.

Craig Hum's speech closely resembled the one he had delivered in 2000, only without reference to the silence between Rebecca and Jose in the backseat of a police car.

Ed Murphy told jurors that the prosecution had not proved its case against Rebecca Cleland. She had driven her two cousins to the site for a confrontation with Bruce over his sexual advances to Arturo, but she was totally shocked, he asserted, when she saw Jose kill her husband. Murphy asked them to find her not guilty. To court observers, Judge Perry seemed to pay even closer attention than usual.

After again appealing to the judge for a mistrial, Gary Meastas focused on alibis and eyewitness identification. Jose's mother had been right, he said, in asserting that he couldn't have done it.

The final turn always belongs to the prosecutor, and Craig Hum stepped up to deliver his rebuttal argument, when another thunderclap struck inside the courtroom.

Judge Perry had thought long and hard about the antagonistic defense issue, and the motion for a mistrial submitted by Gary Meastas. To everyone's surprise, the judge interrupted proceedings to announce his decision. Perry granted a mistrial in the case against Jose. The jury would deliberate only on the guilt or innocence of Rebecca. A new trial would be held for Jose right after the holidays.

The twelve panelists rejected Rebecca's new story and took only a short time to convict her of murder in the first degree. They also found true the special allegations of murder for financial gain and of lying in wait. Rebecca again received a sentence of life in prison without the possibility of parole.

Two expensive trials had put two killers away. Now it would be necessary to conduct yet a third trial for disposition of the case against Jose Quezada.

In a 2008 interview, Craig Hum described what happened next. "Judge Perry made his decision just before I put on my final rebuttal argument. He recognized the serious conflict between defenses in that second trial. According to statements from Rebecca's lawyer, we thought she would testify, but she didn't." With a sly grin lighting up his face, Hum said, "I like to think that she was afraid to be cross-examined by me."

He continued, "When her lawyer decided to argue that Jose did it, Judge Perry declared a mistrial and we started the new one in a couple of weeks after the Christmas holiday. It was really difficult for me because my dad was sick up in Northern California at that time.

"In the third trial, it was our position that we needed to show motive and all the facts, not just Jose's involvement. We had to put in all in context. The fact they were cousins was a strong factor—not like Rebecca had hired a stranger. We put on exactly the same trial in [the] third case as in the second. Same witnesses. And they all were very cooperative. Especially since they had testified just six weeks earlier. It went really fast in Judge Perry's court, a little less than three weeks. The second trial had taken about four weeks."

* * *

As had happened twice before, the jury found Jose Quezada guilty of murder in the first degree, with the same special circumstances. Judge Perry sentenced him to life without the possibility of parole.

Rebecca appealed again. The same appellate court that had previously overturned the verdicts against her, and Jose, affirmed Rebecca's conviction on July 21, 2008. It happened just five days before the eleventh anniversary of Bruce's death.

Alvaro Quezada, found guilty once, Rebecca Cleland, twice guilty; and Jose Quezada, also guilty two times, remain in California prisons, where they are condemned to spend the rest of their natural lives.

On a serene, picturesque slope of the Rose Hills Cemetery, near the southwestern edge of Whittier, Bruce and Patricia rest, side by side. Their parents, Harold and Theda, are a short walk away, in a peaceful dell. All four members of the Cleland family are together again, for eternity.

Acknowledgments

As always, we find ourselves deeply indebted to numerous people who helped us in researching and developing this story. We are especially grateful to some who went the extra mile, such as Karen Corwin, the extraordinary librarian who knows where to find everything.

Finding a suitable subject for a true-crime book is not as easy as it sounds. Ron and I had sifted through scores of cases, and had nearly exhausted the possibilities. As he sat one day at his dining-room table with his wife, Rosemarie, telling her of our problem, she suggested, "What about Rebecca, the woman who took her husband to the cleaners and then had him killed?" *Bingo!* Without Rosie's help, this story might never have reached you, our terrific readers, to whom we owe the greatest thanks.

Elizabeth Lamb gave us generous, courteous, and lively interviews, as well as gracious permission to use photographs she had taken. Beth's courage significantly helped this case culminate in justice, for which she deserves admiration. She is not only a model citizen with a wonderful sense of humor, but a terrific lady as well.

Bertha Awana invited us into her lovely Arizona home, and also came up with great photographs. She spoke frankly and extensively about her long relationship with Rebecca, and held back nothing. Bright and gregarious, with a sparkling personality, Bertha supplied invaluable input to the story. Alma Arias, her sister, joined in the illuminating conversations, and contributed great slants on several incidents. We hold them both in high regard.

Deputy DA Craig Hum met with us for lunch, and ran through the trials, legal issues, tactics, and personalities in this complex tale. He is truly one of the brightest and most talented trial lawyers in the L.A. District Attorney's Office.

Private detective Walt Zwonitzer gave us a welcome hand with research.

Once again, Michaela Hamilton, executive editor at Kensington Publishing Company, not only gave us the green light to proceed with this book, but smoothed out the long road with her suggestions. Michaela's colleague, Mike Shohl, also aided us in hurdling obstacles. Literary agent Susan Crawford provided the usual solid bridge of communication.

To the best of our ability, we have told a completely factual story. Because it took three trials to finally send Rebecca, Alvaro, and Jose to prison, we needed to avoid taking readers through all of them in repetitious detail. So we have used a modicum of literary license to interpose testimony into the first trial, and thereby reduce the narrative lengths of numbers two and three. However, we have neither altered nor embellished the essential facts. Quoted conversations are derived from interviews and trial testimony. To protect privacy and safety of several characters, we have changed their names in the text.

—Don Lasseter and Ronald Bowers, 2009

MORE MUST-READ TRUE CRIME
FROM PINNACLE

MORE SHOCKING TRUE CRIME
FROM PINNACLE